MW00912252

The Miegunyah Press

This is number fifty-four in the
second numbered series of the
Miegunyah Volumes
made possible by the
Miegunyah Fund
established by bequests
under the wills of
Sir Russell and Lady Grimwade.

'Miegunyah' was the home of
Mab and Russell Grimwade
from 1911 to 1955.

Clearings

Clearings

*Six Colonial Gardeners
and their Landscapes*

Paul Fox

THE MIEGUNYAH PRESS

THE MIEGUNYAH PRESS
An imprint of Melbourne University Publishing Ltd (MUP Ltd)
PO Box 1167, Carlton, Victoria 3053, Australia
mup-info@unimelb.edu.au
www.mup.com.au

First published 2004
Text © Paul Fox 2004
Design and typography © Melbourne University Publishing Ltd 2004

This book is copyright. Apart from any use permitted under the
Copyright Act 1968 and subsequent amendments, no part may be
reproduced, stored in a retrieval system or transmitted by any
means or process whatsoever without the prior written
permission of the publishers.

The botanical appendix was prepared by Margaret Brookes.

National Library of Australia Cataloguing-in-Publication entry

Fox, Paul.
Clearings: six colonial gardeners and their landscapes.

Includes index.
ISBN 0 522 85086 3.

1. Landscape gardening—Australia—History.
2. Gardeners—Australia—History.
3. Gardens—Australia—History.
I. Title.

Publication of this book was assisted by a Publications Grant
from the University of Melbourne.

Acknowledgements

This book brings together a multitude of stories about landscapes and places—stories told by my family and friends, as well as those I have ferreted out of the archives and libraries.

I have drawn inspiration from the memory of my maternal grandparents' garden, with its Waterhouse camellias, fruit trees and giant willow, where we lounged in cane divans during summer. My grandmother told me stories of the Australian countryside and sparked my interest in photography by showing me her uncle's letters and photographs from South Africa, where he had laid out the telegraph system. The first political act I remember was at a flower show, where she signed a petition against the development of Victoria's Little Desert. She also gently pricked Melbourne's pretensions. Once, on passing a statue of a local notable, she said, 'His father was nothing more than a cattle duffer'.

My parents have sustained each other and their six children for over fifty years. In particular, I am grateful to my mother for her gift of music. One of my primary-school memories is of a house filled with the sound of her playing Debussy's Images. My father too has been a source of wonder. He could count sheep in paddocks at a glance, and spot a well-run farm with a flick of the eye. Before family holidays, each of us children was assigned a task: one of my sisters read the maps, while I read the local history. We grew up in the suburbs hearing about the seasons, of the farm my father had left behind and his extended family, which he loved.

My aunt used to say that her father recited poetry while he ploughed, scattering words over furrowed ground. My uncle George loved Henry Handel Richardson's *The Fortunes of Richard Mahony*, and evoked its landscape with a great passion. It was he who first took me to the great reading room at the State Library of Victoria; so began my love of the library's collections. My cousin Michael and his wife Anne have also sustained me through their friendship.

Then there was Great-aunt Kate of Mornington (whose laugh I can still hear today) and her son, James, another reader of maps, who remembered hearing my great-grandmother describe seeing Melbourne as a tent city, and watching Burke and Wills at Royal Park, taking leave of Melbourne. James also told stories of racehorses, and of great-uncles who rode into hotels on horseback. With James's daughter Leonie and her children I have discussed the environment, landscape and the law, continuing a 130-year conversation within the family.

It was James who rediscovered family places in distant Ireland, where each of us travelled in our own way. There, on Fox land, Mr Eustace (arrayed in cheetah mittens willed to him by a bishop) showed me where he had built fences so foxes could escape the hunt. Lady Mount Charles too showed many kindnesses to the Australian cousins of the Irish Foxes she had visited as a small child. In County Meath, on the steps of a house designed by Francis Johnston, I stood thinking of the transformations migration engenders, and decided to write a book.

Gardening creates great friendships. The hospitality of Margaret and Clive Windmill has carried me on my way for over twenty years. Grace Fraser, landscape architect and conservationist, told me at our first meeting that I should continually look at the landscape—advice that has reverberated through my life. John Stevens infused me with his great love of plants; Paul Thompson inspired me with his enthusiasm, creativity and encyclopaedic knowledge of Australian flora. Clive and Penny Blazey have enriched the whole community with their delight in plants and gardening. Anne Latreille, who accepted my early writings for the Melbourne Age, taught me how to write for a general readership.

Gael and Danny Spooner have invited me to come and stay, sharing their music, garden and wonderful meals, and allowing me to be frolicsome when I chose. Mike Daffey displayed great hospitality and good nature on the many Sunday afternoons during which this book was edited. I am also grateful to John and Ros Martin and their children for their friendship, and John's metaphysical reading of landscape.

Jennifer Phipps has transported me with her great visual gifts. To stand in front of a painting with her is to see what one has never seen before. Anyone who knows Christine Downer's work in creating the picture collection at the State Library of Victoria cannot but be in awe of her energy, integrity and passion for the State's visual culture. I thank her for her inspirational friendship.

Dr Leon van Schaik, now professor of architectural innovation at RMIT, encouraged me to become a conceptual thinker, and it was through him that I came to lecture in architectural theory at RMIT, an experience that helped me to develop a spatial reading of history by exposing me to wondrous students, architects and ideas.

Dean Boothroyd, Peter Brew, Michael Markam, Ian McDougall, Allan Powell, Alex Selenitsch and Roger Wood have also informed the making of the book through their passion for architectural space. I am indebted to Peter Corrigan for his far-ranging conversations and for championing this book.

The late Grant Featherston and Mary Featherston have taught me much about what creates perfectly conceived spaces.

Members of the Australian Garden History Society, especially the Victorian branch, have also given me invaluable encouragement. I would especially like to thank Nina Crone for the twinkle in her eye when I read the Macarthur chapter to the Society; Suzanne Hunt, whose strength in adversity has provided inspiration to many people; Helen Page, the organisational genius of the Victorian Society;

ACKNOWLEDGEMENTS

Christine Reid, who generously looked at the Veitch catalogues in London for me; and Georgina Whitehead,who has provided friendship over many years. I would also like to pay tribute to Janet and Lachlan Gordon for the tact, energy and love of landscape they have shown in restoring the dream of Guilfoyle's garden at Turkeith, and to Mrs Rundle for sharing the wonders of Glenara with me.

Richard Aitken and his wife Georgina Binns have offered encouragement during the years of writing. Richard generously made information available to me while he was editing the *Oxford Companion to Australian Gardens*; for this I am much indebted.

Others have generously shared their knowledge with me. Barney Hutton gave me access to his research on Thomas Lang. Eve Almond shared details of William Guilfoyle's early life, and Clare Gervasoni and Susan Paterson went with me one Easter, maps in hand, looking for the farms Josiah Mitchell judged around Smeaton. The Historic Houses Trust of New South Wales provided me with an exhibition research grant, which allowed me to locate the Macarthur–Veitch correspondence in the Mitchell Library.

Thanks also to the staff of the State Library of Victoria for answering my endless enquires. In particular I would like to thank Gayle Veal, whose enthusiasm and service at the General Reference Desk has gone well beyond anything a user of the library might expect; Sandra Burt, Gerard Hayes, Lois McEvey and Jock Murphy of the Manuscript Collection; Judy Scurfield of the Map Collection; Kerry Agnew, Fiona Jeffrey, Madeleine Say and Olga Tsara of the Picture Collection; and Des Cowley of Rare Books. The kindnesses of Dianne Reilly and Shane Carmody have paved the way for this book.

At other cultural institutions, I have to thank Jason Benjamin of the University of Melbourne Archives; Richard Barley, Helen Cohn and Jill Thurlow of the Royal Botanic Gardens, Melbourne; Elizabeth Ellis, Mitchell Librarian, State Library of New South Wales, and Alan Davies and Margo Riley of the Mitchell Library; Leanne Fitzgibbon of the Bendigo Art Gallery; Simon Jacks of the Central Highlands Regional Library; Danny McGowan of the Hamilton Art Gallery; Jennie Moloney of the National Gallery of Victoria; Peter Perry of the Castlemaine Art Gallery and Historical Museum; Dr Elizabeth Rushen of the Royal Historical Society of Victoria; Mrs Meralyn Roberts and Mrs Jane Salmon of the Friends of the Geelong Botanic Gardens; Cheryl Timbury of the Geelong Heritage Centre; Roger Trudgeon of the Ballarat Gold Museum; and the staff of the Public Record Office of Victoria.

Mrs Pat Glass and Mrs Marigold Gregory Maclean have generously granted me permission to use their families' collections. Vivienne Mehes photographed material for the book with great patience and care, and Graeme Kinross-Smith graciously agreed to photograph an image in Geelong.

I owe the abundance of images in this book to a grant from the University of Melbourne's Publication Sub-committee, and for this I am extremely grateful. I would especially like to thank Associate Professor Kate Darian-Smith, director of the university's Australian Centre; Kate has a rare combination of vision, humanity and consummate skill in facilitating the talent that can effect change.

Others who have contributed include Laurence Aberhardt, Natalie Adamson, Professor Weston Bate, Tony Birch, Dulcie Brookshaw, Naomi Cass, Bruce and Kate Commins, Tom Darragh, Harriet Edquist, Anne Finch, the American cousinage Ripley and Denise Fox, the late Pam Gullifer, John Hawker, Michael Hiscock, Timothy Hubbard, Roderick McIvor, the late Sir Thomas Ramsay and Lady Ramsay, Diane and Bill Routt, Andrew Saniga, Rosemary Simons, Faith Smith, Margaret Stones, Ray Tonkin and members of the Landscape Advisory Sub-committee at Heritage Victoria, the late Dr Norman Wettenhall and Joan Wettenhall, and Maureen Dagg, Robert Gray and Helen Sharpley, whose many kindnesses when I was working in Strategy at Australia Post were greatly appreciated. I am especially grateful to Margaret Brookes for checking the botanical names and creating the botanical appendix.

At Melbourne University Publishing, I would like to thank Tracy O'Shaughnessy for her energy, professionalism and patience, and especially for the collaborative spirit in which she has approached the publication process. Thanks also to Hamish Freeman and Klarissa Pfisterer for the wonder of creating a coherent and distinctive design, and to Guy Holt for producing the maps.

I owe a special debt of gratitude to two people. For more than twenty-three years, Hilary McPhee has encouraged me to write, and this book would never have been written without her conversation and support. Jenny Lee has not only offered me friendship for many years, but has also edited the book with great commitment, energy and expertise.

And how should these acknowledgements end? While I have been writing about landscape, my brother and his wife have bought a block of uncleared land between the Little Desert and the Great Desert in north-west Victoria. So my father and mother travel to visit my brother's land, not far from the Mallee, where my father farmed with his father. Here, my father reflects on the clearing with an equanimity of mind as elegant as the bow room in his ancestors' Irish house—the house from which his grandfather stole forth to work his passage across the ocean, jump ship in Melbourne, lose himself in the bush and gift his descendants a great attachment to the land of Australia.

ACKNOWLEDGEMENTS

Contents

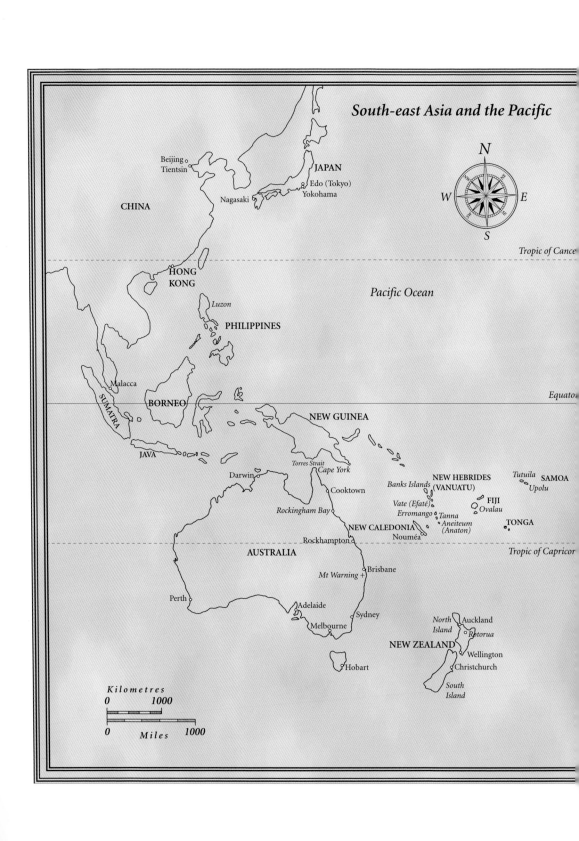

South-east Asia and the Pacific

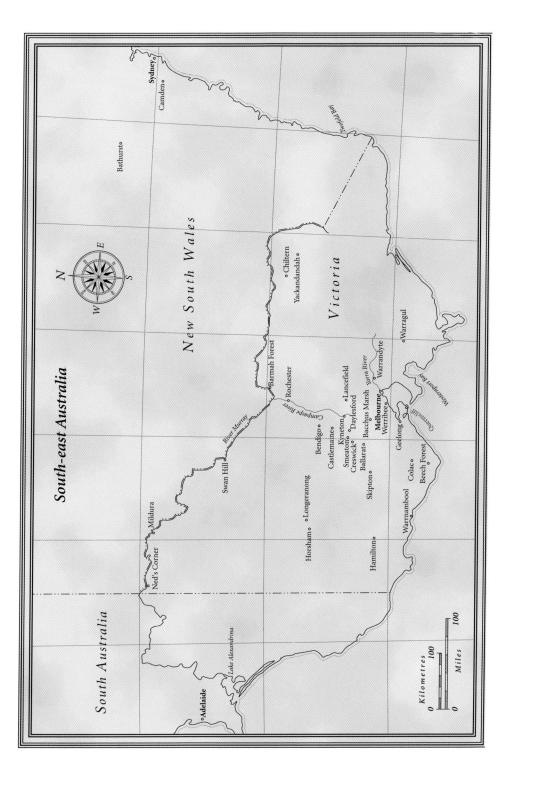

South-east Australia

South Australia

New South Wales

Victoria

Adelaide

Lake Alexandrina

Ned's Corner

Mildura

Swan Hill

River Murray

Horsham ○ ○Longeranong

Hamilton○

Bendigo ○

Campaspe River

○Rochester

Barmah Forest

○Chiltern
Yackandandah ○

Castlemaine○
Kyneton○ ○Lancefield
Smeaton○ ○Daylesford
Creswick○
Ballarat○ Bacchus Marsh
Skipton○

Warrnambool
Colac○
Beech Forest

Geelong○

Melbourne
Werribee○

Yarra River

Warrandyte○

○Warragul

Queenscliff○

Port Phillip Bay

Bathurst○

Sydney○
Camden○

Twofold Bay

N
W E
S

Kilometres 0   100
Miles 0   100

A Wardian case

From Nathaniel Ward, *On the Grow
of Plants in Closely Glazed Cases*, 18
Copy inscribed 'To Ferdinand Muel
Director of the Melbourne Botanic
Gardens', Archives of the Royal
Botanic Gardens, Melbourne

Introduction

This book is dedicated to the Wardian case, a modest invention that revolutionised the movement of plants around the globe. From the 1840s onwards, miniature glasshouses full of living plants could be found on the decks of the ships that plied the mercantile trade routes to and from Europe. The resulting flood of exotic plants transformed European horticulture. In London, which was the epicentre of this trade, professional nurserymen and wealthy gardeners alike were consumed by desire for the latest horticultural novelty. English gardens and conservatories filled with a medley of plants: pines from California, Guatemala, Mexico, Japan and India, orchids from South America and the shores of the Pacific, rhododendrons bred from Indian stock, and fabulous lilies from Japan.

The plant trade was governed by unequal relationships between England and the colonies. Few colonial nurserymen had the power to contest the hegemony of their British counterparts, though some tried. The centralisation of scientific botany in England meant that most new plants had to be sent there for identification; in effect, British botanists became gatekeepers to the plant trade. To get the better of the London nurserymen not only required substantial means and business acumen, but also local access to taxonomic knowledge.

The growth of the plant trade had far-reaching consequences on the other side of the world. In the Australian colonies, the exotic plants unpacked from Wardian cases would colonise the country as surely as the settlers who imported them. Professional nurserymen played an active part in this imperial project as intermediaries between wild places and cultivated Europe. The garden more than any other site expressed the transformations inherent in colonialism.

But first the land had to be cleared. To make a clearing in the colonies was to erase what existed in nature in order to write a new narrative. Nurseries and botanic gardens offered ideal landscapes by which colonists could glimpse what their settlements might eventually become. The clearing became a stage on which competing versions of Australian colonisation were played out.

Colonial gardeners did not create facsimiles of English gardens, although they employed the same plant species. In Australia, glasshouse plants could be grown outdoors in combinations that seemed improbable to English eyes. Here, it was plain to see that the colony was different from the mother country. In time, this became the basis of a distinctive Australian horticultural aesthetic.

This book examines how all these factors played out in the lives of six colonial gardeners. It is not only concerned with elucidating their individual contributions but also with exploring the larger issue of the success or failure of the garden as a metaphor for the changes in the colonial landscape. Each of these gardeners' stories has a different inflection; there is no one grand narrative to explain the settlement of colonial Australia. Rather, we see a multiplicity of places created by settlers to make sense of where they are—in the nursery, the botanic garden, the farm and the forest.

The colonial landscape was always a contested site. Just as the clearing was an attempt to expunge the pre-European landscape, so too colonisation attempted to imagine away the country's indigenous peoples, along with their knowledge. The devaluation of Aboriginal understandings of country in turn opened the way for the settlers' contemptuous treatment of many indigenous plants.

There was also a lack of shared understanding of the settled landscape. In the rural areas, this was epitomised by the colonists' divergent attitudes to trees. For the selector on the small farm, clearing indigenous trees was an official prerequisite for gaining title to land and a practical necessity for gaining a livelihood. By contrast, large sheep-owners who had secured their holdings planted belts of trees (often exotic) as a visible sign of their determination to stay on the land for the long term.

In this contest, the garden came to represent a harmonious vision of the future occupation of the land. This representation owed much to the influence of professional gardeners and nurserymen, many of whom became respected members of the self-improving urban middle class. Through their land-scapes and their writings, colonial gardeners promoted the ideal of a land intensively shaped by disciplined human activity. This ideal was bound up with a moral imperative towards self-improvement, which in turn gained potency from the imperial narrative of progress and enlightenment. In this order of things, the ethical gardener could claim moral hege-mony over the whole landscape.

The story of the clearing is seminal to European settlement in Australia. It is the story of colonial gardeners who created one landscape as they destroyed another. In their nurseries, botanic gardens, farms and forests, they manufactured visions of country that have become second nature to most Aus-tralians. In a sense, we still inhabit the clearings they made.

Sir William Macarthur

The Colonial Grandee

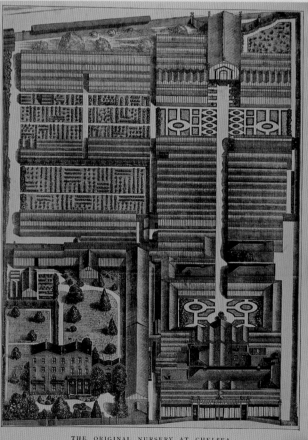

THE ORIGINAL NURSERY AT CHELSEA

The Colonial Grandee

Sir William Macarthur (1800–1882) was a colonist in the grand manner, and gardening was his passion. He was renowned as having 'by far the best' collection of plants in New South Wales. As owner of Camden Park, a 30000-acre estate west of Sydney, he could indulge his desire for all the latest plant discoveries from around the globe.[1]

Sir William's search for rare plants led him to the enterprising English firm of Veitch and Son, proprietors of a fifty-acre nursery at Exeter. He first wrote to the Veitches in 1849, ordering a large consignment of plants and seeds.[2] His timing was opportune: four years later, Veitch and Son acquired the celebrated Exotic Nursery in Chelsea, London, where they gained royal patronage and swiftly established themselves as nurserymen to men of means throughout the Empire.[3]

To the Veitches, Sir William was just such a client, 'a most enthusiastic amateur in horticulture'.[4] Significantly, he was also a potential source of exotic plants for the London market. No demand was too great; to displease a horticultural gentleman was to risk losing his patronage. They cultivated their colonial client as they would a rare new plant.

In a thirty-year correspondence, the Veitches unfailingly addressed Macarthur as 'My Dear Sir William', and used all their wiles to encourage his horticultural enthusiasms. Their correspondence was as familiar as the English class system would permit. Amid the business of selling plants, intimacies were traded, family achievements were reported, and Macarthur was kept abreast of a world that was much larger than Sydney.

In their letters, the elder Veitches discreetly boasted about the plant-hunting activities of John Gould Veitch, a fourth-generation member of the firm and graduate of botanical studies from University College, London.[5] In 1860 Sir William learnt that John Gould Veitch was on his way to China with Lord Elgin, and had survived a shipwreck in Ceylon.[6] The letters did not mention the purpose of Lord Elgin's voyage, which was a punitive expedition sparked by the Chinese government's failure to ratify the 1857 Treaty of Tientsin. Before

Sir William Macarthur
and his family, c. 1865
Macarthur Family at Camden Park,
albumen print, Macarthur album,
Mitchell Library, State Library of
New South Wales

John Gould Veitch
From James Veitch, *Hortus Veitchii*,
James Veitch & Sons, London, 1906,
Archives of the Royal Botanic
Gardens, Melbourne

James Veitch & Sons' Royal Exotic
Nursery, Chelsea, London
From James Veitch, *Hortus Veitchii*,
James Veitch & Sons, London, 1906,
Archives of the Royal Botanic
Gardens, Melbourne

Nagasaki, where John Gould Veitch
began his Japanese adventures

*At the Entrance to the Bay of
Nagasaki*, from Aimé Humbert,
Le Japon Illustré, Paris, 1870, vol. 1,
State Library of Victoria

An expedition for the purpose
of 'recreation and observation':
the ascent of Mount Fuji, 1860

Ascent of Fusiyama, from Rutherford
Alcock, *The Capital of the Tycoon*,
vol. 1, opposite p. 425,
State Library of Victoria

Elgin's forces left, they set fire to the Chinese emperor's summer palace.

From China, John Gould Veitch went on to Japan, which had been opened to trade with the West only seven years before by the gunboat diplomacy of Commodore Perry of the United States Navy.[7] Europeans were hungry for information about the unique flora of this mysterious country. Veitch had a perfect opportunity to publicise his botanical discoveries in a series of letters to the English *Gardeners' Chronicle and Agricultural Gazette*.

His first port of call was Nagasaki, where he spent two weeks rambling around the surrounding hills, accompanied by a Japanese interpreter. Unknown to him, the distinguished German botanist Dr Philipp von Siebold was living near by, 'entirely away from Europeans', and writing a major series of works on the flora of Japan.[8] Veitch's ambition to 'get together all the plants I can' was curtailed by restrictions on the movements of foreigners,[9] so he paid a Japanese intermediary to collect plants and seeds for him. To transport his spoils to London, he employed a Japanese carpenter to build a Wardian case. Veitch was pleased with the result, although the little glasshouse quite bewildered the Japanese.[10]

Veitch was grateful when the British consul, Sir Rutherford Alcock, appointed him honorary British botanist in Japan. 'You may imagine I at once grew six inches taller', Veitch wrote on hearing this news.[11] This freed him to travel to places usually forbidden to Europeans, and also satisfied Sir William Hooker, the director of the great imperial botanic gardens at Kew in England, who was eager to add Japanese plants to the national collection.[12]

John Gould Veitch could now explore the 'really wonderful' imperial city of Edo (Tokyo), where he even gained entry to the royal nurseries. Under the consul's aegis, he then travelled to snow-capped Mount Fuji, joining a European expedition to the mountain for 'the avowed purpose of recreation and observation'.[13] The expedition was prompted by Sir William Hooker, who had suggested that it would be 'of great interest

SIR WILLIAM MACARTHUR

LE PAPENBERG, ILE A L'ENTREE DE LA BAIE DE NAGASAKI.

S. J. Gower, delt.   Hanhart, lith.

ASCENT OF FUSIYAMA.

Wild hydrangeas captivated
European plant-hunters in Japan

Hydrangea otaksa, from Philipp
von Siebold, *Flora Japonica*, Leiden,
1835–70, vol. 1, plate 52,
State Library of Victoria

to botanists to learn something of the mountain vegetation of Japan'.[14]

In fact, the party often seemed more interested in recreation than in observation. When the climbers (including Alcock's scotch terrier, Toby) reached the top of Mount Fuji, they drank a champagne toast to the health of Queen Victoria, Rutherford Alcock and 'absent friends in Europe'. They then used their revolvers to give a 21-gun salute, hoisted the British flag, gave three cheers 'such as only Englishmen can give', and gave a rousing rendition of 'God Save the Queen'.[15]

Nevertheless, Veitch emerged from this expedition 'laden with many new ferns, and other specimens of interest'.[16] The way to Mount Fuji was a plant-hunter's paradise. Every hill and mountain was clothed in 'a dense mass of luxuriant foliage' of autumn-tinted oak, maple, beech, alder and chestnut, and the mountain banks were covered with the large lilac, blue and white flower clusters of wild hydrangea. Temple gardens too held rare and beauteous plants, and there were spectacular avenues of pines (*Pinus massoniana*) and Japanese cedars (*Cryptomeria japonica*).[17]

By collecting these plants, Veitch captured Japan for his European readership. The foreign landscape was reduced to a series of horticultural tableaux of conifers and crimson maples. In particular, Japan's great variety of conifers fuelled the European mania for pines.[18] Veitch came away from Mount Fuji with the seeds of twenty-five different species.[19]

In spite of all these successes, the 'practical botanist ... [and] son of the well-known London horticulturalist' was firmly reminded of his place in the hierarchy of empire. When Veitch discovered a variegated *Thujopsis dolabrata* at the foot of Mount Fuji, Alcock ordered that it be sent to Hooker because until recently the Veitches had had the only specimen of *Thujopsis dolabrata* growing in England.[20] The commercial interests of Veitch and Son must yield to the imperial scientific demands of Kew.

Science also informed Veitch's understanding of what he saw on Mount Fuji. The German traveller Alexander von

SIR WILLIAM MACARTHUR

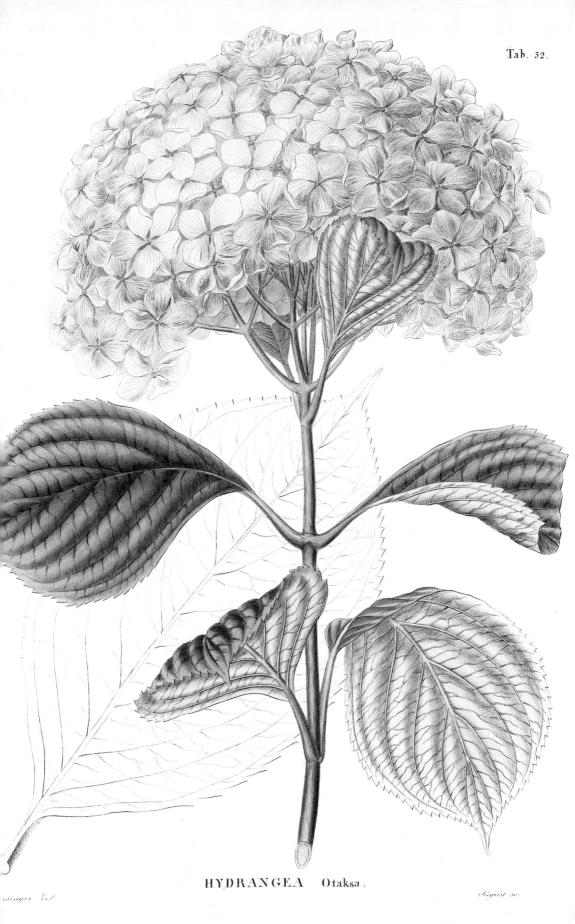

Tab. 52.

HYDRANGEA Otaksa.

Pinus massoniana, which lined
the avenues on John Gould Veitch's
journey to Mount Fuji

Pinus massoniana, from Philipp
von Siebold, *Flora Japonica*, Leiden,
1835–70, vol. 2, plate 114,
State Library of Victoria

John Gould Veitch's sketch of Mount
Fuji shows how vegetation changes
with different elevations

John Gould Veitch, 'Vegetation as
noted at the different elevations
of Mount Fuji Yama, the highest
mountain in Japan', *Gardeners'
Chronicle and Agricultural Gazette*,
22 December 1860,
State Library of Victoria

Veranda of the English
Legation in Yedo (Tokyo)

From Aimé Humbert, *Le Japon Illustré*,
Paris, 1870, vol. 1, State Library of
Victoria

Humboldt had advanced a scientific theory about the relationship between plants and altitude in his popular book *Cosmos*, and Veitch drew on its example. He made a sketch, similar to the one illustrated in the *Cosmos*, detailing the types of plants he found at different altitudes on Mount Fuji.[21]

Veitch also constructed European gardens in the foreign landscape. At the British legation in Edo, he began by planting a kitchen garden from seeds sent by his father.[22] Then, even though he admired the legation's 'very fine and beautiful' Japanese garden and shrubbery, he proceeded to redesign it 'on English principles'.[23]

Veitch continued to map new vegetation and cultivate botanical exchanges with the consuls of empire. On a side-trip to Luzon in the Philippines, he undertook an arduous 7500-foot mountain climb to determine the altitude at which orchids grew.[24] He also stopped in Hong Kong on his return voyage to England, and presented a case full of Japanese plants to the botanic gardens recently established by the Territory's governor, Sir Hercules Robinson.[25]

Back in England, John Gould Veitch spent 'long hours' in the glasshouses and nursery beds at his father's establishment, sorting and cultivating the many new plants he had collected on his travels.[26] A few years later, he set off travelling again; this time Sir William would have an opportunity to meet the renowned plant-hunter and learn of his adventures at first hand.

On 26 January 1864, the firm's principal, James Veitch, matter-of-factly informed Sir William: 'John Veitch hopes to come to Australia in the year'.[27] True to his father's word, John Gould Veitch left Plymouth in August on the passenger ship *La Hogue*, armed with a letter of recommendation from the Admiralty entitling him to travel on Her Majesty's naval fleet. He travelled with a Wardian case filled with 'plants intended for distribution among friends in Sydney', and spent the 95-day voyage studying the plants' progress.[28]

Within two weeks of arriving in Australia, he was on his way to Camden Park. His initial impression of the country between

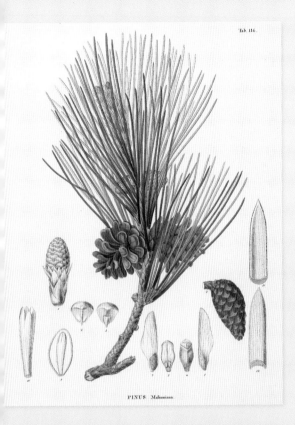

Tab. 114.

PINUS Massoniana.

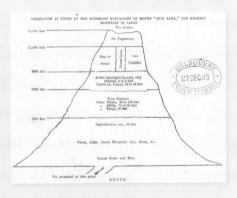

VEGETATION AS NOTED AT THE DIFFERENT ELEVATIONS ON MOUNT "FUSI YAMA," THE HIGHEST MOUNTAIN IN JAPAN.

MELBOURNE
27 DEC 83
PUBLIC LIBRARY

VÉRANDA DE LA LÉGATION ANGLAISE, A YÉDO.

Nerium oleander *Album*.

Plumbago capensis.

Sydney and Camden was extremely unfavourable. He was disconcerted by the eucalypts, whose 'white and light brown peeling bark, and brown foliage' made them seem half-dead:

> The first idea of a person coming from England is, that all the trees are dying, or that each specimen has been struck by lightning. The barren, desolate appearance this produces, deprives the country scenery of all beauty, or semblance of luxuriance.[29]

After this alien scenery, Sir William's garden seemed the epitome of luxury. No expense had been spared to assemble 'the best varieties in each class' of plant, and together the collection was 'by far the best' he had seen in the colony. Veitch was delighted to find that 'even our most recent strawberries are thriving here', not to mention the numerous conifers his father had supplied to Sir William.

The garden was divided into two parts. The area near the house was 'laid out in lawns and shrubberies, with an orange grove ... and two greenhouses for the purposes of propagation', while the lower garden was 'devoted chiefly to vegetables and fruit', although it also contained several flowering shrubs and 'a large collection of bulbs', including 'numerous hybrids raised by [Sir William] himself'. Veitch's only criticism was that the approach to the house was 'poor, and not in keeping with other portions of the grounds'.

If the plants were familiar, however, the planting combinations were not. Here oleanders from the West Indies grew in the open ground beside Chinese elms, *Magnolia grandiflora* from the southern United States, the variegated *Arundo* from the Mediterranean, several species of ficus and the Cape of Good Hope plumbago. In this topsy-turvy world, plants classified in England as stove and greenhouse species could be found growing in riotous profusion. The northern side of the house was covered with bougainvillea and other creepers. 'There are few sights more beautiful', Veitch wrote, 'than the side of a large house covered with these bright mauve-coloured and scarlet flowers'. The only plants that required 'special treatment' were the numerous rhododendrons and

The house in the clearing:
Camden Park in 1843,
before the garden

Conrad Martens, *Camden Park*, 1843,
watercolour, Dixson Galleries,
State Library of New South Wales

The West Indian oleander,
a favoured planting in Australia

Nerium oleander, from *Loddiges
Botanical Cabinet*, vol. 7, plate 700,
State Library of Victoria

Plumbago capensis from
South Africa

Plumbago capensis, from *Loddiges
Botanical Cabinet*, vol. 3, plate 295,
State Library of Victoria

azaleas, which were 'mostly grown in pots'. The colonial garden-esque so challenged the prescriptions of English horticultural fashion that Veitch fell back on the only certainty left to a nurseryman who knew the value of plants: the cost of the Camden plantings.[30]

Veitch was grateful to Sir William for taking 'an especial interest in my visit to his country'; the colonial grandee had made Veitch's time in Australia more interesting 'in many ways'. James Veitch too wrote Sir William a letter conveying appreciation for the 'kindness and the trouble you have taken to let John have anything which can be of service to him'. Exactly what Sir William had provided to the peripatetic nurseryman we do not know. Yet clearly Veitch had not come to the colonies simply to see how plants sent from Chelsea acclimatised there. He had come to profit from new plants that could be collected in the wild or obtained from colonial nurseries. London nurserymen assumed the right to gather plants from all over the world.

Veitch wasted no time in taking the opportunity to explore the frontier of empire. From Sydney, he boarded HMS *Salamander* with four empty Wardian cases, bound for Somerset, near the tip of Cape York. His first collecting expedition was at Cardwell on Rockingham Bay in Queensland, where he met John Dallachy, a plant collector for the Melbourne Botanic Gardens. There was trouble in this plantsman's paradise. 'All Europeans' carried arms in the bush, while Aboriginal people were forbidden to enter the town. When Veitch reached the Cairness islands, sixty miles south-east of Cape York, 'two natives, neither of whom had a vestige of clothing on', greeted the crew by 'waving a green branch', universally recognised as a 'signal of peace'. Yet they were frightened off by 'the report of a gun', leaving our well-travelled collector to gather eucalyptus, casuarina, erythrina, ficus and *Pancratium amboynense*. Here then was paradise before and after the fall.[31]

Veitch's northern explorations would introduce London collectors to new orchids such as Lord Egerton of Tatton's dendrobe (*Dendrobium tattonianum*) and other flowering plants such as the Australian wild turmeric (*Curcuma australasica*).[32] But he did not stop there. On his return from northern Australia, he heard that Commodore Sir William Wiseman was about to depart on HMS *Curaçao* for 'the various groups of the Polynesian and Melanesian Islands'. Although a Pacific island excursion was not part of his itinerary, Veitch applied for a passage on the advice of Charles Moore, the director of the Sydney Botanic Gardens, who had visited some of the same islands in 1850. 'Such an opportunity offered too many advantages to be thrown away', Veitch wrote.[33]

Veitch contemplated his coming excursion 'with mingled feelings of expectation and satisfaction [such] as are only known to those who have experienced the infinite pleasure of lighting upon some fine plant previously unknown to English gardens'—and, of course, to his competitors. His travelling companions were to include the naturalist Julius Brenchley and the photographer Henry Kerr.[34] Before leaving Sydney in June 1865, Veitch filled eight Wardian cases with soil and gathered hatchets, knives, fishhooks and red cloth for barter.[35]

Yet often Veitch could not use these trade items because relations with the local people were so tense. On Vate (Efaté) in the New Hebrides, a local chief was held hostage on board a Presbyterian missionary ship to secure Veitch's safety while he was collecting on shore.[36] Even when he did get to shore, he was often so pressed for time that it was 'difficult to form large collections'. This was the case at Aneiteum (Anatom), 'a rich botanical field ... likely to produce many ornamental plants which would be highly valued in European gardens'. At times it was too dangerous even to land. At Tanna, 'a magnificent island teeming with vegetation', Veitch watched from the ship while the Commodore engaged in some routine gunboat diplomacy. As John wrote to his father: 'it is very vexing to see these places and not be able to explore them' for want of 'the natives' being 'friendly'.

Veitch believed there was 'a rich botanical harvest in store for some future traveller', but only 'at some future day [when] the Melanesian islands will doubtless be civilised'.[37] His view

5537.

W.Fitch,del.et.lith.

Vincent Brooks,Imp.

5690.

W.Fitch,del.et.lith.

Vincent Brooks,Imp.

Tab. VII.

W.Fitch,del.et.lith.

Vincent Brooks,Imp.

Elæocarpus Storckii, Seem. *(sp nov)*

of the islanders was shaped by popular Victorian racial theories, but his shipboard companion Julius Brenchley saw it differently. Where Veitch saw only a lack of civilisation, Brenchley detected patterns and connections that helped to create a sense of the indigenous place. On Vate (Efaté), for example, Brenchley was not perturbed when he found his path barred by a split coconut leaf fixed across two sticks stuck in the ground; rather, he recorded that the indigenous people used this as a sign to indicate that the coconut trees in the vicinity were tabu. Later, meeting a group armed with spears, clubs, hatchets, bows and poison-tipped arrows, Brenchley expressed his admiration of their handiwork, and was delighted when they agreed to 'part with some of their arms for a trifle'. He had literally disarmed people whom the authorities considered so dangerous that they would kill the two collectors unless a chief were taken hostage.

Only in places where European missionaries had 'civilised' the heathen did Veitch feel able to explore and collect unhindered. On Samoa, he attributed the abandonment of 'heathenish practices' and 'respect for life and property' to successful missionary work over the previous thirty years. Having ascertained that almost all the Samoans were 'nominally Christians', he happily spent three days in the forests on the island of Tutila 'under the guidance of a native'. By following the 'native tracks', Veitch found specimens of *Dracaena terminalis ferra*, fruit of pawpaws and Malay apples, and some of the island's 150 ferns and 90 mosses.[38]

Veitch's description of Fiji indicates how far his collecting depended on the presence of European missionaries:

> The inhabitants of these islands were at one time as savage and barbarous as any people in the world—the worst of cannibals . . . Now happily these fearful vices are ceasing. The Wesleyan missionaries are gradually Christianising the whole group . . . Europeans are established on many of the islands, and are successfully planting coffee and cotton. The flora is rich and varied.[39]

Lord Egerton of Tatton's dendrobe, *Dendrobium tattonianum*

From *Curtis's Botanical Magazine*, vol. 91, tab 5537, State Library of Victoria

Australian Wild Turmeric

Curcuma australasica, from *Curtis's Botanical Magazine*, vol. 93, tab 5620, State Library of Victoria

'The flora is rich and varied': *Elaeocarpus storckii*

Elaeocarpus storckii, from Berthold Seeman, *Flora Vitiensis. A Description of the Plants of Viti or Fiji Islands*, London, 1865–73, plate 7, State Library of Victoria

Oralau — Gulf of Curaçao. 1865

SCENE IN BANKS ISLANDS.

DRACÆNA ROBUSTA.

DRACÆNA REGINA.

CROTON HOOKERI.

Although the *Curaçao* stayed only a few days in Fiji, Veitch felt he could safely 'write volumes about the many novelties one sees when visiting such an interesting group of islands'.[40]

In the Banks Islands, Veitch found that 'the natives, although far from being Christians, are quiet and treat white men civilly', a circumstance he attributed to the influence of Bishop Patterson of Melanesia. The *Curaçao* was therefore able to land on the northern islands. Here Veitch took a 'short' walk of five or six hours (sometimes wading through swamps up to his armpits), and collected an extraordinary number of new plants: palms, ferns and mosses, coleus, Chinese hibiscus, crotons, a fine *Dracaena* with half the foliage white, and several pandanus, some growing thirty feet high.[41]

Veitch used these plants to advantage when he returned to Sydney. There was 'a grand flower show in the Botanic Gardens', where his Pacific acquisitions inspired general excitement.[42] This was a foretaste of what he would experience in Europe. In November 1866, he wrote to 'My Dear Sir William' from Chelsea to announce that his South Seas collection would be exhibited in Paris during the coming year.[43] What Paris saw prompted the French government to award John Gould Veitch the Legion of Honour in recognition of his contribution to European horticulture. An orchid was also named in Veitch's honour: Mr John Gould Veitch's orchid (*Dendrobium johannis*), collected on the north-east coast of Australia.[44] His younger brother, Harry, commented laconically to Sir William Macarthur, 'This is of course very gratifying'.[45]

While Veitch was acclaimed at home, he longed for the climate of Sydney. Writing to Sir William in the English winter of 1868, he confided: 'I feel that I should be another man in such a place as Sydney as the damp atmosphere and winter of England tries one sorely'.[46] Intimacies, confidences and a wistful longing to recapture the fleeting good fortune of youth momentarily fill a correspondence normally characterised by the promotion of the firm's business.

The next year it fell to John to inform Sir William of the unexpected death of his father, James Veitch: 'He retired to bed

In Fiji, John Gould Veitch wrote, 'I could write volumes about the many novelties one sees when visiting such an interesting island'

Henry Kerr, *Ovalau, Cruise of the Curaçao*, albumen print, 1865, Macarthur album, Mitchell Library, State Library of New South Wales

In the Banks Islands, Veitch waded through swamps up to his armpits to collect new plants

Scene in Banks Island, Julius Brenchley, *Jottings from the Cruise of the Curaçao among the South Seas Islands*, London, 1873, State Library of Victoria

Mr John Gould Veitch's orchid, *Dendrobium johannis*

From *Curtis's Botanic Magazine*, vol. 91, 1 October 1865, tab 5540, State Library of Victoria

What Paris saw: from left to right, *Croton ovalifolium, Croton hookeri, Dracaena mooreana* and *Dracaena regina*

Dracaena mooreana, from *Florist and Pomologist*, October 1872, p. 233; *Dracaena regina*, from *Florist and Pomologist*, March 1872, p. 63; *Croton hookeri*, from *Florist and Pomologist*, September 1871, p. 199; *Croton ovalifolium*, from *Florist and Pomologist*, January 1875, p. 8, State Library of Victoria

Plants sent to London by Sydney
nurserymen: *Dracaena baptistii*
(bottom) was named after a Sydney
nurseryman who corresponded with
the Veitches, while *Croton disraeli*
(top) was sent to the Veitch
nursery by A. H. McPhee of Sydney

Croton disraeli, from *Gardeners'
Chronicle*, vol. 4, 1875, p. 420;
Dracaena baptistii, from *Florist
and Pomologist*, March 1875, p. 52,
State Library of Victoria

at 10.00 pm cheerful and as far as we could see well, and at 4 am was dead'. Yet even in bereavement, his letter had a tone of business as usual; he reassured Sir William that 'our establishment is as much at your service as in my father's day'.[47] The old proprieties continued: a few days later, he thanked Sir William for offering to send some Lord Howe Island palms, and in exchange he offered a Wardian case filled 'with any plants you most wish for'.

John Gould Veitch's time managing the firm was short. His health was already weak; for several years, he had suffered from tuberculosis, and after his father's death he was advised to recuperate at Hyeres in the south of France.[48] In 1870, however, he died, and his brother Harry took over the running of the business.

In his business dealings with Sir William, Harry was far more direct than his father and elder brother. In 1873 he wrote bluntly about the threat posed by Sydney nurserymen sharing new plant discoveries with Veitch's competitors in London: 'It is a pity that the South Sea Island plants find their way into so many hands at Sydney and several people here in Europe also'. But with the help of Sir William and other friends in Sydney, the firm had managed to be 'as early in the field as anyone with all the good novelties'. For this the firm was greatly indebted to the colonial grandee.

Harry also shared business intimacies with his New South Wales customer. In terms worthy of Mrs Grundy, he pronounced: 'A conceited gardener is about the worst man that can be met with in my idea'.[49] The clear inference was that Sir William was not that sort of chap.

Rather, Sir William was an enthusiast who would do anything to keep up with the latest European horticultural fashion. During 1872, Harry sent him a copy of B. S. Williams's *Orchid Grower's Manual* in the hope that 'it may be of some service to you'—not to mention what it might do to help the firm.[50] Two years later, Harry sent dried specimens of crotons and dracaenas, with written descriptions and woodcuts, to ensure that what Sir William sent to London was new.[51]

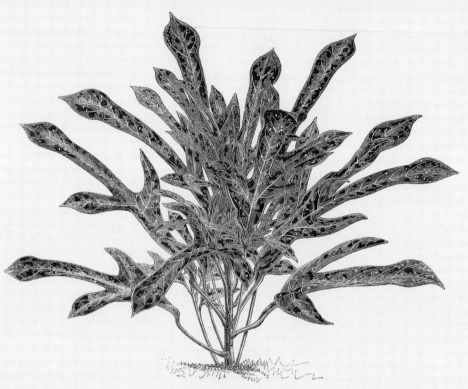

CROTON DISRAELI, VEITCH.

DRACÆNA BAPTISTII

By this means the Veitches cultivated the colonial grandee's energies, resources and on-the-ground knowledge for the benefit of their trade.

But it takes two to play these games. Harry often had to prod Sir William when he was slow to fulfil his end of the bargain. In response, Sir William would knowingly suggest that he send something that was already plentiful on the London market, so that Harry had to suggest alternatives.[52] Months might pass before Sir William attended to the matter. Tact was called for: the Veitches could never allude to Sir William's measured inaction as tardiness.

This assiduous cultivation of the client was to pay handsome dividends. The Veitches used the colonial grandee's local influence to safeguard their competitive advantage in the London market. They emphasised that plants 'should not get into the hand of two or three firms'. When a transgression occurred, the Veitches recruited Sir William to deal with it. At one point, Harry informed Sir William that a local plant collector had sent Mr Bull's London nursery specimens of some crotons that Sir William had also supplied to the Veitches. Sir William summoned the offender and upbraided him, not only to satisfy London but also to protect his own role in the trade.[53]

Sir William's correspondence with the Veitches was driven by a shared passion for collecting. While each letter from Chelsea carried intelligence about the secrets of the international plant trade, Sir William's letters kept the Veitches up to date with the doings of colonial collectors. In 1874, for example, Harry was gratified to learn that Sir William had accumulated a collection of fifty-three sorts of crotons.[54] He was even more delighted to procure specimens of all these plants the following April, as well as the palm *Kentia wendlandiana*, 'which I have never heard of before and which I think must be new to the country'. This was not an isolated incident. In 1875 Harry again thanked Sir William for 'letting us have plants from your collections before anyone else'. In return, Sir William received the latest Indian orchids and other valuable specimens.

Both parties sent plant collectors to untrodden places. After the success of John Gould Veitch's expedition, the Veitches went 'very heavily into collecting', sending collectors to Java, New Granada, Peru and Guatemala. Soon their Exeter nursery had plants from California, Peru, Chile and Patagonia growing in open beds alongside those of the Khasia Hills, Java, Malacca, the ghauts of Malabar and the provinces of Tenasserim.[55]

Sir William emulated their efforts on a smaller scale. In 1875 he despatched his gardener, Mr Reedy (who could be trusted to keep a secret), on an expedition to New Guinea. This venture was the brainchild of William Macleay, a Sydney scientific gentleman who was prepared to devote 'a portion of the riches which a smiling fortune has shed on him, to add to the world of knowledge'.[56]

News of this initiative sparked an immediate response from Harry, who hoped that the expedition would supply novelties to which the Royal Exotic Nursery would have exclusive rights. Europeans knew little of New Guinea, and Harry saw the expedition as an opportunity to 'learn something very definite' and clarify 'the varied opinions as to the New Guinea Flora'. He anticipated 'very great results from the mission'.[57]

The expedition also captured the imagination of the Victorian government botanist, Ferdinand von Mueller, who told Sir William he was particularly eager to acquire alpine plants from 'that wondrous large island', New Guinea. Von Mueller proposed a wildly optimistic timetable for the expedition. He suggested that the explorers send out an armed party and enlist the aid of the 'almost civilised' Malayan population of the north-east coast to guide the expedition 'through the lowland jungles'. He believed the collectors could ascend the mountains in three days. On the fourth, Reedy and his assistant could 'pick up any kind of plants in flower or fruit from a moss to a branchlet of a tree'. They would return on the fifth day and rest on the sixth.[58]

What was to follow was a tale of youthful naïveté and colonial cunning, of avarice in equal measure on both sides, and of the breakdown of the Veitches' artifice in cultivating Sir

CROTON MACULATUS KATONI.

THE ILLUSTRATED SYDNEY NEWS

AND NEW SOUTH WALES AGRICULTURIST AND GRAZIER.

No. 12—Vol. XI. SATURDAY, MAY 29, 1875. Price 1s. Ann. Subscription, 13s.

IMMIGRATION.

The question of immigration is likely to become a prominent one in the legislation of the leading Australian colonies. It is occupying the columns of all the chief colonial papers, and is an important part of the programme of almost every Colonial Ministry. The ambition of Queensland, the audacity of New Zealand, the hopeful tenacity of South Australia, and even the possible repentance of Victoria are all tending in the same direction, and if New South Wales will not lead the way, at least the force of circumstances will compel her to follow. Already our Legislature has been occupied with the subject, and Mr. Piddington's resolutions will probably prove of more lasting importance than Mr. Robertson's fragment of Land Reform. Whether the present session will afford an opportunity for their discussion is extremely doubtful; but the time is auspicious and the condition of the colony favourable, and therefore both the measure and the men to carry it out are almost sure to be forthcoming. The resolutions themselves need not be accepted as a full and adequate statement of the case. One of them proposes the establishment of an Immigration Board, under whose direction the funds shall be expended and the whole business conducted. Against this proposal it was forcibly argued that a Board withdraws some portion of public business from that direct control of Parliament which is one of the most essential requisites of Representative Governments. It is of the utmost importance that government should be encouraged in these colonies, in the form of municipal institutions, wherever possible; but for national purposes the interposition of intermediate Boards between a responsible

NEW GUINEA EXPEDITION.—SKETCHES ON THE DEPARTURE OF THE "CHEVERT."

1. HOME, SWEET HOME!   2. RECEPTION OF MR. MACLEAY ON BOARD THE "COONANBARA."   3. A BLOW AFTER LUNCH.   4. THE LUNCH.
5. EMBARKING ON THE "CHEVERT."   6. THE LAST FAREWELL.

NEW SOUTH WALES STATE LIBRARY STAMP

William. Yet the story began full of promise and high hopes. The plant collectors left Sydney for New Guinea on the *Chevert* in May 1875. Also on board were Sir William's nephew, Captain Macarthur Onslow, and the sponsor of the expedition, Mr Macleay.

For all Macleay's scientific erudition, one inconvenient fact had been overlooked. It was the dry season in New Guinea, and the Fly River was low. As a result, the *Chevert* had to beat an early retreat.[59]

Although his mission was cut short, Macarthur's gardener, Mr Reedy, diligently collected plants and specimens whenever he could. He brought back pressed specimens from Darnley and Yule islands in the Torres Strait, and from the Katan and Baxter rivers in New Guinea.[60] He also collected hundreds of potted plants and several small trees. Laden with this booty, the *Chevert* returned to Sydney in December 1875.[61] All these plants came into Sir William's possession.

But what were these plants? To find this out, Sir William sent Reedy's pressed specimens to Melbourne for von Mueller to describe. An unnamed plant, after all, was of little value. Later that year, von Mueller obliged by publishing his *Descriptive Notes on Papuan Plants*, which included *Elaeocarpus reedyi*, named to acknowledge Reedy's contribution.[62] Von Mueller was profuse in his tribute to Sir William, who 'still preserved a youthful ardour for scientific and especially horticultural research', despite being 'in the autumn of a long laborious life, spent for the pastoral, agricultural and industrial interest of Australia'.[63]

Amid this mutual congratulation, the English journal *The Garden* kept a level head about the value of Sir William's collection. With true metropolitan disdain, the *Garden* sniffed that von Mueller's descriptions of the plants Reedy had collected contained 'almost nothing new'. The first-time efforts of a colonial gardener could not be compared to the discoveries of the Italian plant-hunter Odoardo Beccari (1843–1920), whose 'magnificent Borneon collections' had already 'enriched' many a herbarium. *The Garden* was sure that Beccari's most

A photograph of Harry Veitch later in life

From James Veitch, *Hortus Veitchii*, London, 1906, Archives of the Royal Botanic Gardens, Melbourne

Croton maculatus katoni, one of many plants sent to the Veitches by Sir William Macarthur

From *Florist and Pomologist*, February 1879, p. 27, State Library of Victoria

The *Chevert* leaves Sydney for New Guinea

New Guinea Expedition. Sketches on the Departure of the Chevert, from *Illustrated Sydney News*, 29 May 1875, State Library of New South Wales

recent voyage to Dutch New Guinea would 'add much to our knowledge of the flora of that interesting region'.[64]

Even so, news of Sir William's New Guinea collection created enough interest in England to induce other London nurserymen to sound him out about selling plants to the London trade. Information about his intentions was keenly sought. Soon the knight of Camden was receiving solicitous letters inquiring if these new plants might be seen or purchased.

Among Sir William's new correspondents was a would-be plant collector, Andrew Goldie, 'just arrived from England'.[65] Goldie had been engaged by B. S. Williams, proprietor of 'one of the largest of the London nurseries' and author of *The Orchid Grower's Manual* (the same book Harry Veitch had sent Sir William in 1872). Goldie had been instructed 'to purchase or make arrangement with any gentlemen hear [*sic*] to exchange for plants they may have got'.[66] If this was not possible, Goldie asked Sir William if he might see 'the plants just come from New Guinea' to give him 'an idea of what is in that unknown island'.[67]

Harry Veitch too had been considering a voyage to the colonies; in 1874 he had wistfully written to Sir William 'I live in hope of seeing you in Sydney'.[68] In the event, however, he sent his younger cousin Peter.[69] Peter Veitch disembarked in Sydney after Sir William had received the first consignment of Reedy's collections, but Peter seemed reluctant to visit Camden. The South Seas beckoned. Peter set sail for Fiji almost immediately in the schooner *Renard*, and then secured a passage on a South Seas trading vessel in February 1876.[70] The only communication Sir William received from this botanical wanderer was a note expressing Peter's desire 'to hear further particulars about Reedy' and see Sir William's orchids.[71] This was a far cry from the intimacies and intelligence Sir William had received in earlier times from John Gould Veitch.

Sir William for his part was determined to recoup every penny of the £500 he had spent sending Reedy to New Guinea —and to make a profit.[72] The Veitches had taught him how to play the game of talking up new plant discoveries, and he easily outmatched the inexperienced Peter. The old fox began by taking up von Mueller's offer to 'name any new orchids from the South Sea islands or elsewhere' in the Camden conservatories.[73] Von Mueller identified one of the orchids Reedy had collected as a new species, which he called *Dendrobium sumneri*. Next, Sir William sought von Mueller's opinion of the orchid's commercial value, and was told that 'as yet *Dendrobium sumneri* has not entered European conservatories where . . . it would be regarded as a very showy one'. In general, von Mueller was of the view that plants from New Guinea 'surely ought to be of high value in London'.[74]

Armed with this knowledge and aware that nurserymen were prone to irrational enthusiasms, Sir William decided to extract full value from the Veitches. Knowing well that unfulfilled desire would boost the price of a new plant on the market, he held out the intoxicating prospect of unknown plants from an unexplored region. Yet Sir William already knew from Charles Moore that Andrew Goldie had sent off 'six cases of plants . . . collected on the very ground' where Reedy had obtained his specimens.[75] If this intelligence perturbed Sir William, he did not show it. Instead, he gambled that Peter would not find out until after they had made the deal.

When their agreement was concluded in September, Peter displayed unprecedented largesse, offering Sir William plants valued at £800.[76] Peter also ordered a large consignment of *Dendrobium bigibbum* and *D. sumneri*—'a thousand of each kind to commence with'.[77]

For all his inexperience, Peter well knew the secrecy that surrounded securing plants for the London market. He reminded Sir William: 'I believe you promised, and Reedy as well, that none of the New Guinea plants shall be given away to anyone until such time as my friends are able to send them out in England and get some return for their outlay'. Sir William was told the state of play directly: 'You know I presume . . . that if only one plant of any of the species reach England before we send it out, it will materially alter our sale'.[78]

Drawn from Nature & on Stone by R.D.Fitzgerald F.L.S

DENDROBIUM bigibbum

Printed at the Department of Lands Sydney N.S.W. Feb.r 1891

Secure in the knowledge that Sir William would honour his agreement, Peter now set out in search of still more plants. In October 1876 he went to Brisbane, encouraged by Charles Moore; next came Bathurst and Mount Victoria in New South Wales, and then a trip to Melbourne in November.[79] By January 1877, Peter was writing from New Zealand, where he was collecting ferns and visiting the Lake District. He told Sir William that he had called on Andrew Goldie 'to find out what he has sent Home'. At this point, Peter presumably discovered the information Sir William had withheld. Peter now had doubts about the transaction: 'I almost fear I promised too much', he told Sir William. 'The price is good, in fact on second consideration I am afraid it is too high'. Brushing aside these reservations, however, Peter decided to 'let it remain as it is'.[80]

In the event, Peter was right to have misgivings. Sir William's New Guinea crotons sold badly, 'there being so many good kinds at Home'. To make matters worse, the first consignment did not travel well. When the Wardian cases were opened, Harry gave 'a very indifferent account of their contents'. All the crotons apart from *reedyi* had lost their leaves, while the palms were 'as yellow and dried in foliage as if they had been in an oven'.[81] Harry was at a loss 'to account for so great a number of deaths': some of the cases were too dry, but the plants were 'just as bad in the cases which are damp'. He expressed the hope that 'they may turn out better than they look but I really fear they will not'.

Despite this setback, the correspondence between gentleman and Chelsea nurseryman was all politeness. Harry adopted a conciliatory tone, tempered by practicality; he named 'the sorts we most wish to receive again'. In his letter to Peter, however, he privately expressed his dismay at the price offered for the plants; and it was Peter, lacking his cousin's business acumen, who told Sir William that the Veitches were concerned about the profitability of the project.[82]

Experience may have contributed to Harry's *sang-froid*. This was not the first time that plants from foreign climes had arrived in a parlous state. It was best to remain level-headed—

'It would be regarded as a very showy one': detail of *Dendrobium sumneri* (also known as *Dendrobium phalaenopsis*)

From R. D. Fitzgerald, *Australian Orchids*, Sydney 1882–1893, Archives of the Royal Botanic Gardens, Melbourne

Peter Veitch ordered a large consignment of *Dendrobium bigibbum*: 'a thousand . . . to commence with'

From R. D. Fitzgerald, *Australian Orchids*, Sydney, 1882–1893, State Library of Victoria

DENDROBIUM GOLDIEI.

to point out the needs of the London market and hope the orchids sent under different cover would arrive safely.

Still, Harry was concerned to recoup the firm's investment. In 1877 he auctioned a new orchid, the purple-flowering *Dendrobium superbiens*, which Professor Reichenbach had described as 'a most striking novelty', 'easily distinguished' from the more common *Dendrobium bigibbum*. By auctioning this plant, they broke their agreement with Sir William, which had stipulated that on no account were small numbers of new plants to be released on the London market. Furthermore, the catalogue had the temerity to tell the whole world that Sir William had consigned only six of the plants, which were 'unfortunately very rare'. The catalogue also quoted Reedy's opinion that it was the finest dendrobium he had ever seen, being a very free flowerer and having twenty flowers per spike.[83] By scientifically verifying the orchid, publishing it as a new species and exhibiting it at the Royal Horticultural Society (where it was awarded a first-class certificate), the Veitches turned colonial hyperbole to their advantage at the expense of 'My Dear Sir William'. In this way London translated colonial discovery into a profitable commercial language.

The reaction? Indignation on Sir William's part, a spirited defence on Harry's. Reminding Sir William of the competitive state of the London market, Harry wrote:

> Can you blame us for getting as much as we could for these six, knowing more were to follow, and not knowing how soon Mr Goldie might send some to Mr Williams or Mr Bull might get some from his correspondent . . .? I really think not.[84]

At last the real intent of the thirty-year correspondence between grand signor and metropolitan plant trader was revealed. The salutation 'My Dear Sir William' could no longer mask the toughness of those who profited from selling botanical novelties. The enthusiasm and deference that oiled the friendly correspondence of old had now given way to plain writing.

What Goldie sent 'Home': *Dendrobium goldiei*

From *The Garden*, 14 September 1878, plate 140, State Library of Victoria

'A most striking novelty':
Dendrobium superbiens

From F. Sander, *Reichenbachia: Orchids
Illustrated and Described*, London,
1888, plate 36, State Library of Victoria

Inside the dendrobium house at
James Veitch & Sons' nursery, 1883

*Messrs James Veitch & Sons'
Dendrobium House*, 1883, from
Gardeners' Chronicle, 7 April 1883,
p. 441, State Library of Victoria

At the same time, Harry Veitch had hardly been impetuous. It required patience to bring new plants to market. Specimens from distant climes arrived without flowers, and often without foliage. They had to be nursed back to health, and more time had to elapse before flowers would bloom. Even when they did, the blooms had to satisfy fickle fashion.

Before he wrote his less-than-temperate epistle to Sir William, Harry had been patient. He waited for the *Tapeinochilus* to flower before concluding that this 'shy blooming plant of not good habit' would never be of any value. Similarly, when Reedy's crotons had returned to full vigour after their travels across the oceans and the equator, he dismissed them as inferior to varieties already in cultivation such as 'Lord Derby', 'Disraeli' and 'Wiseman'. There is nothing a nurseryman abhors more than an unsaleable plant.

Sir William had promised much, and the Veitches had been tantalised by the prospect of the rare and the new. They had hoped for a business bonanza, but their expectations had been disappointed. Even orchids soon lost their allure in London; by the time Harry wrote to Sir William in November 1877, *Dendrobium bigibbum* was 'a drug on the market', while *D. superbiens* had reached 'another London firm this week'. Peter's arrangement with Sir William had proved 'a dead loss, there is no doubt, as we shall never make the cost price of the plants'.[85]

Sir William's protests were met with a mixture of honesty and prevarication. On one hand, Harry boldly declared: 'My cousin made a bad bargain and we must abide by it, but I want you to see we really have reason to lose by the affair'. On the other, old habits died hard; Harry expressed sincere regret that Peter's visit had 'caused a less friendly feeling to exist between you and ourselves than had been the case for many years'. He tried to salve the sore by emphasising the firm's loyalty to their longstanding client, but his letter was also a lesson in commercial realities.

FIG. 66.—MESSRS. JAMES VEITCH AND SONS' DENDROBIUM HOUSE. (SEE P. 440.)

Sir William was already aware of the disquiet felt in Chelsea. Peter had let the cat out of the bag several months earlier, when he wrote:

> It was only the day before yesterday that I received my cousin's letter saying how very disappointed he felt that there were not a greater variety of genera among the plants and again remarking . . . that Crotons were altogether at a discount.[86]

Peter was already afraid that 'we shall lose money by the transaction'. He was dismayed at his own lack of acumen, concluding: 'I am afraid Harry will be very downhearted with my trip'.

Throughout the letter, Peter assumed that Sir William knew what was happening in Chelsea: '[Harry] has no doubt written to you in very much the same strain as he wrote to me so I do not therefore need to particularise his objections to my purchase'. Harry, however, had done no such thing. Tact rather than truth was his guiding principle. It was not until November that he wrote to Sir William broaching the subject of his cousin's unsuccessful commercial arrangements.

Receiving two different stories from his London suppliers, Sir William must have been cognisant of the ill feeling that had arisen. This may have contributed to his feeling that he had acted generously but was being wronged. After all, he had given the Royal Exotic Nursery first option on the plants Reedy had collected in New Guinea. The point was not disputed by Harry, who wrote in his epistle of woes: 'Did I not thank you for offering us the New Guinea Plants? and have never withdrawn that?' Harry closed by reminding Sir William of his contractual obligations. He must destroy all excess stock and ensure that no plant of any kind was let out of his hands, as 'plants when once distributed get spreading in so mysterious a way'.[87]

And who had the last word? Harry or Peter Veitch? It was the straight-shooting Peter who ended the firm's thirty-year correspondence to Sir William Macarthur in July 1879 with a wonderfully upfront and defamatory statement: 'Sydney gardeners are great thieves'.[88] This was a far cry from the honeyed words his forebears had used to woo 'My Dear Sir William', the colony's leading amateur gardener. In horticulture as elsewhere, the English visitor could always gain the ascendancy by taking the high moral ground. There's the colonial rub.

Thomas Lang

The Million~Plant Man

Verbenas
1. Foxhunter. — 2. Fairest of the Fair.
Plate 182.

The Million-Plant Man

Thomas Lang (1815–1896) was a remarkable nurseryman. In the twelve years to 1870, he brought almost a million living trees, shrubs and vegetables to Victoria and propagated them in a clearing in the forest outside Ballarat.[1] In the opinion of his fellow Ballarat nurseryman George Smith, Lang was 'one of the most enterprising men we ever had in introducing new plants for experimental purposes'. 'If there is any man in the colony we are indebted to for introducing new plants', Smith added, Thomas Lang was that man.[2]

Lang introduced colonial gardeners to 'a great variety of European, Asiatic and American ornamental fruit trees', including 150 varieties of apples, 150 pears, 60 plums, 50 cherries, 115 gooseberries and 50 grapes, as well as new sorts of apricots, peaches, figs, Spanish chestnuts and walnuts. All these were tested 'to assess their suitability to colonial conditions'.

He claimed to have been first to import many plants. In 1853, a year before he migrated to Australia, he became the first nurseryman in Scotland to sell the Kilmarnock weeping willow (*Salix caprea* var *Pendula*). Ten years later, he introduced this willow to Victoria.[3] He also claimed to have introduced colonial gardeners to the Californian redwood, a tree whose stupendous size fired the nineteenth-century imagination. Among his other introductions were the golden spruce, the silver poplar, the purple laburnum, the rich-leaved Corstorphine plane and two varieties of weeping elm.[4]

Living plants arrived from London by means of the Wardian case. Lang related the history of this revolutionary invention in an 1862 lecture to the Ballarat Horticultural Society 'On Wardian or Plant Cases'.[5] He had first encountered a Wardian case in Scotland when he visited his friend James McNab (1810–1878), son of the curator of the Royal Edinburgh Botanic Gardens and himself an active collector.[6] In McNab's parlour, Lang saw 'a very neat miniature greenhouse containing a number of beautiful plants growing vigorously and flowering profusely'. He was astonished to learn that these specimens had spent twelve months in the case without water or fresh air.

If there was 'any man in the colony we are indebted to for introducing new plants', Thomas Lang was that man

Mr and Mrs Thomas Lang and family on their golden wedding day c. 1882, Castlemaine Art Gallery and Historical Museum

'Foxhunter', a verbena of the 'richest and brightest scarlet', released in 1861

Verbena Foxhunter, from the *Florist*, November 1861, plate 182, State Library of Victoria

The Wardian case had come to public attention in 1842 when its inventor, Dr Nathaniel Ward (1791–1868), published a treatise *On the Growth of Plants in Closely Glazed Cases*.[7] Since then, 'many thousands of Wardian cases filled with plants had been transported to the most remote quarters of the globe'. As a result, the gardens of England and Europe were now 'decorated with gorgeous plants of Brazil, the rich novelties of Japan and Borneo'. Chinese curiosities too had been 'introduced alive into the pleasure grounds of our countrymen at home'.

To illustrate his lecture, Lang showed his audience two Wardian cases recently arrived from England. The standard case was like an open-roofed greenhouse with wire netting to protect the glass, and stood on little feet to steady it on the ship's deck. The other was a newly patented flat-roofed model that had arrived only three months earlier on the *Great Britain* (the ship in which Lang had sailed to Sydney in 1854[8]). In it were 'a large number of the latest and choicest acquisitions to English horticulture', planted in 'a general soil bed of mixed peat and sand' instead of the customary pots. This kept the soil humid and the plants healthy.[9]

There was no doubt in Lang's mind that Wardian cases promoted 'the comfort, the pleasures, the commercial interests, the happiness of mankind'. He cited the case's greatest success: in 1853, the plant-hunter Robert Fortune had sent 100 000 living tea plants from China to Calcutta, establishing the Indian tea industry and breaking the Chinese monopoly. Lang's introduction of plants into Victoria, while not on quite the same heroic scale, would also help to transform a colonial territory and enhance its economic value to the Empire.

Lang had begun his business modestly in 1856, when he established a seed store and adjoining nursery in Main Street, Ballarat East, selling everyday plants such as sage and thyme.[10] He also acquired a half-acre block in Ballarat West, on the corner of Lyons and Eyre streets. Here he expended 'much time and care' in cultivation, using his garden as an experimental plot.

He began his garden in July 1857, planting an orchard of peaches and plums. In October of the same year he sowed seeds of the Victoria rhubarb, which were harvested in March 1859. He also had high hopes for a Chinese yam, which grew and grew for three full summers, reaching a height of sixteen feet. Yet its crop of roots was not commensurate with its gargantuan size.

His flower garden was luxuriant, with choice varieties of roses, gladioli, fifty or sixty different hollyhocks and 120 types of dahlias, all imported from England. Nothing could suppress Thomas Lang's enthusiasm; it seemed there was always room for at least one more plant. Today it might be *Aralia japonica*, a 'very pretty shrub' that had of late become a 'great favourite' of the Queen; tomorrow, *Tritona media*, a bulbous plant with sword-like leaves, which Her Majesty had planted at her Isle of Wight residence. In his rare moments of leisure, Lang could gaze on these floral emblems of loyalty and feel pleased to be so connected to his monarch.

His enthusiasm for new plants was constantly fired by news of what was available in London. From 1848 until at least 1867, he subscribed to the *Gardeners' Chronicle* and the *Florist* (from which many of the illustrations in this chapter are drawn).[11] He scoured the British horticultural press for the latest hybrids and plant discoveries. Among these were 'Foxhunter', a verbena of the 'richest and brightest scarlet', launched by the London nurseryman Hugh Low in 1861,[12] and the double-flowering 'Matthieu' petunia, greatly admired for its purple-rose flowers spotted with white when it was exhibited in London during 1862.[13]

Not to be forgotten were those arbiters of mid-Victorian taste, the conifers. In spring 1857, Lang sowed Italian stone pines (*Pinus pinea*), which within two-and-a-half years were five feet tall. He pronounced the stone pine to be 'both useful and ornamental'.[14]

Encouraged by this success, the indefatigable horticultural-ist planted at least ten more varieties on that ever more crowded half-acre, including 'a very fine plant of *Cupressus*

Pinus Pinea

Araucaria imbricata

macrocarpa' and as many araucarias as he could. Others included the black Austrian pine (*Pinus austriaca*) and the Scots pine (*Pinus sylvestris*), both 'well adapted to our country'. Amid all this dark green, he planted golden spruce (*Thuja aurea*).[15]

William Elliott, who became Lang's business partner in November 1860,[16] also recognised that the Australian climate limited what the ambitious gardener could grow. He outlined some of these limitations in 1865, when he addressed the Ballarat Horticultural Society on the subject of 'Deciduous Trees Adapted to the Climate'.

Deciduous trees, Elliott argued, had both economic and ornamental value; yet, 'being natives of temperate climates', they were not 'generally adapted to bear the heat of countries where the temperature rises so high as in these latitudes and where the air during summer is so extremely dry'.[17] In Europe, the linden (*Tilia europea*) grew to ninety or a hundred feet, but in Victoria it would only succeed in a 'very sheltered' situation. Similarly the horse chestnut, 'one of the largest sized and handsomest of trees, remarkable for the beauty of its flowers', could not bear Ballarat's hot summer winds.

It was difficult to judge if the new trees imported over the previous decade would grow as tall in the colonies as they did in their original habitats. So much remained unknown. Would the tulip tree (*Liriodendron tulipifera*), 'one of the most magnificent trees of the temperate zone', reach 120 feet in Victoria, as it did in North America? After careful observation of twenty liriodendrons imported in May 1861, Elliott was not convinced they would.[18] He came to similar conclusions about the North American sweet bay (*Magnolia glauca*), which grew in swamps from Massachusetts to Florida, and *Magnolia macrophylla* from the mountains of South Carolina, a plant Lang had imported in 1861.[19] Requiring moisture, deep soil and humid air, these magnolias could not be 'expected to thrive in this climate except in very peculiar situations'.

Lang sowed Italian stone pines in his garden during the spring of 1857

Seeds of Pinus pinea, from Aylmer Bourke Lambert, *A Description of the Genus Pinus*, 1832, State Library of Victoria

A young Chilean monkey puzzle tree—just right for Lang's half-acre garden

Araucaria imbricata, from Aylmer Bourke Lambert, *A Description of the Genus Pinus*, 1832, State Library of Victoria

Magnolia glauca (now *Magnolia virginiana*) grew in swamps from Massachusetts to Florida, and did not acclimatise to the colony except in 'very peculiar situations'

Margaret Stones, *Magnolia virginiana*, private collection

Elliott compiled a list of the imported trees he thought were suited to the colony. He singled out plane trees as 'the finest . . . we have'. Both the western plane (*Platanus occidentalis*) and the oriental plane (*Platanus orientalis*) would 'thrive equally well in this country'. He also believed that English oaks would grow successfully, as they would 'thrive in any kind of soil'.[20] But the hot Australian summers remained the real enemies of the nurseryman's dream of planting Australia with foreign flowers and fruits. Indeed, Elliott observed that a brief exposure to the colony's hot winds could do more damage than the long sea voyage from London.[21]

Lang too was aware of the need to protect tender plants from the 'vehement assaults of the hot winds of summer'. To this end, in October 1857 he had planted a shelter belt of quick-growing blue gums along the north-western boundary of his suburban garden. Even so, he struggled to raise trees from cold climates. Only one out of 10 000 'vigorous seedlings' of the Norway spruce (*Abies excelsa*) survived the summer heat. A similar fate befell the European larch (*Larix europaea*), a native of the elevated regions of Switzerland. In spring 1859, Lang sowed a liberal amount of larch seed. When the summer heat arrived, he was well prepared: he watered the seedlings copiously and covered them with calico awnings, which he removed only after sunset if the weather was cloudy. Despite this cosseting, by autumn 1860 only 2000 plants survived, and even these were reported to be 'in imminent danger from the fervid rays of the sun'.

By the late 1850s, Lang was finding his Eyre Street property too small for the extraordinary number of plants and seeds he raised, so he took up twenty acres at Mount Warrenheip, five miles from Ballarat in the Bullarook forest,[22] in a clearing 'surrounded with timber on every side'.[23] Here, he established a bedding-out nursery to acclimatise imported plants. In 1865, when John Gould Veitch visited Warrenheip, he pronounced it 'one of the few Australian establishments' planted on a large scale 'with the order and method of an English hardy nursery'.[24]

The climate and soil were 'everything that could be desired'; almost every class of plant was found to thrive. There were 'fruits of every description' (even oranges) and 'a great many forest trees of all sorts'.[25]

Lang would later describe developing his nursery as 'an arduous and expensive undertaking', and one 'fraught with anxiety'. In Ballarat town, he had a seed warehouse and greenhouses to accommodate 'new European introductions and a collection of soft wooded plants'.[26] By 1866, he had outlaid £5000; his expenses exceeded sales until 1865.[27]

With all these new facilities, Lang could indulge his enthusiasm for introducing 'new races' from the 'old world'.[28] In 1860 he ordered pelargonium seed from the Belgian nurseryman Louis van Houtte, who had collected plants in Brazil.[29] The following year, he obtained 'a parcel of East India seeds from the shoulders of the Himalayan mountains', including the sacred cedar (*Cedrus deodara*), the lofty Bhutan cypress (*Cupressus torulosa*) and other conifers. At the same time, a collection of seeds arrived from Shanghai. Lang cannily displayed these in the window of his shop with Chinese labels to entice Chinese market gardeners. In 1858 he encouraged customers by offering them 'a few' free seeds of exotic-sounding melons: the Early Sugar Melon, Portugal Black Rock Melon, Persian or Odessa Melon, and the red-and-black-fleshed Maltese Melon.[30]

Lang was quick to recognise the commercial possibilities of the mushrooming colonial gold towns. His *Monthly Calendar* (first issued in hundreds and then thousands) sought to 'show how the garden . . . can be turned to the greatest profit with the least possible expense'.[31] He realised that the miner's allotment could be transformed through ornamental plantings in the front yard and utilitarian ones in the back, creating the suburban villa allotment so familiar today. At the same time, beyond the boundary of these villas, the planting of street trees and the provision of parks could create a coherent urban vision amid the disorder created by mining and mass immigration. Lang's ideas here betray the influence of British urban reformers, who since the 1830s had championed

Ballarat in 1870. In the distance is Mt
Warrenheip, where Lang established
his nursery in a clearing

Eugene von Guérard, *Ballarat from
the Tower of the Western Fire Brigade*,
La Trobe Picture Collection,
State Library of Victoria

The 'Scarlet Pearmain' apple,
which Lang advertised for sale
in 1870, had partial resistance
to American Blight

David Boyle, *Scarlet Pearmain*,
Archives of the Royal Botanic
Gardens, Melbourne

the virtues of the suburban villa allotment and public parks in industrial towns.[32]

For Lang, gardening was a public pursuit that enriched the civic domain. In July 1860, he assumed the 'honorary and honourable office of superintendent of municipal plantations' in Ballarat East.[33] He undertook to have these plantations growing within a year. Remembering that blue gums had grown rapidly in his home garden and wanting to elevate them to 'the dignity of municipal trees', he wrote to the Melbourne Botanic Gardens asking Ferdinand Mueller for seeds of these trees. Lang complemented these blue gums with lightwoods, which he grew from seed collected in 'the dark forest' of Bullarook, outside Ballarat. In November he reported that 'some plants of both species had made their appearance above ground while others were just preparing to burst the clods which covered them'.

Yet Lang had failed to reckon with 'the attacks of the inhabitants who dwelt in the neighbourhood of the gardens'. With mock seriousness, he detailed how 'the canine race' had broken down fences and 'waged fierce war upon one another inside the very precincts of the municipal enclosures', making a battlefield of 'land which was destined for more peaceful purposes'. Then there were cats, those 'feline tribes', which 'exhibited their taste for gardenesque and picturesque scenery' by indulging in 'nocturnal rambles over the freshly dug soil'.

Dogs and cats, however, could not match the havoc created by 'man and the children of men'. Armed with dangerous metallic missiles such as salmon tins and sardine boxes, the denizens of Ballarat East attacked the tender young trees from a distance, pelting some to death. Lang was outraged that even 'woman, the sweet companion of man' had 'endeavoured to influence the destinies of some of the young plants by bestowing upon them a shower of water heated to the temperature of 212 degrees Fahrenheit'. He attributed these 'wicked deeds' to 'hatred toward young trees'. The more Lang puffed, the less the residents responded. They were unmoved by the prospect that

THOMAS LANG

Scarlet Pearmain

Ripe in the end of April

Grown by the Author

in Numawading 1879

Pyrogenium.

their houses would 'forever remain exposed to the scorching rays of the infuriated sun'.

To protect the municipal plantations from these 'barbarians', Lang recommended that 'the peaceful and cultivated' form an association to 'restore to the district the honourable character of civilisation and taste'.[34] In Lang's mind, people were distinguished by intellect and merit, not social rank. In 1862–63 he became president of the Ballarat Mechanics Institute, a temple to the virtues of self-improvement.[35] His resourceful wife, Matilda, appears to have shared these values. She established a school for young ladies in Ballarat, and also invented a washing machine to end domestic drudgery.[36]

Lang insisted that he had established his business 'not only from selfish and mercenary motives' but out of a desire to contribute to the 'public good'.[37] These values informed his attempts to solve the problem of American apple blight, a disease caused by the introduction of an aphid (*Aphis lanigera*), which threatened Victorian apple production. After reading George Lindley's *Guide to the Orchard*, which mentioned that Majetin apple stock was resistant to the blight, in 1863 Lang imported twenty-four Majetins from Norwich and proceeded to 'cultivate and propagate them on a large scale', advertising them for sale in his 1870 catalogue. He also offered several varieties of apple with partial resistance to the blight, among them the 'Scarlet Pearman'.[38] At a time when 'the culture of fruit was becoming extremely precarious', Lang's Majetin stock enabled Victorian orchardists to 'continue their operations with satisfaction and profit'.[39]

These efforts were publicised by the agriculture writer W. H. Treen, FRHS, who had been the proprietor of Victoria Nursery in Ruby, Warwickshire, before emigrating to Australia.[40] At Warrenheip, Treen saw 700 Majetin roots, 'all perfectly clean and very healthy', and resolved to make the results of Lang's experiments known through a detailed story in the Melbourne *Weekly Times*.[41] Lang was long remembered for his part in ameliorating the 'fearful destruction caused by American blight', and was honoured by a public testimonial in 1886.[42]

Lang's belief in self-improvement and public duty was strongly influenced by his upbringing. His father, Major Andrew Lang (1779–1870), son of a Scottish clergyman, had gone to the West Indies, intending to become a sugar planter.[43] In the event, he had settled on the island of St Croix, where he established an observatory for navigational purposes and maintained it at his own expense. Thomas Lang told Sir William Macarthur that his father 'used to give the time to the shipping daily and the shipmasters . . . used to bring their chronometers regularly to him to rectify their time'.[44] For this 'life of honourable usefulness', Major Lang was knighted by the King of Denmark, whose dominions included St Croix.[45]

Lang was sent back to Scotland to be trained by his uncle, the nurseryman Thomas Sawson. Here, he was exposed to new ideas about social reform, especially the movement known as phonography, which advocated the introduction of phonetic spelling as an aid to universal literacy. Lang became excited by the 'beautiful details' of this system in 1842, when he heard a lecture by Benn Pitman, brother of the inventor of Pitman's shorthand, at the Kilmarnock Philosophical Institute. Lang eventually joined the Phonetic Council, whose members included William Gregory (1803–1858), professor of chemistry at Edinburgh University, and the naturalist Sir Walter Trevelyan.[46]

Lang preached the phonetic gospel to all who would listen. He gave a weekly lecture at the Kilmarnock New Academy, disseminated his ideas in the *Phonetic Journal* and placed extracts from the journal in the Kilmarnock press.[47] He was also treasurer of the Kilmarnock Library in 1851, and attended the Kilmarnock Philosophical Institute.[48] He even conducted pedagogical experiments, inviting friends who were bankers, lawyers, clergymen, doctors—'educated men in fact'—to observe him teaching 'ragged boys entirely ignorant of reading' to read phonetically, a task he successfully accomplished in six weeks. His own eldest daughter learnt to read by perusing elementary phonetic books prepared by a missionary to the Micmac people of Canada, and by retiring to a corner

Cupressus lambertiana was among
the plants Thomas Rivers sent
to Lang in 1858

Cupressus lambertiana at Osborne,
from Edward Ravenscroft, *The
Pinetum Britannicum*, Edinburgh,
1884, vol. 2, plate 33, State Library of
Victoria

Camellia 'Countess of Derby',
which Lang imported in 1864

Camellia Countess of Derby, from the
Florist, November 1859, plate 157,
State Library of Victoria

Thomas Lang's town nursery in
Ballarat, showing the greenhouses

*View of Lang's Nursery, Corner of
Dana and Albert Sts Ballarat*,
albumen print, *c.* 1865, Ballarat
Historical Parks Association

at home and immersing herself in *Chambers' Edinburgh Journal*.[49]

In Lang's vision of a social meritocracy, gardeners were intellectually 'in a class above the mere hewer of wood and drawer of water'. Yet in his dealings with the great houses of Scotland and Ireland, he had observed that the British landed classes tended to treat the gardener as 'an uneducated unintelligent labourer'. If landowners persisted in this attitude, he warned, gardeners would become 'rebellious, dissatisfied and disagreeable'.[50]

When Thomas Lang emigrated, he left this prejudice behind. In Victoria, he could realise his aspirations in a more fluid social milieu. He built up an extraordinary network of contacts with the leading British nurserymen of the age.

His first consignment, sent on New Year's Day 1858, came from the famous Thomas Rivers (1789–1877) of Sawbridgeworth in Hertfordshire, renowned for his fruit trees and roses. Aware of the commercial potential of the overseas trade, Rivers had devised a unique method of packing his plants in Irish peat charcoal inside their Wardian cases.[51] Lang's consignment included cherries, pears and plums, Manetti rose stock, two species of holly and pines from all parts of the globe.[52] From South America there were monkey puzzles (*Araucaria araucana*), from India sacred cedars (*Cedrus deodara*) and from California *Cupressus lambertiana*.

Rivers's second consignment in May 1860 contained a dazzling array of fruit trees—precious commodities in a colony starved of fresh produce. There were hundreds of grafting stock, as well as pears ('Prince Albert', 'Winter Nelis' and 'Beurres'), plums ('Rivers' Early Prolific', 'Purple Gage' and 'Ettiene'), cherries ('Empress Eugenie', 'Governor Wood' and 'Ohio Beauty'), an apple ('Cox's Orange Pippin') and a single peach. To 'prove their adaptability to the climate and correctness to name', all these were planted at Warrenheip.[53]

By this time, Lang was obtaining conifers from another eminent English nurserymen, Hugh Low (1793–1863) of Clapton.[54] Low's first order included six Californian

CYPRESSUS LAMBERTIANA.
AT OSBORNE.

Camellia.
Countess of Derby.
Plate 157.

redwoods, thirty sacred cedars and sixteen monkey puzzles.[55] The orders steadily increased in size. In 1862, Low sent a hundred sacred cedars and yet more redwoods, and in 1866 Lang paid £10 for a thousand monkey puzzles, which were shipped in two Wardian cases on the *Dover Castle*.[56]

From Low, Lang obtained plants within months of their release in England. In July 1861, Low advertised the Californian Douglas fir and Western red cedar, both new introductions raised from seed collected by the renowned Californian plant-hunter William Lobb. Both arrived in Ballarat in August 1862.[57] In the same year, Low sent new pines from Mexico, as yet unnamed.[58]

If these consignments from Low arrived safely, others did not. Disaster befell Lang's first major consignment of camellias, ordered in 1864. Only 140 of 260 plants survived, representing thirty-five varieties. The survivors included *Camellia* 'Imbricata', 'Double White', 'Fimbriata' and 'Beali'—already considered old-fashioned in England—along with newer hybrids such as the 'Countess of Derby', which James Veitch had imported from Italy in the autumn of 1856.[59]

Despite these mishaps, by 1870 Lang was boasting that he had the finest collection of camellias in the colony. This opinion was shared by a Melbourne journalist who reported that by 1871 Lang's Ballarat greenhouses contained 'over 160 named varieties, including English novelties of great merit'.[60] More knowing colonists were less effusive. In 1873 the new director of the Melbourne Botanic Gardens, William Guilfoyle, compared Victoria's camellias unfavourably with those of New South Wales, suggesting that they were 'very expensive', small and unreliable 'as to sorts'.[61]

Lang's collection of rhododendrons would become indisputably Victoria's best, though it too required perseverance. His first consignment of thirty-two varieties from Low arrived safely in 1863, but three years later an entire consignment from Veitch and Son was pronounced dead on arrival.[62] This did not deter Lang from adding to his collection, even if he did so more slowly. In October 1866, for example, the Veitches

THOMAS LANG

sent a mixed consignment that included only six rhododen-drons, four of which survived. Among these was the celebrated *Rhododendron dalhousiae*, described as the 'noblest species of the whole race' by Joseph Hooker, who collected it on the Nepalese frontier in 1847–52.[63]

The rhododendrons that most attracted Lang's attention, however, were the new, improved varieties bred by John Waterer (1784–1868), of the American Nurseries in Bagshot, and his brother Anthony. In November 1866, Lang ordered fifty-five rhododendrons from Low, including many of John Waterer's new varieties: the fragrant white 'Princess Alice', 'Giganteum', with its immense trusses of deep rose flowers, 'Sir Isaac Newton', 'Sir John Russell', and the conjugal couple them-selves, 'John Waterer' and 'Mrs John Waterer', released in 1855.[64] By 1868, these plants had sufficiently 'recovered from the effects of the voyage' to be offered for sale.[65]

Lang kept his rhododendrons in greenhouses, even though he appears to have selected the hardier types.[66] By 1871, he had more than eighty named varieties, and in 1874 he exhi-bited 'the largest and most varied collection of these beautiful flowers' ever seen in the colony—an exhibition comparable to 'the grand displays of this noble flower' once seen at John Waterer's nursery.[67]

For roses, Lang turned to the celebrated English rose grower William Paul (1822–1905), who had established a nursery at Waltham Cross outside London in 1860.[68] In 1862, Paul sent Lang sixty-three roses of different varieties, which arrived in the colony in March 1863. Although the timing was intended to give the plants a whole winter to recover from the voyage, all but nine had died by May.[69]

Paul was a great populariser of roses, particularly 'half blown, deeply-cupped or globular flowering' European varieties, which had previously been little known to English growers. He pro-moted these new hybrids through the horticultural press and in his illustrated *Rose Annual*. Paul's writings drew Lang's attention to other hybrid perpetuals such as *Rosa* 'Empereur de Maroc', described as possessing 'rich velvety maroon flowers';

J.D.H. del. Fitch lith.   Reeve, Benham & Reeve, imp.

RHODODENDRON DALHOUSIÆ, Hook. fil.

Rhododendron.
Dalhousiæ, album.

and the 'splendid but uncertain' variety 'General Washington', a hybrid perpetual with 'bright, rosy red flowers of large size'.[70] Another source of rose intelligence was the *Florist* magazine, which in January 1861 recommended 'Prairie de Terre Noire' ('Meadow of Black Earth') to enthusiasts with a penchant for 'hard and absurd names'.[71] By May 1862, Lang had obtained all these varieties from the Hertford rose grower Edward Parke Francis (*c*.1802–1869).[72]

Lang also developed a strong network of Australasian suppliers. In August 1859, J. J. Rule of Richmond supplied him with 'Isabella Gray', a new climbing tea rose with deep yellow flowers, introduced into England two years earlier.[73] In 1863, Lang ordered New Zealand veronicas (hebes) and variegated European hollies from Otago nurseryman George Matthews (1812–1884), who was known for his 'love of rare and fine plants'.[74]

Lang showed great persistence in pursuing the plants of his desire. Among these was the golden-rayed Japanese lily (*Lilium auratum*), which John Gould Veitch had brought back from the hillsides of Japan. This lily's spectacular flowers, nine to ten inches in diameter, 'created a sensation' at the Royal Horticultural Society's fête in July 1862.[75]

Having read about the lily in the horticultural press, Lang became determined to possess it. In 1863, he paid James Veitch £2 for a single bulb, which arrived together with five smaller bulbs in February 1864.[76] (A rival nurseryman, John Smith of Riddell's Creek, had already raised the lily in Victoria.[77]) In 1865, Lang ordered a dozen more for the considerable sum of £5.[78] But when Lang tried to order yet another consignment, the English trade refused to come to the party, saying that they did not have enough to supply the demand in the home market, let alone the antipodean one.

Lang then set out to import the lily directly from Japan, with disastrous results. All but one of 10 000 'large and beautiful bulbs' were cooked during the voyage. Lang was 'extremely mortified', but he concealed his loss for the sake of saving face. Most people, he conceded, would think it 'a fine joke'.[79]

'The noblest species of the whole race': the Himalayan *Rhododendron dalhousiae*, imported by Lang in 1866

Rhododendron dalhousiae, from Joseph Hooker, *Rhododendrons of Sikkim-Himalaya*, London, 1849, plate 2, State Library of Victoria

The fragrant white rhododendron 'Princess Alice', which arrived from England in 1867

Rhododendron Princess Alice, from *Florist and Pomologist*, November 1862, vol. 1, State Library of Victoria

The rose 'Isabella Gray', introduced into England from South Carolina in 1857 and acquired by Lang two years later

Tea Rose Isabella Gray, from the *Florist,* 1857, plate 127, State Library of Victoria

The Japanese Golden-rayed Lily, which 'created a sensation' in London in 1862

The Golden-rayed Lily, Lilium auratum, from *Curtis's Botanical Magazine,* October 1862, vol. 88, tab 53338, State Library of Victoria

Nevertheless, Lang exhibited a semi-double golden-rayed lily when he opened the Melbourne branch of his business in 1868.[80] Whenever the lily was shown, it excited attention. In 1871, a journalist who saw it in Lang's Ballarat greenhouse described its 'charmingly sweet-scented and elegantly-coloured' flowers as having a 'silent beauty more eloquent than words'.[81]

In the 1860s, Japanese plants were all the rage in London, and Lang was swept up by the craze. John Gould Veitch's epistles in the *Chronicle* had made him aware of the many new Japanese plants arriving at the Royal Exotic Nursery in Chelsea.[82] Having already learnt so much about the Veitches, he welcomed the opportunity to meet John Gould Veitch in Ballarat in 1865. As 'one of the first settlers in the district . . . having seen the formation of the town from its infancy', Lang showed Veitch 'all the objects of interest' in the rising city.[83] Their meeting spurred Lang to order more Japanese plants from the Royal Exotic Nursery, and in May 1866 three cases arrived in Ballarat. Lang advertised these plants to the public in May 1867.[84] The list included Japanese laurels, cedars, juniper and cypresses, among them the Hinoki cypress, *Retinispora obtusa*.[85]

It seems likely that Veitch mentioned Sir William Macarthur's Japanese plant collection to Lang during his visit. Soon afterwards, we find Lang writing to Sir William enquiring about the availability of new Japanese plants. In July 1866, Sir William sent Lang a large selection of these novelties, including 'a Cryptomeria new from Japan', a 'very beautiful' new holly, another Hinoki cypress, a Sawara cypress, two species of fir (*Abies alcoquiana* and *A. polita*), an osmanthus, a clematis and five unnamed bamboos. Lang listed all of these for sale in his catalogue of new Japanese plants during 1867.[86]

Four years later, the *Weekly Times*' travelling horticultural correspondent visited Lang's Mount Warrenheip nursery and saw the 'noble tree' *Abies alcoquiana*, named after Sir Rutherford Alcock, the former British consul in Japan. The sight of this tree prompted the journalist to recount the story of how it had been discovered in September 1860, 'during a trip taken

5338.

W.Fitch, del. et lith.   Vincent Brooks, Imp.

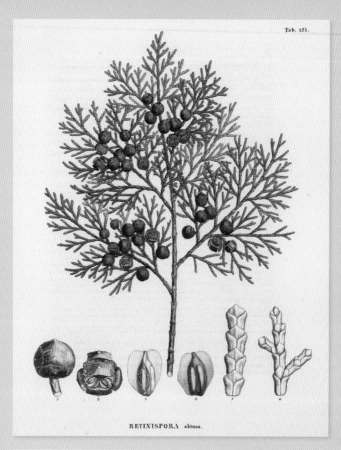

Tab. 121.

RETINISPORA obtusa.

Tab. 111.

ABIES polita.

by Her Majesty's Minister at the court of Jeddo, in company with Mr Veitch, upon the mountain of Fuji Yama'.[87] The tale of imperial adventure infused a place as distant as Mount Warrenheip.

Over time, Lang came to understand every nuance of the imperial plant trade. In the 1860s, for example, he found that his colonial customers preferred London-bred gladioli to the bulbs he had 'very carefully' bred in his nursery. He contemplated overcoming this prejudice by sending his seedlings to Europe, having them named there, and then re-importing them with London's endorsement.[88] In the following decade, he tentatively began to bypass the London nurserymen. As well as his unsuccessful bid to import the golden-rayed lily, in 1879 there was talk of having a friend help him bring in a thousand new date plums (*Diospyros lotus*) from Yokohama. Here, Lang followed the example of Sir William Macarthur, who had imported this plum from Tientsin.[89]

Given the scale of his business, Lang looked to 'the landed proprietors of the colony' to support his enterprise.[90] In particular, he hoped that landowners would 'bear their part in enforesting the country' and so ameliorate the climate.[91] To this end, in 1865 he supplied squatter Andrew Chirnside with 200 pines for a shelter belt across his Carranballac property near Skipton in western Victoria. The pines selected were the stone pine (*Pinus pinea*), Scotch pine (*Pinus sylvestris*) and black Austrian pine (*Pinus nigra*)—the very ones Lang had raised in his Ballarat garden in 1857. Ten years later, Lang and Company despatched twelve pounds of acorns to Western District wool baron Niel Black with the advice that 'they should be sown in autumn'.[92]

The vision of the garden as a force for ameliorating land and society remained part of Lang's understanding of the world into his old age. In the early 1890s, when the Melbourne land boom crashed and the colony slid into depression, Lang used his writings to remind hard-pressed readers of the virtues of the garden. He wrote gardening columns for the *Kyneton Guardian* in 1893, 'to assist those who have been

The Hinoki cypress, *Retinispora obtusa*, which Lang received from the Veitches in May 1866

Retinispora obtusa, from Philipp von Siebold, *Flora Japonica*, Leiden, 1835–70, vol. 2, plate 121, State Library of Victoria

The Japanese fir *Abies polita* was sent to Lang by Sir William Macarthur in July 1866

Abies polita, from Philipp von Siebold, *Flora Japonica*, Leiden, 1835–70, vol. 2, plate 111, State Library of Victoria

deterred from entering upon the formation of a garden . . . by the want of knowledge of how to start'.

To help his readers make a success of their gardens, Lang coupled practical wisdom with scientific knowledge. He enlisted Professor Ellery of the Melbourne Observatory to provide him with information about local climate, rainfall and frosts. In this way, Lang's readers learnt that less than an inch of rain had fallen in January, February and March 1893, whereas the average for those months was 5.68 inches. At the same time, Lang's 'life long training' provided a wealth of anecdotal information for the would-be gardener. While chastising the slothful, he reassured upright gardeners that three hours a week in the garden would produce 'more vegetables and fruit . . . than an ordinary family can consume'.[93]

Even city-dwellers could join in the bucolic quest for 'the well being of man' that arose 'out of the earth', and share Lang's vision of the soil as 'the greatest producer of wealth when labour is rightly used'. This vision owed much to the English Romantics, who saw rural labour as morally uplifting and hoped to 'improve' urban life by importing rural values to the towns. In Lang's view, gardening ennobled the labourer and contributed to a sense of social equipoise; his ideal social order was one in which 'the success of the capitalist found its reflex in the employment of the sturdy labourer'.[94]

This understanding was bound up with Lang's political dreams, which he enumerated a year before his death as a tribute to Australia's leadership in achieving progressive reform:

Australia set the example of registering the titles to land in a correct and satisfactory manner; it has been so when the adoption of the ballot box in political elections was shown to be possible and advantageous; it was so when the eight hours movement was proposed and carried in Victoria; it will be so when the advantages and blessing of admitting women to a share in the political rights has been demonstrated before all mankind.[95]

Lang envisaged the colony and its inhabitants transformed in the image of that wellspring of change, the colonial nursery. Through horticulture, he believed, ambitious men of small means could not only engage in self-improvement, but also play a part in the defining story of Australian national identity: battling the elements to create wealth for self and country.

II. Daniel Bunce

The Man on the Edge

The Man on the Edge

Daniel Bunce (1812–1872) was a man of uncertain reputation. He claimed to have learnt botany in the England of his youth, yet there were many who doubted him.[1] When he arrived in Van Diemen's Land in 1833, Bunce set out to make his livelihood as a nurseryman. By 1835 he was working at Lightfoot's nursery in Hobart's New Town Road. He soon took the place over and renamed it the Denmark Hill Nursery.[2] Here, he laid out the plants according to the taxonomic systems of the Swedish botanist Carl Linnaeus and the Swiss Augustin-Pyramus de Candolle.

For Bunce, the ameliorative power of gardening was an article of faith. When he came to Hobart, he found a society where horticulture was a 'thing of little moment, or deserving very remote attention'. Five years later, he was pleased to report that gardening had risen to pre-eminence as 'a source of domestic comfort, convenience and health'.[3]

He viewed the Tasmanian vegetation with a gardener's eye. Writing in his *Manual of Practical Gardening Adapted to the Climate of Van Diemen's Land*, published in instalments during 1837 and 1838, he predicted that 'native plants ... would become a handsome ornament to shrubberies, provided a little taste was displayed in planting them according to their size, and habits of growth'. For the edge of the border, he recommended 'low growing plants from the top of Mount Wellington', and for intermediate planting, those found halfway up the mount. Although he knew that colonial gardeners were in the habit of furnishing their gardens by digging up plants in the wild, he was adventurous enough to include Australian plants in his 1836 nursery catalogue.[4] As his travels through Van Diemen's Land grew more extensive, he began advertising 'native seeds collected by himself ... in some of the most unfrequented parts of this island'.[5]

He was also deeply involved in the exchange of plants and seeds between the colonies and London, corresponding with 'the well known establishment of Messrs Whitley and Osborne of Fulham' to bring Van Diemen's Land its 'first importation of English forest trees and other choice British shrubs and

Daniel Bunce

Albumen print, Royal Historical Society of Victoria

plants'.[6] By 1837, he was sending indigenous plants to the Horticultural Society of London,[7] and he also sought to raise private subscriptions to publish the results of his botanising as a book.[8]

Bunce tried to impress Hobart society with his knowledge of scientific botany, but some doubted his claims.[9] Foremost among his detractors was Ronald Gunn, the leading Tasmanian botanist of the time, a learned man who corresponded with William Hooker of Kew Gardens and subscribed to French journals such as the *Annales des Sciences Naturelles*.[10] In Gunn's opinion, Bunce was a charlatan who would give '*any* hard name to *any* unknown plant in his nursery'.[11] The campaign to discredit Bunce reached a climax when his book *Hortus Tasmaniensis* was withdrawn from sale after the publisher was alerted to the egregious errors it contained. Among the colonial cognoscenti, Bunce's name soon became a synonym for ignorance.

If Bunce had many failings as a botanist, he was an acute observer of the aftermath of frontier conflict in Van Diemen's Land. He had come there only three years after the Black War, in which the authorities had organised a sweep of the 'settled' districts to round up the remaining indigenous people and banish them to Bruny Island. This was the culmination of years of violence.

On his botanical excursions, Bunce travelled a landscape where terror was remembered at every step. The 25-mile point outside Hobart marked the spot where 'Mrs Gough and child with Ann Gray were killed by blacks'; further on, Bunce passed a place where a bushranger had 'barbarously shot' Mary, 'the native black girl' with whom he had lived with for many months. At Quamby's Bluff, not far from Westbury, a 'black native' had been surprised by Europeans kangaroo hunting; in 'a melancholy accent', he exclaimed 'Quamby', which the settlers believed to mean 'Mercy!' or 'Spare me!'[12] Continuing his journey, Bunce crossed Black Man's River, named for an incident in which 'natives' had murdered a number of herdsmen, whose graves were to be seen at the end of the bridge.[13]

Bunce was not content merely to record his journeys; he sought to understand why the violence had occurred. He recoiled when Dr Ross told him the story of a stockman who had captured an Aboriginal woman and chained her to a log. She managed to escape, only to have him pursue her 'upwards of five hours, through copse, vale and thicket, up-hill and down-hill'. After hearing this tale, Bunce concluded: 'even worse treatment than this by white stock keepers in the earlier periods of the colony was the chief and original cause of the hostility which the Aborigines have indiscriminately shown the whites'.[14] Opinions of this kind were not fashionable in Hobart Town, and probably added to Bunce's unpopularity among its settler class.

In 1839, bankrupt and in disgrace, Bunce left Tasmania in the *Lord Hobart* and crossed Bass Strait to the fledgling settlement of Melbourne, which had been founded by John Batman and John Pascoe Fawkner in 1835. Bunce would later recall his first trip up the Yarra Yarra River, its banks thick with vegetation, including a tree (most probably a kind of melaleuca) with 'long heavy branches . . . [that] hung in massive graceful arches over the river's side'. This tree was known to local Aboriginal people as the good mother, '*monomeeth parbine*', because its seeds remained on the branch after flowering, and Bunce referred to it by this name.[15]

It almost seems that Bunce's failings as a conventional botanist made him receptive to indigenous views of the natural world. Soon after landing in Port Phillip, he met a well-known Aboriginal man called Benbow, who lived with his wife Kitty in a corner of John Batman's garden. Bunce visited Benbow at his home, a 'small hut of his own constructing', which Bunce reported was 'clean and in good order'. In this garden setting where European and Aboriginal resided, Benbow deeply impressed Bunce. 'He was not only an intelligent native', Bunce remarked, 'but a really worthy fellow: an evidence that the aborigines of Australia are not, as has been so frequently stated by various writers, incapable of being civilized'.

Epacris impressa

Bunce also met several other Aboriginal people and soon set off with them on his first collecting trip, travelling overland towards Western Port Bay, south-east of Melbourne. As the trip progressed, he learnt more of the local language and became more relaxed in Aboriginal company. Initially, he viewed the local flora in terms of European taxonomy. At Brighton he hazarded Latin names for the plants of the sandy heathlands, including the tea-tree (*Leptospermum*) and the red and white flowering heath (*Epacris impressa*). He readily admitted that at this stage he had 'a very imperfect acquaintance' with Aboriginal languages and customs; it was the first time he had ever 'camped for the night in company with aborigines', and his first impression of them was 'by no means favorable'. After dining on possum, which he found 'very strongly tinctured' with the volatile smell of gum leaves, he spent the greater part of his first night trying to decipher his companions' cheerful conversation.

On the second day, he awoke to a different world. His companions began to assist him by bringing him plants and naming them. He added the specimens to his collections, together with their indigenous names.[16] The party's destination was Mount Koronth Marabool, a small mountain divided from the main chain of the Dandenong Ranges. As they walked, Bunce continued to observe the country scientifically, attempting to relate plant distributions to geology and soil type. For example, he noted that large arborescent banksias occurred wherever there was sandy soil.

Having reached the mountain, they camped beside a creek lined with tree ferns. Bunce learnt that the Aboriginal name for the tree fern was 'Quambee Jack', and described how the heart of the tree fern was cut out for food. All that was new was carefully recorded; Bunce began to understand how well his companions lived off the land. The women in the party brought in large, white grubs to be grilled and eaten; they soaked the gum of the black wattle tree (*korong*) and prepared it as a relish; and they dug up long, finger-like roots called '*myrnong–myrnongatha*', meaning 'hand'.[17]

'Mr Gunn's Olearia' was named to honour Bunce's arch-enemy, the Tasmanian naturalist Ronald Gunn

Mr Gunn's Olearia (Olearia gunniana), from *Curtis's Botanical Magazine*, vol. 78, tab 4638, State Library of Victoria

Flowering heath, as seen by Bunce near present-day Brighton

Epacris impressa, Loddiges Botanical Cabinet, vol. 17, plate 1691, State Library of Victoria

John Batman's garden, with Benbow's 'small hut of his own constructing' at lower right

W. F. E. Liardet, *John Batman's House*, La Trobe Collection, State Library of Victoria

With each passing day, Bunce's understanding grew. He learnt that the lightwood trees on the range were named for the purposes to which people put their timber: *weenth kalk kalk* (meaning 'fire stick') and *thaal kalk*, the sounding sticks used to accompany the corroboree. From Jemmy, who acted as the party's guide, he learnt the name of the lyrebird, 'Bullen Bullen', and discovered its extraordinary powers of mimicry.

One morning, Bunce was left in the company of a few of the younger men and the 'interesting and astonishing lovely female occupants' of the camp. How was he to make conversation? The answer was a language lesson. His instructor was 'Little Sally Sally', Jemmy's 'affianced bride', and there was general merriment at Bunce's 'clumsy attempts at pronouncing their soft Italian, although somewhat guttural idiom'.[18]

Bunce's journey toward Western Port allowed him to see and speak about plants in a new way. His growing interest in ethnography also drew him to a small group of like-minded Melbourne settlers. Among them was the merchant William Hull, author of *Remarks on the Probable Origin and Antiquity of the Aborigines of New South Wales*, an armchair speculation based on George Grey's reports of Aboriginal rock paintings on the Western Australian coast. Hull became one of Bunce's patrons.

No amount of patronage, however, could save Daniel Bunce from misfortune—some of it of his own making. In his recollections, he was conspicuously silent about what happened after his return from the bush in 1839. He had a volatile relationship with his wife, Sarah, and he was soon caught up in the serious economic crisis that beset the Port Phillip District in the early 1840s. At one point, he was reduced to borrowing a tent and camping on Port Melbourne beach.

There were scandals as well. In 1842, Bunce and his wife were charged with disorderly conduct for assaulting a former patron and giving him a black eye and 'concussions to the head'. Although the charges against Sarah were dropped, Daniel was brought before the courts. The case went no further, but the damage was done: the couple's private affairs—her infidelity, his violent behaviour and evident want of charac-ter—were placed before an eager reading public. To make matters worse, in July 1843 Bunce was charged with embezzle-ment. By 1845, he had become known as 'the notorious Mr Bunce', and in that year he was passed over for the position of curator of the Melbourne Botanic Gardens.[19]

Just when Bunce's fortunes had reached their nadir, William Hull engineered a reprieve, recommending the beleaguered plantsman to Ludwig Leichhardt, who was assembling a party for his second expedition across northern Australia. By this stage, the calamities of the previous few years had taken their toll on Bunce. He was only thirty-six years old when he joined Leichhardt in 1846, but he was prematurely aged; a wit in the party described him as 'an old rake of a gardener'.[20]

Going bush gave Bunce an opportunity to escape the oppro-brium of Melbourne society and share in Leichhardt's reflected glory. He sailed for Sydney with 'three red shirts, three mole-skin trousers, and many stockings'. After a brief meeting with Leichhardt, he was sent to drive the expedition's goats and cattle to Moreton Bay.

Yet Bunce's passion for botany would cause conflict with the autocratic Leichhardt. Even before the expedition began, they quarrelled about how much time was to be spent collecting plants. Leichhardt refused to allow Bunce more than half a ream of the paper used for interleaving specimens. He also decreed that Bunce would only be permitted to keep specimens for himself if they were available in triplicate, and only then if they could be carried. Any unique specimens would belong to Leichhardt, who intended to pass them on to the proposed Sydney herbarium. This did not deter Bunce in the slightest. On one day alone, 29 December 1846, he collected some thirty kinds of grasses.[21]

On one occasion, Leichhardt tried to stop Bunce collecting bottle-tree seeds, but Bunce defied him. The expeditionary party surprised a group of Aboriginal people, who ran away and left twelve bottle-tree seeds behind; naturally, Bunce seized the opportunity to collect them.[22]

Dr Leichhardt with a bottle tree, the
seeds of which Bunce collected from
an unattended Aboriginal camp

J. F. Mann, *Dr Leichhardt*, c. 1846,
Mitchell Library, State Library of
New South Wales

On 13 January 1847, the party encountered a group of
Aboriginal people who were waving a wattle branch, the customary way of greeting a new tribe. In response, Bunce waved
a bunch of specimens he had in his hand. This initiated an
extended exchange: Bunce held up his plants one by one, and
the Aborigines began to name them. The cymbidium orchid
was '*N'yangan*', the nettle '*Parree*'. When they came to the plant
they called '*N'gneera*', they indicated by signs that its juice was
highly poisonous.[23] The language of plants had momentarily
bridged the gulf between Aboriginal people and European
explorers.

As Bunce collected, he arranged the specimens in his note-
book 'according to their natural affinities'; he recorded when
and where he found them and the nature of the soil in which
they grew, and compared them with the flora of Port Phillip
and Van Diemen's Land. He hoped to publish the results in a
book; in his mind, he had already named it *Flora Terrae
Indigina Australis*.

Bunce placed great store in his hard-won collections. Even
when he fell dangerously ill with a fever, he seems to have been
more concerned about his plants than himself. At the height of
the fever, he called out in the night to another member of the
expedition: 'Mr Perry, take care of my specimens'. Two days
later, he was rejoicing in his deliverance and had begun collecting again.[24]

The expedition, however, was a failure. Plagued by illness
and constantly distracted by the need to round up absconding
horses and stock, the party became bogged down in one insect-
infested camp after another. When their privations were at
their worst, Bunce, the inveterate gardener, planted mustard
and cress to supply the invalids with greens, only to have
Leichhardt harvest the food for himself, 'a sore disappointment to the poor helpless invalids'.[25]

In early June, Leichhardt was forced to abandon his plans
and turn back. On the return journey, most of the party were
extremely weak, and there was grumbling about the lack of
medical supplies. Matters would have been far worse were it

DANIEL BUNCE

TURNER & HENDERSON, LITH.

not for Bunce, who harvested native melons he had planted during the expedition's advance.[26]

The failure of the expedition led to animosity between Leichhardt and the rest of the party. When Leichhardt set out on his fatal third expedition across the continent, he chose a new set of companions. He was reluctant to take Bunce because he had discovered that the plantsman 'bore a very bad character in Port Phillip'.[27]

Leichhardt and Bunce never met again. At the close of the expedition, Leichhardt returned to Sydney, taking many of Bunce's specimens with him. He sent 'a good number of seeds' to his friend Sir William Macarthur, including those of the bottle tree, which was 'unknown to the European horticultural world'; he suggested that Macarthur share these specimens with the newly appointed curator of the Sydney Botanic Gardens, John Bidwill (1815–1853).[28] Leichhardt also forwarded duplicate specimens to William Hull, Bunce's patron down south.[29]

Leichhardt suggested that Bunce remain in Moreton Bay, as there were 'many trees and seeds' that 'had not as yet been sent home'—enough to keep Bunce busy collecting for several years.[30] The explorer waxed lyrical about 'the brush that covers the mountain over an area of fifty English miles long and ten miles wide', where Bunya Bunya pines grew like pillars supporting the sky.[31] Bunce was already aware of the Bunya Bunya brushes. Leichhardt's expedition had encountered 'many tribes of natives' on their way to collect the fruit of these 'large and magnificent trees'.[32] Leichhardt had asked the Aborigines what lay beyond these brushes, and had been told that at Wide Bay there was another araucaria, which they called 'dandajom'.[33]

The prospect of collecting things new to Europe while living on the grace and favour of the local squatters was enough to keep Bunce in Queensland. He spent 1848 collecting plants, which he forwarded to the Sydney Botanic Gardens.[34] After this, he felt confident enough to return to Melbourne. His expedition with Leichhardt had rehabilitated his reputation and literally put his name on the map—although he was

DANIEL BUNCE

disappointed that the only geographical features named after him were 'completely hidden from view' in remote country near the Comet River. As the Melbourne *Argus* observed, the 'worthy Bunce' felt that more could have been done to preserve his name for posterity.[35]

Within a year of returning to Melbourne, Bunce decided to go bush again, following the Murray River to Adelaide. The *Argus*, which published his account of his travels, trumpeted it as 'an exploratory and botanising expedition'. In reality, Bunce avoided the dangers of uncharted country, keeping to known tracks and pastoral runs.[36] He was so carefree about this reconnoitre that he agreed to take along a new chum whose idea of roughing it was to load his double-barrelled gun with alcohol and drink it through the nipples. To make up for this inexperience, Bunce invited his 'old and tried aboriginal friend' Yammabook, alias Jemmy, whom he had known since his earliest days in Port Phillip.[37]

In the event, the expedition became an odyssey into a world peopled by the survivors of European settlement. For this reason, Bunce recorded every detail. 'Anything relating to a race of people, who there is every reason to believe will in the course of the next few years disappear from the face of the earth, cannot fail to be interesting', he wrote.[38]

In November 1849, the party left Melbourne and travelled to Bacchus Marsh so that Jemmy could take leave of his country. Bunce observed the leave-taking ceremony. Weeping, Jemmy held out his hand to the oldest and nearest of his kin, covering his eyes with his other hand and bending his head. He held this pose for five minutes. Then, with two sharp jerks of their hands, both men walked away in different directions without looking at one another.

Bacchus Marsh lay on the Werribee River, where eels were to be found in great numbers, providing an important source of food for Aboriginal people. Bunce described the surrounding countryside as being closely timbered with trees peculiar to very good soils, including blackwood, black wattle, native cherry, she-oaks and bull oaks. He made no mention of

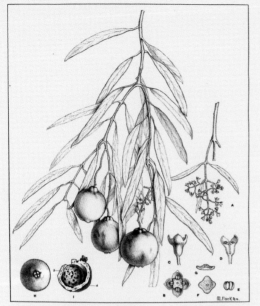

QUANDONG.
(Fusanus acuminatus, R.Br.)

M.Flockton

N.° 678.

Acacia longifolia.

G.C.Fec.t

Melaleuca Ericifolia, or Heath-leaved Melaleuca

herbage or yams, although according to the son of Captain Bacchus, the settlement's founder, the native grasses there had 'once had been long enough to conceal a flock of sheep a few minutes after they had been turned out of the yard'.[39]

On leaving the Werribee, the party traversed romantic gorges and park-like country crossed by goanna tracks before coming on terrain of 'a more northerly aspect'. At every stage along their way, they spoke with the Aboriginal people they encountered; and everywhere Bunce looked, he learnt more about how they used plants. He observed an abundance of smaller flowering plants growing in the sandy soil, including the *Myrnong* yam with its yellow flowers. He also recorded the presence of prickly wattle, which was used by Aboriginal people as far north as Port Essington to poison fish. During a conversation at the head of the Campaspe River, he was surprised to learn that Aboriginal people thought of the Melbourne Botanic Gardens as a signpost to a burial ground.

Travelling light, Bunce and his companions were sustained by the generosity of Aboriginal people. On the Campaspe, two Aboriginal men known as Long Bill and Mr Thomas made the party a bark *gunya*, and Bunce retired there to write up his journal while the rest of the party went fishing. Unfortunately, the *gunya* collapsed and pinned the diarist to the ground. It was some time before his companions heard his cries for help, and by then he was so thoroughly buried that they took some time to find him. The misadventures continued the next morning, when a dog stole the party's only piece of salt beef. Bunce observed that the dog belonged to a painted Aboriginal man, two women and a child (the first child he had seen during the trip).[40]

Bunce's diary recorded his emotional responses to the country as he passed through it. The sight of a quandong tree aroused a feeling that 'none but a lover of plants could fully appreciate', but his spirits fell when he encountered violent winds on the 'dusty looking' saltbush terrain of the Terrick Terrick Plains. This country was 'dreary, treeless, stoneless, grassless and waterless', and there were few specimens

Pidthegul or quandong

From J. H. Maiden, *The Forest Flora of New South Wales*, part 4, Sydney, 1903, State Library of Victoria

To Kitty, Bunce's Aboriginal informant, this plant was *N'gloora*; Daniel Bunce identified it as *Acacia longifolia*

Acacia longifolia, from *Loddiges Botanical Cabinet*, vol. 7, plate 678, State Library of Victoria

The melaleuca known as *Eherrook* or 'good mother'

Melaleuca, from Robert Thornton, *The Temple of Flora*, c. 1812, State Library of Victoria

to be had. Only near waterholes (locally called 'dead men's graves') could the botanical explorer add to his herbarium.

The 'uninteresting and cheerless' plains gradually gave way to 'scrubby country', which continued until they reached the Murray River early in December 1849. Here was more of interest to the collector, and Bunce could call on the assistance of 'a black fellow and his gin', known as Mr and Mrs Campbell, and another Aboriginal woman called Kitty, who 'appeared to have a name for most of the plants on this run'.

Kitty drew Bunce's attention to many inconspicuous plants that he might otherwise have overlooked, and he transposed her knowledge into his own. He identified her *N'gloora* as *Acacia longifolia*; *Merri Meeroom*, a stackhousia; *Pidthegul*, the quandong; *N'gooreek N'goreek*, a small-leafed acacia; *Burk Burke*, an arboreal hakea. Some edible finger-like bulbs were called *Binyong Binyong* (from *Binyongata*, meaning hand), while the melaleuca was known as *Eherrook* or 'good mother'. Kitty distinguished between the dwarf species of native cherry, *Popeenyong*, and its larger shrubby counterpart, *Goodtheemoonth*. The Aboriginal people of this district called sheep *Booboorn*, which Bunce thought was probably derived from *Boobornyong*, their name for the 'abundance of round balls of a kind of silk or cotton' produced by a local saltbush.

The Aborigines still treated the country as their own, despite European occupation. Both sets of proprietors welcomed the itinerant botanist. One day Mr and Mrs Campbell were showing their country to Bunce; the next day their European namesake, squatter Mr Archibald Campbell, took Bunce on a tour of 'his' Gunbower run, which covered the same territory. Along the way, squatter Campbell and Bunce were cheerfully hailed by the Aboriginal Mr and Mrs Campbell. In these circumstances, whose land was Bunce being shown?

Bunce's party travelled from station to station along the Murray. From Gunbower, they went on to Reedy Lake, then crossed 'plains of wretchedly poor country' to Mr Beveridge's station, near present-day Swan Hill.[41] While exploring the district's mallee scrub, Bunce made 'a considerable addition to his Hortus'. The next stage of their journey was along the billa-bongs and branches of the river; the party took several days to reach their next staging post, a station belonging to Mr Garnat, a Scottish Highlander, and his wife. After another 'Jim Crow's dance around sundry boggy lagoons' and across a sheep bridge built by Aboriginal station hands, Bunce was delighted to call on his next host, a squatter by the name of Crawford, who 'appeared to take a great interest in the study of Botany'.

Crawford offered the services of 'an old blackfellow' to carry the wandering botanist across creeks. Not far from Mount Dispersion, they came upon an 'aboriginal place of sepulchre' strewn with human bones. Perhaps intending to collect some relics, Bunce picked up 'a nearly perfect skull of an infant'. At this, the old Aboriginal man objected, repeatedly saying 'no good—no good'. Bunce immediately dropped the skull; he wrote: 'I have always, at least to them, apparently respected the prejudices of these people'. The old man then pointed in the direction of Mount Dispersion and said '*Midgell, Midgell*', from which Bunce deduced that the old man might have seen Sir Thomas Mitchell on his expedition in the mid-1830s, when his party was 'said to have had an encounter with the natives' at Mount Dispersion.[42]

Bunce departed from Crawford's station on Christmas Day; the next day his new-chum travelling companion left the party, while Bunce and Jemmy continued downstream. At a place called *Milleura* (Mildura), Bunce and Jemmy met a group of Aboriginal people, who took them to a spot where a dam had been erected for catching fish. On the way, an Aboriginal man kept Bunce's plant specimens dry by carrying them across the river.

From here, Bunce headed for Captain Bagot's station, Ned's Corner, in the far west of the colony. Their route took them across whole plains of mesembryanthemum, colloquially known as pig's face.[43] They left Ned's Corner on 3 January 1850 with four new companions: Mr Colman, the station overseer; another European by the name of Jamieson; Toby, 'Mr Jamieson's blackfellow'; and the Reverend Mr Tickam, 'a native of the mallee scrubs', from whom Bunce endeavoured

Geelong

to obtain 'as much information relative to the locality as possible'. To his disappointment, the only useful information Mr Tickam offered was about how to obtain water from the roots of the mallee tree. Bunce assessed Tickam as being 'very stupid … like most of the middle aged Blackfellows', but Tickam may have been deliberately avoiding giving an itinerant traveller details of his country.

When Bunce arrived in Adelaide, he received a warm welcome. A 'sort of levee' was held at a tavern, and many people arrived to see 'Mr Bunce the explorer'.[44] After resting for a short time, on 18 January Bunce and Jemmy set off on their return journey to Melbourne. They made their way past Lake Alexandrina, near the Murray mouth, to 'a series of long lagoons called Reedy Creek'. Here, they met an Aboriginal couple known as Mr and Mrs Lillycrop. Bunce had heard that the couple was wanted for trying to spear a publican who had allegedly been involved in abducting a young Aboriginal woman.

When Bunce told the fugitives that the police were after them, they took the news in their stride. They were well aware of the injustice of colonial law enforcement. 'Supposing black fellow to have stolen white woman', they said, 'wouldn't he be hanged?' Bunce was 'overwhelmed' by the logic of this remark; he responded by inviting 'this gentleman and lady to join in a pot of tea and Johnny cake'.

Over their tea, Mr and Mrs Lillycrop asked him to put their case to the governor. Bunce could see that his tea-party companions were 'very sore', but he did not share their faith in the Queen's representative. If they referred the case to the Port Phillip District, redress was very unlikely. While 'nothing could justify kidnapping the girl against the wishes of herself, and the knowledge of her friends and relatives', Bunce knew only too well that 'in this transaction, as in almost all others where disputes occur between blacks and whites, the latter was [judged] the aggressor'. When they parted after 'luncheon', Mr and Mrs Lillycrop's last words were, 'You yabber Gubbernor Anglice'.[45]

Continuing on their way, Bunce and Jemmy eventually crossed the South Australian border and returned to Port

Bunce arrived in Geelong Botanic Gardens to find a curator's residence on 'a treeless, naked and bleak headland' overlooking Corio Bay

Horace Burkett, *Limeburner's Point, 1856–February 1857*, Geelong Heritage Centre

Cape Wattle was planted to protect the Geelong Gardens from sea gales

Acacia lopantha, from *Loddiges Botanical Cabinet*, vol. 8, plate 716, State Library of Victoria

A botanical park with 'bold and wide carriage drives'

Eastern Park, albumen print, c. 1864, Geelong Botanic Gardens

Phillip late in February 1850. They traversed 'an immense, apparently endless expanse of undulating plains . . . dotted with she-oak and lightwood trees' and made their way to Wando Vale, the pastoral run of John Robertson, a Scottish squatter whom Bunce had met some years before at Norfolk Plains in Van Diemen's Land. Robertson was 'greatly attracted to the study of entomology', and was also a plant collector, having supplied Bunce's arch-critic, Ronald Gunn, with 700 species of plants from around Wando Vale. Robertson also had an Aboriginal name; Jemmy called him Wyeeboo N'gamojitch Anglice, 'little [English] man'.[46]

Seduced by the 'neatly laid out and well kept fruit and flower garden' at Wando Vale, Bunce was oblivious to the changes in the natural landscape that had occurred since pastoral occupation. Robertson, however, was only too well aware of the deterioration in the country. On his arrival in 1840, he had found Wando Vale a beautiful 'park with shade for sheep and cattle'. He had counted thirty-seven varieties of indigenous grass, and also remarked that there was none of the silk grass that was destroying the pastures of Van Diemen's Land. Four years later, however, calamity struck: a severe frost killed nearly all the 'beautiful blackwood trees' and the *Acacia glutinosa*. Within weeks, the remnants were completely destroyed by fire. Herbaceous plants disappeared; annuals died after a few days of hot weather and did not return until the following winter.

As 'the long deep rooted grasses' died, the soil began to slip. Robertson wrote in 1853: 'when I first came here, I knew but two landslips . . . now there are hundreds'. The country was criss-crossed with ruts 'seven and eight feet deep and as wide'. With only silk grass growing 'year after year', Robertson believed the 'carrying capacity of the country would decrease substantially'; only fencing would prevent further losses. Robertson believed these problems would not be rectified through cultivation: 'The day the soil is turned [to sow English grasses], that day the pasture is gone forever'.[47]

Bunce was also unaware of the meanings and stories the Aboriginal people attached to their land. From Wando Vale, he returned through Port Phillip's Western District, past Terrinallum (Mount Elephant) to Mount Buninyong, near present-day Ballarat, without realising that these two volcanic landmarks were linked by Aboriginal stories of country. In Aboriginal cosmology, the mountains were created as a result of a fight between two men, Terrinallum and Buninyong. Terrinallum threw his handspear at Buninyong, forming the crater on the western side of the mountain, then was himself felled by a blow that formed the spectacular Mount Elephant crater.[48]

At Buninyong, Bunce and Jemmy 'fell in with another mob of black men and women', many of whom were Jemmy's 'relatives as well as friends', and they all travelled together as far as Bacchus Marsh. Here, Jemmy took leave of his people, just as he had when the expedition began.[49]

By contrast, Bunce's reception in Melbourne was cool. Much to his disappointment, the colonists refused to concede that he had made any new discoveries. After all, his critics said, he had been travelling through country that had been occupied by settlers for well over a decade. He was publicly mocked as a self-seeking ignoramus. One sceptic, signing himself 'Jemmy', expressed surprise at discovering that 'Buggins has a mind'. Another lampooned Bunce's pretensions in satirical verse:

> A voice prophetic whispered once
> In the ear of Mr Bunce:
> 'Would you win a glory great,
> A brilliant fame in spite of fate?
> Go down the Murray, cross the punts,
> And write your travels learned Bunce; . . .
>
> Each wise man and each scribbling dunce,
> Shall lavish praise on the travelled Bunce;
> And they shall say, the shine he took
> Out of Leichhardt—with a hook.
> He fished the Murray—wrote a book';
> Then take the path to fame at once:
> Oh, go to glory!—Mr Bunce.[50]

This hostile reception gave an added poignancy to Bunce's complaint: 'I am received in every place better than I am in Melbourne. What is the reason of this? It is a question I cannot answer.'[51]

Nor was Bunce's reputation restored by the publication of his *Hortus Victoriensis* in 1851. His old foe, the respected botanist Ronald Gunn, wrote:

> If length of residence and extended travels in any country would constitute a botanist Mr Bunce has perhaps every claim to the title, but we think we can show that neither the one nor the other have given him much insight into the Botany of Victoria . . . After careful examination we find that the whole *Hortus Victoriensis* has . . . been compiled from a list of Tasmanian plants written by Mr. James Backhouse, and published by Dr. James Ross in his Hobart Town Almanack and Annual for 1835![52]

Bunce had no choice but to return to his old trade. He had already advertised seeds and botanical specimens from his 'long journey in the interior'.[53] He now offered to 'lay out on landscape principles' designs for 'gentlemen possessing Gardens and Villas or those who are desirous of forming the same'. He hoped that his stock of indigenous trees, along with the English forest trees he had 'introduced from England . . . by the *William Hyde*', might earn him the trust of those who held his name in disrepute.[54]

If Bunce failed to win the regard of the worthies of Melbourne, he was attuned to Aboriginal people in a way most settlers were not. In his *Language of the Aborigines of the Colony of Victoria and Other Districts*, also published in 1851, he challenged the generally held settler belief that Aboriginal people had 'little of the intellectuality' possessed by 'their more favoured brethren', the Europeans. This notion was 'unjust'; 'few people possessed closer reasoning power' or had 'observing faculties of a higher order' than the Aborigines of Victoria.[55] Here was a man at odds with his society.

Bunce was also ambivalent about the discovery of gold and the resulting influx of settlers to Victoria. Although he was among the first on the Clunes field,[56] by the end of 1851 his enthusiasm had waned. It was 'pretty much the same thing' to him, he wrote, whether he drove to the diggings or stayed behind and drove 'the few men in Melbourne mad' by reciting botanical names to them. By December 1851 he was back collecting plants, this time in the Yarra Ranges beyond the Anderson Creek diggings (near present-day Warrandyte). Walking over the 'black and scorched' earth resulting from the calamitous Black Thursday fires of February 1851, he noticed a 'great variety of dwarf annuals and herbaceous plants' in flower.[57] He was especially struck by the bright blue flowers standing out against the fire-blackened soil. When he looked skyward, the 'giants of the forest', 'the tall stringy bark and other lofty species of eucalypt' were covered with 'youthful branches, adhering as closely as ivy to some colossal monument'.

After several years of wandering, alternating between plant-hunting and gold-seeking at Bendigo,[58] Bunce returned to Melbourne in 1855 and settled down to write and edit *The Rural Magazine*. Readers who remembered his advertisements of five years before, when he had proudly announced the arrival of trees from England to stock his gardens, might have been surprised to learn that Bunce now disapproved of imported trees. Yet this apparent volte-face was based on observation. He had realised that foreign plants fared better in the colony if they were raised from seed: they were 'acclimatised from birth' and consequently became 'more indigenous than exotic in their habits'.[59]

Bunce wrote a column, 'Journal of a Naturalist', in which he indulged his penchant for lyrical descriptions of colonial scenery. In August 1855, for example, he described the wattles between Geelong and nearby Lake Connewarre as forming 'one uninterrupted cloth of gold . . . as agreeable to the sight as their delicious and fragrant scent is to the sense of smell'. He also observed the 'strange but pleasing feature' of the parasitical mistletoe hanging from the eucalypts, whose white flowers were 'an agreeable contrast' to their 'showy compeers the golden wattle'. By this stage, Bunce's circle of acquaintances appears to have become more respectable; at Lake Connewarre, he was staying at the house of the mayor of Geelong.[60]

In September 1857, Bunce's prospects finally took a turn for the better. He was appointed curator of the Geelong Botanic Gardens, a reserve of 300 acres on the eastern edge of the township, overlooking Corio Bay. Bunce described it as 'a treeless, naked and bleak headland'. Into this unprepossessing landscape came the gardener who had traversed much of eastern Australia to settle, propagate plants and create an imaginary world.

Bunce confounded the pessimists who said nothing would grow on such a site. He began by creating plantations to provide protection from the sea gales; he ploughed the garden's perimeter to a depth of three to four inches, then broadcast seed of the exotic Cape Wattle and other trees. Next, he ploughed the garden's most elevated portions and planted 'belts and clumps of the same hardy and swift growing vegetation'. These plantings were intended to provide shelter for the 'better kinds of trees' that would form the permanent plantation.[61]

Over the next eight years, the nurse planting was gradually removed to reveal an English park planted with numerous types of pines, including some sent by Walter Hill, the superintendent of the Brisbane Botanic Gardens.[62] According to a *Ballarat Star* journalist who visited the gardens in 1865, the result was more like 'a botanical park than a botanical garden'. The gardens boasted miles of 'bold and wide' carriage drives and winding paths through shrubberies, affording glimpses of the sea and a two-acre artificial lake.[63]

Whose dreams did Bunce realise in creating this landscape? The *Ballarat Star* journalist provided a clue when he reported that Bunce knew Humphry Repton (1752–1818), the landscape gardener responsible for many of England's great estates.[64] Bunce may have adopted Repton's gardening style, but Repton had died when Bunce was six years old. Either Bunce was a precocious gardener or he told a tall story to a naïve listener who was eager to learn about important men.

Bunce established a five-acre nursery in a hollow sheltered by hedges, with white pegs marking 'seeds of rare plants lately received from Kew and other gardens', including a seed of the prized Californian redwood.[65] The site was well protected from cold winds and rain, and the vegetation growing there had 'almost a tropical aspect'. Here Bunce laid out his nursery beds according to botanical systems, planting two or three of each species as propagating stock. In 1859 he added a glasshouse erected to his design, in which the soil was heated by hot water running in pipes.[66]

What did Bunce first plant in his nursery? In order of planting, there were tulips, babianas, watsonias, gladiolus and oxalis, as well as narcissus with names such as 'States General' and 'Grand Monarque'. Larger plants included rock roses (*Cistus*), mock orange (including *Philadelphus coronarius*), berberis, cotoneaster, lilac, viburnum, crab apples, privet, ribes and clematis, along with stone, Weymouth and Aleppo pines.[67] Foxgloves were planted later; the white foxglove bore the number 1360 and the yellow variety was 1413, while roses, including *Rosa* 'Souvenir de la Malmaison', were catalogued last. As well, there was an extensive list of Australian plants, including the Huon pine, hakea, bottlebrushes, the dragon blood pittosporum, boobialla, she-oak, native laburnum, kurrajong, native dogwood, melaleuca, the indigenous mint bush and pine, and forty newly discovered Western Australian plants catalogued without names.[68]

When the plants multiplied, Bunce sent specimens to 'various establishments and private individuals throughout the colonies', hoping for reciprocal donations. Thanks partly to these efforts, he collected 2325 different plants between September 1857, when the gardens were opened, and January 1860, when he published his *Catalogue of Plants under Cultivation in the Botanical Gardens, Geelong*.

'A five-acre nursery in a hollow
sheltered by hedges', the cradle
of the Geelong Botanic Gardens

Geelong Botanic Gardens, albumen
print, *c.* 1870, Ballarat Historical
Parks Association

Babiana tubiflora, the second plant
Bunce introduced to the Geelong
Botanic Gardens

Babiana tubiflora, from *Curtis's
Botanical Magazine*, vol. 22, tab 847,
State Library of Victoria

Oxalis hirtella, another of Bunce's
early plantings in Geelong

Oxalis hirtella, from Nikolaus Joseph
von Jacquin, *Oxalis: Monographia
Iconibus Illustra*, Vienna, 1794,
State Library of Victoria

Each year from at least 1859, Bunce advertised that he would supply plants free of charge to public parks and institutions in the Geelong district, as well as to 'gentlemen possessing gardens and villas'.[69] The response was overwhelming. In 1859, the gardens distributed 29 576 trees and shrubs, 1035 herbaceous plants, 1503 parcels of seeds and 2130 cuttings.[70] Nine years later, the tally was 38 208 plants, consisting principally of trees and shrubs, including many fashionable pines. Among the areas planted were the grounds of Barrabool's shire hall and the Church of England section of the Geelong Cemetery. Bunce suggested that 'the gratuitous distribution of trees and plants' was of 'national benefit' and deserved government funding.[71]

Bunce's plants were also used for the public reserves and private gardens of the nearby seaside town of Queenscliff. In 1866 he supplied the borough council with a 'large quantity of young trees' and personally superintended their planting on the public reserve above the sea cliffs.[72] Among the other Queenscliff recipients was the Anglican minister, Henry Wilkinson, who requested hedging plants, creepers, 'a packet of seeds and bulbs' and any other 'choice things most suitable for Queenscliff' to plant in the parsonage garden.[73]

Geelong acted as a gateway to the Western District. Here the squatters needed trees that would survive dry conditions, and Bunce obliged by delivering a lecture on 'A List of Plants Capable of Resisting Long Drought' to the Horticultural Improvement Association of the Western District in 1862. He went there again on a collecting tour in 1866, travelling as far as Mount Noorat, the station of the wool baron Niel Black.[74]

Further afield lay the Wimmera, where Bunce's tender plants met an indifferent fate. Desperate to grow fuchsias in spite of the hostile climate, in 1864 squatter Henry Nicoll had a wooden slatted shade house built at his station on the Richardson River and planted it with climbers to provide shade; in the Wimmera heat, there was no need for a glasshouse. Despite these elaborate precautions, Bunce's cuttings of twenty-one 'splendid fuchsias' suffered during the 1868 drought, when the thermometer reached 125 degrees

Oxalis hirtella.

N.º 391

Pub. by W. Curtis St. Geo. Crescent Dec. 1. 1797.

3925

1

W. Fitch Del.

Pub. by S. Curtis. Glazenwood. Essex Feb. 1. 1843.

Swan Sc.

Fahrenheit. Nicoll had greater success with Bunce's gifts of 'Banana, Moreton Bay fig, Orange trees, Moreton Bay Chestnut and a great variety of rare plants', which were 'the admiration of all the visitors' to his station.

In return, Nicoll sent Bunce seeds he had received from his brother in India, hoping that they would have 'a better chance of growing by hothouses' under Bunce's care. Nicoll's apparent generosity was also motivated by self-interest: he knew Bunce would send him specimens of these Indian plants if they grew.[75] By such calculations, the gardens' collection multiplied.

Geography was irrelevant to these calculations. Every visitor from distant parts was a prospect. One such was the Western Australian Assistant Surveyor General, Campbell Carey, who visited Bunce in 1867. If patience was a necessary virtue, Carey severely tested Bunce's. His list of requests was importunate. There were not only Californian redwoods, Moreton Bay figs, native cypress, English oaks, laurels, walnuts and chestnuts, but also holly, coloured hawthorns, camellia, azalea, tree peony, abutilon, pineapple, pittosporum and poinciana. Then came a bevy of roses—yellow and white flowering banksia roses, 'Persian', 'Cloth of Gold', 'Empereur de Maroc' and a small Chinese rose for borders. For the vegetable garden, Carey requested strawberries, Jerusalem artichokes and sweet potatoes; for creepers, wisteria, clematis and the leather-leaved creeper of New Zealand. As if this were not enough, he added tea and coffee plants, the 'best cactus, Norfolk Island pine, and seed if you have any to spare'.

All this, Carey emphasised, was 'not for my own sake but for the colony'. Reviewing his list, he admitted it had 'reached such a length I am ashamed to add more, or indeed to ask what I have named'. He left the final selection to Bunce, whom he likened to the 'Great Ferdinand' of the Melbourne Botanic Gardens. Perhaps fearing that gratuitous flattery would not elicit all the plants he desired, Carey added another inducement: a Wardian case of Western Australian plants.[76] On returning to Western Australia, he sent 'a valuable collection of seeds'.[77]

Mock orange, *Philadelphus coronaris*, a later arrival

Philadelphus coronaris, from *Curtis's Botanical Magazine*, vol. 11, tab 391, State Library of Victoria

The yellow flowering foxglove, plant no. 1413

Digitalis lutea fucata, from *Curtis's Botanical Magazine*, vol. 68, tab 3925, State Library of Victoria

The parsonage garden at Queenscliff, ready for planting

View of St George's Anglican Church, Queenscliff, albumen print, *c.* 1866, La Trobe Picture Collection, State Library of Victoria

'Not for my own sake but for the colony': a tree peony, one of the plants Bunce sent to Western Australia

Paeonia moutan, The Moutan or Chinese Tree Peony, from *Curtis's Botanical Magazine*, vol. 29, tab 1154, State Library of Victoria

The Brilliant Fuchsia

Brilliant Fuchsia (Fuchsia fulgens), from *The Botanist*, plate 63, State Library of Victoria. The fuchsia took its name from early botanical writer, Leonhard Fuchs (Fox)

The 'elegantly constructed aviary' (left) in the Geelong Botanic Gardens about 1868

Fred Kruger, *The Aviary, Geelong Botanic Gardens*, albumen print, c. 1868, Ballarat Historical Parks Association

As Carey went west, he alerted other plant-hungry collectors to the Geelong curator's generosity. From the Adelaide Club, he wrote to Bunce introducing Mr Driffield, who had 'rare and valuable collections' superior even to those of the director of the Adelaide Botanic Gardens, Dr Schomburgk. This was a promising contact; Driffield, a florist who believed that 'landscape gardening has more affinity to painting than any other art', had horticultural novelties that would interest Bunce.[78] Carey hoped his two new friends would 'be able to serve each other as well as both colonies in exchanging plants, seeds etc'.[79]

Driffield was not Bunce's only Adelaide connection. Another was an Adelaide bank manager called Tomkinson, who had visited the Geelong gardens with his wife in 1865. Tomkinson had alerted Bunce when the directorship of the Adelaide Gardens fell vacant later that year. Although Bunce did not gain the position, he continued to send Tomkinson plants. In 1870, Tomkinson reported that Bunce's pines were 'doing well at Mount Lofty'; he hoped they would replace the local stringybark, which was 'subject to catch fire in summer' and had 'timber only fit for firewood'. Unfortunately, Bunce's gifts were not reciprocated. Tomkinson seemed embarrassed that he had nothing to offer. 'I wish I could send you something, but of course you have everything that Dr Schomburgk has'.* Nevertheless, on hearing that the Tomkinsons had lost their 'noble little boy', Bunce presented Mrs Tomkinson with a 'very handsome present of a case of fuchsias'.[80]

Bunce's ambitions for the gardens extended beyond botany. He persuaded the gentlemen of the Geelong branch of the Victorian Acclimatisation Society to erect an 'elegantly constructed aviary', and also had English larks released in the gardens. To protect these songbirds from native birds of prey, he offered a shilling for each hawk shot, and he sternly warned visitors not to bring dogs into the gardens 'under any pretence whatsoever'.[81]

*Evidently Tomkinson was unaware that Schomburgk had been sent 100 kinds of seeds from the St Petersburg Botanic Gardens, which the *Geelong Advertiser* had hoped Bunce might be able to obtain. (*Geelong Advertiser*, 21 March 1868, p. 2.)

DANIEL BUNCE

The search for new birds and the search for new plants went hand in hand. In 1866, Bunce donated plants to the Wesleyan missionary ship the *John Williams* in the hope that this would elicit 'a liberal return of seeds and birds from the islands'. He not only sent vegetable and blue-gum seeds, but also filled a Wardian case with primroses, violets, sage and thyme, as well as a liberal supply of trees and shrubs. He added two canaries and ring doves from the gardens' aviary, while pastoralist Thomas Austin of Barwon Park contributed some of his rabbits to this colonial Noah's ark.[82]

Bunce's network even extended to Japan through a former Geelong member of parliament, J. H. Brooke, who had been a patron to the Geelong gardens, donating a statue of Laocoön in 1864. Brooke later left the colony for Japan, where he became editor of the *Japan Daily Herald*. In 1867, when his wife sailed to join him in Yokohama, Bunce took the opportunity to despatch a Wardian case filled with indigenous conifers in the hope Brooke would reciprocate. Sadly, only the Bunya Bunya, *Araucaria bidwillii,* survived the voyage. Brooke was still willing to send a selection of variegated shrubs and bulbs, which he believed would be an embellishment to the gardens, but in the end the lack of reliable transport thwarted Bunce's ambitions.[83]

He was more successful with Dr Tyerman (*c.* 1830–89), director of the Liverpool Botanical Gardens in England. In exchange for shells, seaweed and sponges collected by the citizens of Geelong, Tyerman supplied conifer seeds from Japan and India, and a single seed of 'the very beautiful *Luculia gratissima*'.[84] Earlier, Tyerman had despatched a selection of sought-after plants, only to have them swept overboard.[85] Sending seeds was safer than sending plants.

Bunce's collection continued to grow. The son of the Duke of Marlborough contributed cotton seeds discovered in Africa by the celebrated missionary–explorer Dr Livingstone. In 1864, there were new hyacinths and anemones, while 1865 brought fifty species of ferns, twenty-five camellias and 'a new species of Hoya lately received from Rockhampton'. In 1868, the celebrated English firm of James Carter and Company sent a Wardian case with eighteen of the newest Soulae geraniums and twenty-four of the newest fuchsias.[86]

With gifts from so many countries, the gardens mapped the botanical world. As early as 1838, Bunce had suggested that there was no 'more ready and agreeable means of acquiring a knowledge of geography, of the climate, of the productions of several quarters of the globe, than to learn the native country of the various useful and ornamental plants that botanists and learned societies are everyday introducing into use and note'.[87]

The plants in the gardens also charted Australian exploration. From Cooper's Creek, made famous by the misadventure of Burke and Wills, came 'nardoo seed picked at just the spot where the body of Burke was found'. The well-travelled curator could also point to plants 'raised from seed he had obtained when he was with Leichhardt', and reminisce about his trip through the 'arid and monotonous country' along the Murray, where the mallee root provided water to thirsty travellers.[88]

Indeed, the gardens became synonymous with Bunce the explorer. His reputation expanded with time, helped by the publication in 1859 of his *Twenty-three Years Wanderings in the Australias and Tasmania including Travels with Dr Leichhardt*. The former explorer was now something of a local hero and authority on the colony's early history. He had 'outlived all the difficulties and dangers of past times' and was 'happily settled down'.[89]

Those who promoted the legend of Australian exploration also sought him out. In 1865 the Melbourne photographers Dunn, Wilson and Botherill, 'desirous of making a complete collection of Australian explorers', asked Bunce if he knew where they could find 'an authentic likeness of Flinders, Bass, Cunningham, Mitchell, Strzelecki, Leichhardt or Kennedy'.[90] Five years later, Melbourne photographer Thomas Chuck asked Bunce for help in obtaining portraits of early Geelong settlers for a photo-mosaic of explorers and pioneers. Chuck included Bunce's portrait in his mosaic, *The Explorers & Early*

Tab. 12.

LILIUM *speciosum*.

3946.

Pub. by S.Curtis Glazenwood Essex June 1.1842.

Colonists of Victoria, which was completed in 1872.[91] At the end of his life, Bunce had entered the pantheon of respectable early settlers.

Exploration and settlement heralded the passing of the indigenous landscape. The director of the Kew Botanic Gardens, Joseph Hooker, even suggested that the proliferation of weeds in the colonies was proof of Charles Darwin's theory about the survival of the fittest.[92] To Europeans, introduced birds and plants symbolised an order that would supersede the local flora and fauna.

Yet amid all this triumphalism, some felt a need to commemorate the pre-European landscape. In the 1860s, for example, Geelong saw an ill-starred attempt to plant indigenous she-oaks among the imported pines and cypresses in the park behind the Roman town hall. Three Aboriginal men, Billy, Harry and Jerry, members of 'the once numerous and powerful Barrabool tribe', were coerced into planting the trees. They did so reluctantly, protesting that it would bring bad fortune. By 1872, the she-oaks had died, while the pines and cypresses flourished—a sign, according to the *Geelong Advertiser*, of what would inevitably befall the Aboriginal race.[93]

We do not know whether Daniel Bunce shared the popular belief that the demise of Australia's indigenous peoples was inevitable, but we do know that until the end of his life he continued to acknowledge the presence of Aboriginal people. As the author of *Language of the Aborigines of the Colony of Victoria and Other Districts*, in 1860 he interpreted in court for Governor and Billy, who were accused of murdering another Aboriginal man, Johnny, at Yambuck in the far south-west of the colony.[94] In the imperial world, however, his efforts to collect Aboriginal languages also served other ends. In 1867, Prince Alfred, the visiting son of the British monarch, received Bunce's book from King Billy, widely regarded by Europeans as 'the sole representative of the aboriginal race which formerly owned the district'.[95]

In a world where the princeling of a European people received the words of an indigenous culture, it was common-

Lilium speciosum, one of the most desired Japanese flowers

Lilium speciosum, from Phillip von Siebold, *Flora Japonica*, Leiden, 1835–70, vol. 1, plate 12, State Library of Victoria

A 'very beautiful *Luculia gratissima*' was sent from Liverpool Botanical Gardens in exchange for shells, seaweed and sponges

Luculia gratissma, from *Curtis's Botanical Magazine*, vol. 68, tab 3946, State Library of Victoria

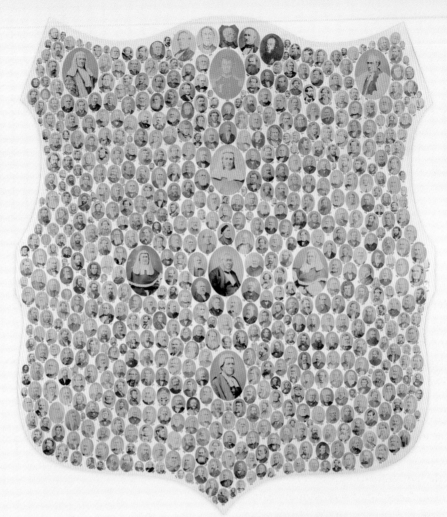

place for Aboriginal remains to be collected and traded. Soon after Bunce's stint as a court interpreter, he received a letter from George Rolfe, proprietor of a private museum in Bourke Street, Melbourne, enquiring about Aboriginal relics. Rolfe hoped Bunce would help him to obtain 'skulls, specimens of hair and implements and any other thing likely to interest' the British collector Joseph Barnard Davis, MRCS FSA, who was writing his *Thesaurus Craniorum: Catalogue of the Skulls of Various Races of Man in the Collection of Joseph Barnard Davis*.[96]

There is no record of Bunce's reply, but his spirited defence of the intelligence of Aboriginal people in his *Language of the Aborigines* suggests he would have rejected the use of skulls to determine a racial hierarchy of intelligence. He had been aware of Aboriginal people's feelings on this issue ever since that incident near Mount Dispersion in 1849, when he had picked up an Aboriginal infant's skull, then dropped it at the behest of his elderly guide. At the time he had written: 'I've always, at least to them, apparently respected the prejudices of these people'. Did Bunce supply Davis with the skulls he sought? It seems unlikely, but there is no conclusive answer.[97] Only the reader can determine if the character found among the fragments and interstices of history has this less attractive side.

When Daniel Bunce died in 1872, a group of mourners assembled at the entrance of the Geelong Botanic Gardens to farewell him.[98] Among them was King Billy, there to take leave of a friend from his country. Bunce's body was laid to rest beside his four children in Geelong's eastern cemetery, 'under the shade of dark green trees' he had planted.[99] These Norfolk Island pines would grow into living obelisks, marking the legacy of a gardener who had distributed thousands of imported trees across the land of his Aboriginal friends.

Thomas Chuck included Bunce's portrait in the photo-mosaic *The Explorers & Early Colonists of Victoria*

Thomas Foster Chuck, *The Explorers & Early Colonists of Victoria*, albumen print, 1872, La Trobe Collection, State Library of Victoria

King Billy (right), a friend of Daniel Bunce

Fred Kruger, *Queen Mary and King Billy*, albumen print, n.d., La Trobe Picture Collection, State Library of Victoria

v. William Guilfoyle

The Colonial Aesthete

v. | William Guilfoyle

The Colonial Aesthete

The Colonial Aesthete

Every man requires a pedigree, and William Guilfoyle (1840–1912) had one ready-made. In England, his father, Michael, had laid out the grounds of the famous Tichbourne estate and was a trusted employee of Joseph Knight at the celebrated Exotic Nursery in Chelsea.[1] In 1849, the family emigrated to Sydney, where Michael established his own Exotic Nursery in Double Bay.[2] These credentials brought him to the notice of Thomas Mort, a prominent landowner and shipping magnate, who employed him to landscape Greenoaks, Mort's residence at Darling Point.[3]

Michael Guilfoyle soon set out to emulate the London nurseries by selling plants internationally. By 1855, he was exporting Australian seeds and plants to South America.[4] His nursery won high praise from John Gould Veitch, who visited it in 1864. Veitch rated it as 'one of the best nurseries in the colony'; he was pleased to report that the former 'long time foreman of Messrs Knight and Perry's establishment at Chelsea', now had 'probably one of the most complete' collections of conifers in New South Wales.[5]

Michael lacked the patronage and influence to attach the 'Royal' prefix to his Exotic Nursery's name, as the Veitches did in London, but he was not afraid to put his case to the New South Wales Legislative Council, a chamber dominated by a bunyip aristocracy of moneybags and sheep-owners. In 1854, Michael Guilfoyle joined with Thomas Shepherd, proprietor of Sydney's premier nursery, to petition the council to protect their trade against Charles Moore, director of the Sydney Botanic Gardens since 1848.[6]

Guilfoyle and Shepherd complained that this man was ruining their business by exchanging rare Australian plants for other botanical novelties without monetary payment. Unlike their salaried nemesis, Guilfoyle and Shepherd needed to make a profit, and they could not do so without a commercial monopoly over the rarer local plants:

> In remote and comparatively young countries, like that of New
> South Wales, the profits of Nurserymen depend very materially
> upon the specimens of rare plants and seeds peculiar to the climate

William Guilfoyle in 1902 with *Phoenix canariensis*, 'undoubtedly the most graceful and beautiful palm'

Garden Gazette, 1902, State Library of Victoria

'At every turn . . . some beautiful
glimpse of jungle scenery
presented itself'

From John MacGillivray,
The *Narrative of HMS Rattlesnake*,
London, 1852, State Library of Victoria

The nurseryman's son painted
the Pacific as an unspoilt Eden

W. R. Guilfoyle, *Untitled*, 1867,
Archives of the Royal Botanic
Gardens, Melbourne

and the soil, with which they are enabled to furnish the nurseries
and private gardens of foreign countries.[7]

The petitioners had outlaid 'a considerable amount of capital';
but alas, investment in nurseries was 'not as speedily repro-
ductive as in other pursuits'. How could a nurseryman prosper
when a stone pine in a four-inch pot could be had for just a
shilling?

Even Moore had admitted that when it came to procuring
'new and rare plants', the private nurserymen of London had
an 'energy and enterprise' that placed them 'far in advance . . .
of any of the purely Botanical Establishments'. Guilfoyle and
Shepherd reminded the Legislative Council of this, and presented themselves as men of just the same 'energy and enterprise'. Evoking the free-trade rhetoric of their age, they asserted
that the exchange of plants between botanic gardens was 'a
direct and unfair interference in their trade'.

The two nurserymen presented the Legislative Council with
a business proposition: every specimen in the botanic gardens
should have a price put on it, and nurserymen should be able
to buy cuttings at a rate that would 'repay the country'. This
would be 'more economical than the present system'; it would
ensure that 'the public could be supplied legitimately' with
the rarities growing in the Sydney gardens; and it would
advance 'the interests of science' by limiting free exchanges to
'those species which are absolutely rich and rare'.[8] The truth
was out: for the commercial nurseryman, every plant had
its price.

Next, Guilfoyle and Shepherd took the high moral ground.
Nurserymen acquired their education through 'laborious
perseverance, diligence and active industry'. In the new world,
their vocation was not only 'calculated . . . to develop the
resources and capabilities of the country', but would also
promote 'the moral and social, as well as the physical arts'. The
growing of plants was 'essential to the material interests of a
country', and was highly valued 'in almost all communities
distinguished by any pretensions to enlightened civilisation'.

T. Huxley, delt.   Hullmandel & Walton, Lithog.

WATERING CREEK, LOUISIADE ARCHIPELAGO.
J & W Boone, Publishers, London, 1852.

Michael Guilfoyle's moral philosophy made him an active participant in colonising the landscape.

Michael also sought to instil this vision in his son William. In a raffish town like Sydney, with its convict pedigree, it was essential that the boy keep good company. A nurseryman's son must be tutored by people with a knowledge of plants. Michael chose William's tutor carefully: William Woolls, a Parramatta schoolmaster, was not only versed in the Thirty-Nine Articles (he became an Anglican clergyman in 1866) but also undertook botanical expeditions to the south coast of New South Wales.[9]

For William's further education, Michael engaged John MacGillivray (1822–1867), whose father was the professor of Natural History at Aberdeen University.[10] MacGillivray had sailed as naturalist aboard HMS *Rattlesnake* during 1846–50, marvelling at the tropics of Australia's north-east coast and New Guinea. He had penned a *Narrative of HMS Rattlesnake*, published in 1852, which imagined the Pacific as a landscape 'never before visited by man'. In this narrative, indigenous peoples were momentarily forgotten. A 'deep silence' pervaded a primeval world of 'tangled bush with very large trees at intervals, and others arching over the stream', where 'at every turn . . . some beautiful glimpse of jungle scenery presented itself'.[11]

From 1852 to 1861, MacGillivray had sailed on HMS *Herald*, collecting plants in the Pacific. His activities were known to the Veitches, and John Gould Veitch credited him with finding 'one hundred ferns, six or eight beautiful Crotons, two new palms, several pretty terrestrial Orchids, some distinct Dracaenas, a red foliaged Musca, several Aroids and Pandanus' on the New Hebridean (Vanuatu) island of Aneiteum (Anatom).[12] Back in Sydney, MacGillivray compiled Michael Guilfoyle's nursery catalogue of 1862.[13]

Young William Guilfoyle grew up listening to Woolls, the scientific gentleman and schoolmaster, and MacGillivray, the plant-hunter with his tales of the South Seas. The two men were to influence him for the rest of his life; his obituary would note their formative influence.

He also sought to advance his prospects by acquaintance with William Macleay, Sydney's greatest gentleman scientist.[14] In the small world centred on Sydney Harbour, Macleay's name carried great weight. At his mansion, Elizabeth Bay House, he gardened 200 acres, where visitors could admire rubber trees (*Ficus elastica*) covered with orchids, exclaim over 'bulbs from every part of the world' or gaze on plants from as far afield as Chile.[15]

By 1867, William had come to the notice of Ferdinand Mueller, director of the Melbourne Botanic Gardens, who viewed this 'young man with some little capital' as a valuable contact for procuring plants in faraway places. In March 1867, Mueller wrote urging William to mount a collecting expedition to the botanically unknown mountains of New Guinea. He admitted that it was 'not safe for a solitary [European] traveller to go inland' in New Guinea, but he thought it might be possible 'to get the natives to bring [plants] down to the mission station at so much the hundred'. The risks to his safety would be outweighed by the wealth to be gained by supplying 'all the large governments in different countries with portions of his gain'.[16]

Mueller's letters may have helped to spark the young nurseryman's plant-hunting passion, but they did not succeed in their immediate aim. In May 1868, William set out for the islands—but not for New Guinea. Instead, he sailed for the South Pacific aboard HMS *Challenger*, commanded by Commodore Lambert. Past disagreements between his father and Charles Moore seem to have been forgotten; William travelled with no less than twelve Wardian cases provided by his father's former adversary. As trade goods, he took a supply of trinkets, pieces of yellow calico and beads of every colour.

He also had a revolver, and for good reason. The *Challenger* was no pleasure boat. It was a man-o'-war, sent to Fiji to teach the islanders the first commandment of European imperialism: 'Thou shall not kill a missionary'.[17] Lambert's aim was to avenge the murder of the Reverend Baker and quell an uprising on the Rewa River, where the Fijians were contesting a land

CORDYLINE GUILFOYLEI.

grab by European sugar and cotton planters.[18] So while the nurseryman's son painted the Pacific as an unspoilt Eden, the introduction of plants from other parts of the globe was changing the islanders' lives.

William was already conversant with the plants of the Pacific, because in the 1860s the Double Bay nursery had built up an impressive stock. The Guilfoyles had 'spared neither trouble nor expense in securing a succession of novelties from Europe and . . . the Australian colonies and the Islands of the Pacific'. By 1866 their collection of 'new plants from the South Seas Islands' was said to be unrivalled in Australia. They could boast ten named varieties of dracaena, including *Dracaena ferrea rosea* and *D. guilfoylei*, and 'a vast number of new unnamed varieties' of ferns 'from the South Sea Islands and elsewhere'.[19]

Yet William was not prepared for the botanical paradise he encountered in the islands. He was dazzled by the garden of the French missionaries on Samoa, with its avenues of bread-fruit and coconut trees, plantations of banana and thickets of pandanus around running streams and small lakes. In Fiji, the hilltop garden of J. B. Thurston, the British consul, served as a vantage point from which to look out upon 'the wilderness of beauty in the valley of Livone with its towering Cocoa-nut-palms and lofty ferns, together with clumps of Plantain and Banana'. Guilfoyle metamorphosed this 'rich and varied vegetation' into 'a garden in fact'.[20] Was this Europe before the Fall?

Time and again, Guilfoyle envisaged the wild in terms of European garden aesthetics. On the Rewa River, his gaze was drawn to the palms and tree ferns growing through 'the rich green mantle which spreads over hill and valley'. The 'bou-quet-like display of certain flowers and foliage' was 'rendered still more magnificent by the sombre green and purple tints of the distant hills and mountains in the background'.[21]

He also aestheticised the gardens of the indigenous peoples he encountered. On Tanna and Vate (Efaté) in the New Hebrides (Vanuatu), the islanders cultivated 'the prettiest variegated plants', including crotons and dracaenas, in the gardens around

Dracaena (Cordyline) guilfoylei
From *Floral World*, 1870, private collection

'A garden in fact': banana and coconut trees in Fiji
Tropical Scene, Fiji, albumen print, private collection

Guilfoyle's sketch of the Rewa River in Fiji
W. R. Guilfoyle, *The Rewa River, Fiji*, University of Melbourne Archives

their houses. These 'naked savages', Guilfoyle opined, shared the European gardener's 'taste for the ornamental and beautiful'.[22]

Yet there were other ways of understanding these gardens. On Upolu in Samoa, Guilfoyle was attracted by a large banana plant with purple leaves and went to take a shoot, but the local people stopped him. No matter how hard he tried to persuade them, they refused to relinquish it. Later, a European settler explained that Guilfoyle had broken a taboo: it was 'customary with the Polynesians to plant ornamental foliage near to their houses in honour of their deceased relatives', and 'to break one of these plants is . . . punishable by death'. Although Guilfoyle read this lack of co-operation as a sign that the islanders were 'generally covetous', the incident perhaps says more about his own cupidity.

In his dealings with Pacific peoples, Guilfoyle's usual strategy was to be 'as jovial as possible'. It was 'an excellent plan', he found, 'to make them laugh'. But there were times when circumstances wiped the smile off his face. He was genuinely afraid when a native informant on Tanna told him, 'S'pose missi-on-a-ry come live on Tanna plenty Tanna man come down kill it missi-on-ar-y like it kill pig'. Guilfoyle was sure 'they would be savage enough to do so'.

On Tanna, danger was never far away. While walking on the island, Guilfoyle was initially overjoyed when a guide pointed to an *Inocarpus* with golden yellow foliage, a plant 'unequalled in the flora of Polynesia'. His hopes, however, were dashed when he found he was unable to collect its seed. Then his guide indicated 'by signs and a few words of broken English' that the same species grew on the far side of the mountain, but he also warned Guilfoyle against going there, because 'were we to venture further the natives would kill me'.[23] The plant collector could go no further. He would need more than a revolver and a stock of trade cloth to cultivate 'a sort of attachment' among the inhabitants of Tanna's interior.

Guilfoyle experienced a different kind of fear when he climbed Tanna's active volcano with two local guides. Their route up the cone took them past many 'heavy masses of red-hot lava almost out of sight but occasionally falling near us'. When they approached the summit, the guides refused to go any further, and Guilfoyle went ahead alone to the edge of the crater. He found himself peering into the maw of the volcano, which heaved with smoke and lava. He was ecstatic at the sight of the inferno and the sound of its 'terrible rumbling'. He only beat a retreat when 'a strong south westerly wind filled the air with dense sulphurous smoke'. He had experienced 'perhaps the most sublime sight Polynesia can present'. It was an experience he would never forget.

He recorded a missionary's version of the local people's story about the volcano's first eruption. It was said that all the people of Tanna were looking down into the chasm when the mountain showed its displeasure with the chiefs by causing 'the side upon which they were standing to give way', so that the chiefs were 'precipitated into the yawning gulf'.[24] This was one of the few times when Guilfoyle showed any ethnographic interest in how the local people saw their landscape.

In describing the islanders, he often resorted to Victorian notions of race. He classified the Tannese as 'mentally . . . superior' to the Fijians, whom he described as having 'the agility of monkeys' when they assisted him to climb huge rock walls in the mountains of Ovalau.[25] By contrast, he regarded the son of the king of Tonga as 'decidedly the most civilised chief we met with during the cruise'. The chief had furnished his home in Western style, complete with sofa, chairs, a Brussels carpet recently acquired in Sydney and some 'pictures representing sacred subjects hung over the mantelpiece'. Guilfoyle remarked on the chief's courtly behaviour, which he attributed to 'the consideration and good will of previous visitors together with assiduous missionary labour'.[26] This explanation failed to give due credit to his host's father, King George of Tonga, who had prevented the establishment of European plantations while introducing European customs and ideas into his kingdom.[27]

The plant-hunter on the *Challenger* was well aware that he was travelling through a world ordered by the gunboat. He

experienced its power indirectly during a confrontation with a group of islanders on the island of Vate (Efaté). Guilfoyle found himself surrounded by 'natives in a state of nudity, some with clubs upon their shoulders, others with bows and arrows in their hands'. When they dared to reach for his revolver, he was speechless with fear. Amid their clamour, Guilfoyle thought he heard the phrase 'man-o'-war'. This seemed to have a salutary effect, and the islanders withdrew.[28]

Guilfoyle too would honour the power of the gunboat. When he found a hibiscus with immense bright scarlet flowers on the Protection and Deception Islands, he named it for HMS *Challenger*; it was later given the scientific name *Hibiscus lambertii*, in honour of the gunboat's commander, Captain Lambert. Guilfoyle observed that when the *Challenger* came into port, it saluted the chiefs with a gun volley. He interpreted this as a sign of 'respect and kindness' that was 'likely to engender good feeling' and 'induce those uncivilised people to throw off their savage character and aspire to a higher humanity'. It does not seem to have occurred to him that the islanders might regard the sound as a portent of European retribution.[29]

Along his way, the voyaging gardener made notes on the islands' potential for commercial agriculture.[30] Yet in the French colony of New Caledonia, the *Challenger's* last port of call, he did not linger at the Model Farm and botanic gardens, both clearings designed to guide settlers in their transformation of indigenous lands. At the farm, he cursorily noted the unusual sight of a rice crop, while in the botanic gardens, he remarked on the 'magnificent' poincianas, the 'gorgeous sight' of the *Dracaena ferra rosea*, and the 'recently discovered Araucarias'. But the lure of the wild mountains was stronger. For half a day he walked over mosses, lichens and fungi, amid ferns, crinums and dianella 'luxuriant beyond description'. Above, the massive green boughs of the forest trees formed a canopy 'profusely ornamented with parasites and epiphytes' and numerous climbers 'beneath which the sun never or seldom gleams'. Guilfoyle was overwhelmed by the scene, and by the new botanical knowledge

The huge rock walls of Ovalau

Ovalau, Fiji, albumen print, private collection

it promised. He left New Caledonia determined to visit it again.[31]

On his return to Sydney, Guilfoyle talked up his discoveries. He had 'no hesitation' in claiming that he had made 'the largest collection of choice and beautiful plants ever yet collected in the islands of the South Pacific'.[32] The contents of the Wardian cases supplied by Charles Moore were shared between the Sydney Botanic Gardens and the Exotic Nursery of Double Bay. It is not recorded what other Sydney nurserymen had to say about Moore's largesse toward their competitor.

Soon after William's return, Ferdinand von Mueller wrote to Michael Guilfoyle enquiring if there were any spare plants among the treasures his 'excellent son' had acquired in the South Sea Islands, and offering to exchange them for rare pines and oaks from America, the Mediterranean and the Himalayas.[33] Michael duly consigned a splendid assortment of plants 'gathered in William's rambles over the Pacific groups', eliciting a letter of thanks to William from von Mueller: 'It is very kind of your worthy father to spare me . . . some of the treasures brought with you from the South Sea Islands. I will gladly send anything in exchange that would be acceptable from here.' As a down payment, he offered to send by 'this day's steamer three species of orchids from the Philippines recently received but not yet named'.[34]

At the same time, von Mueller had not forgotten his idea of having William explore New Guinea. He tantalised William by suggesting that its ranges 'must teem with novelties ten times richer than any of the Pacific Islands'. He mentioned a proposed expedition by a party including the young Edward Pierson Ramsay (later to become director of the Australian Museum). Did William know if any progress had been made toward the expedition, von Mueller asked, or 'what facilities exist of sending a collector to the Mission Stations there?' Von Mueller was certain that in New Guinea 'things of cheapness' could be bartered for plants of 'immense interest' that would be 'the greatest additions to material of modern science'.[35] Where the savant von Mueller could not venture, he would have the likes of Guilfoyle go.

When Guilfoyle did not respond to these inducements, von Mueller sought another means of cementing a valuable contact. He now suggested that Guilfoyle tread the forests of southern New South Wales:

> Since you evidently have a desire to distinguish yourself in botanical science, dear Mr Guilfoyle, I have been reflecting how I could aid you, and it occurred to me that you might render great service and gain simultaneously much solid information if you occasionally made a journey to the southern parts of New South Wales.[36]

He suggested that his young acolyte could make use of one of 'the many coach lines' for this purpose. He emphasised that 'the whole country between Illawarra and Twofold Bay needs a search' because the southern range of the Botany Bay plants had not yet been determined. Guilfoyle's suggested coach ride into the wilds was intended to confirm the suspected geographical distribution of plants for the *Flora Australiensis* that von Mueller was preparing in conjunction with the British botanist George Bentham. (The project was based in England at the insistence of Joseph Hooker of Kew Gardens, to ensure the capture of botanical knowledge of this corner of the empire.[37])

In return for Guilfoyle's assistance, von Mueller undertook to extend the younger man's education. If William collected any species, von Mueller 'would gladly name them always at once'. The exchange would provide William with 'authentic material . . . of immense value' to his 'future independent studies', and would be a source of 'many magnificent plants for your father's garden'. Von Mueller also played on his correspondent's vanity, promising that 'in all my works I always conscientiously quote the name of the collector along with the locality; hence your name would be known in Botanical science'.[38]

When William expressed an interest in travelling to San Francisco, von Mueller offered to provide him with letters of introduction to 'influential friends'. Among these was

Charles Moore's rustic bridge over
a pond filled with water lilies
and papyrus

Rustic Bridge, Botanic Gardens, Sydney,
albumen print, private collection

The older part of the Sydney Botanic
Gardens: 'a monotonous and rigid
uniformity of square beds and
straight lines which offends the eye
at almost every step'

Plan of the Botanic Garden, Sydney,
from *Votes and Proceedings of the
New South Wales Legislative Assembly,*
1870–1871, vol. 4, opposite p. 973,
La Trobe Collection,
State Library of Victoria

Dr Hermann Bohn, who devoted his leisure hours to the study of insects. Von Mueller, the arch and wily collector, suggested that Guilfoyle forward 'any butterfly that may fall into your hands' to this Californian entomologist. In so doing, Guilfoyle would ensure he was 'doubly a friend'.[39]

The trip to San Francisco, however, did not eventuate. Instead, Guilfoyle busied himself with lucrative Sydney commissions. Among his clients was Sir James Martin, Chief Justice of New South Wales, who employed Guilfoyle to beautify his residence, Clarens, with a lavish budget of £20 000.[40] In the process, William was developing a landscape design philosophy.

His emerging ideas can be seen in an 1870 newspaper article about the 'artistic beauties' and 'impressive grandeur' of Sydney's botanic gardens, which he believed 'could not be realised in any other in the world'. Here was a 'pleasure garden' spreading over a hundred acres, where pictures presented themselves 'at every turn': the gothic Government House embowered in botany; a picturesque bridge over a pond filled with water lilies and papyrus; the Brazilian *Jacaranda mimosaefolia*, 'the prince of flowers'; and the quarter-acre rockery, with its 'masses of waterworn rock and stumps of trees of rustic manner'. These elements were distributed in an 'artistic manner' among the gardens encircling Farm Cove—'one of the many charming indents of the magnificent harbour of Port Jackson'. To Guilfoyle the Sydney Gardens were 'an Eden of which Australians should feel proud'.

Guilfoyle's vision of the ideal botanic garden was based on what he saw in Sydney. Although he had no first-hand experience of European gardens, he was aware of what set Sydney apart. The rarities of Kew, Chatsworth and 'other great gardens of Europe' required 'so much careful treatment under glass', whereas in Sydney plants could be found growing in the open. Here, the 'plants of Britain, America, Madagascar, China, Japan, Polynesia, and Australia' could be seen 'vying with each other in their beauty and magnificence'. As well, the gardens had a collection of 'noble specimens of indigenous trees' dating back to the tenure of Charles Fraser, the founding director,

appointed in 1828. For Guilfoyle, the entire ensemble was 'a sight as novel as it is glorious'.[41]

Yet Guilfoyle was highly critical of Fraser's design for the inner garden, with its 'monotonous and rigid uniformity of square beds and straight lines which offends the eye at almost every step'. It was the outer gardens, landscaped by Charles Moore, that caught his imagination. He drew attention to the 'beautifully varied surface and tasteful arrangement of exotic shrubs', and emphasised how 'the slopes, levels and gentle undulations harmonise[d] with the charming aspect of the bay'. For Guilfoyle, 'all Nature is a garden', and the landscaper's task was to create scenery that 'might be mistaken for that of nature'.

In Guilfoyle's eyes, Moore's design of the gardens was a picture to which 'only a painter or poet could do justice'. In this landscape, vision tricked the eye. Shrubbery obscured the entrance of a cove, transforming Sydney Harbour into a lake. Elsewhere, a 'rustic octagonal summerhouse' thatched with the leaves of the Australian grass-tree peeped through palms, pandanus and banana, suggesting 'a South Seas Islander's house'.

Yet the colonial aesthete, nurtured by Sydney gentlemen of science and sensibility, was also a practical nurseryman's son. He recognised that the gardens were almost beyond the understanding of a community 'who feel not the sublimity of nature and art, and in whom the most noble picture, or even the most gorgeous flower will fail to excite admiration'. Knowing this, Guilfoyle set out to address these philistines who lacked 'a love of the beautiful' and sought only to profit from the landscape. He spoke to them in their own language. The gardens offered 'a lesson we might profit by'. They were 'richly clothed', 'an exquisite and interesting picture', and were likened to 'rarely acquired' luxuries available to only the few. This juxtaposition of acquisitive and aesthetic language hints at an inner tension between Guilfoyle's poetic inspiration and the mercantile considerations of running a nursery.

WILLIAM GUILFOYLE

In 1870, Guilfoyle traded the pleasure of the Sydney gardens for frontier life. He went north to join his father, who had taken up a 250-acre selection on the Tweed River in the far north of New South Wales. The Tweed River settlement had a pioneering quality, with its 'patches of cultivated land in the midst of the dark green of the primeval forest foliage'.[42] The new landholders had planted sugar, corn, coffee and tobacco on recently cleared forest land. Guilfoyle's eye, however, was drawn beyond these 'models of pioneering enterprise' to the land beyond the clearing.

The move gave William first-hand experience of a wild Australian rainforest. This experience, combined with his South Seas voyaging, was to produce a unique poetic vocabulary that went far beyond anything the fashionable English garden writer William Robinson, author of *The Wild Garden* (1870) and *The Subtropical Garden* (1871), could have imagined from the cold English countryside.[43] On the Tweed, Guilfoyle looked from the edge of the clearing into the forest, where the vegetation was found 'in its original grandeur'. It was at this boundary that he metamorphosed the wilderness into a sublime garden full of 'showy flowering or fruiting trees and shrubs'. The forest vegetation was 'too varied and too beautiful for description'. A *Ficus macrophylla* became a 'fantastic monster of the forest' interlaced with 'gracefully drooping lianas'. The lilly-pilly *Syzygium moorei* was a tree of unequalled beauty, seventy or eighty feet high, its upper branches clad with deep crimson flowers, giving it 'the appearance of rich velvet'.[44] Guilfoyle turned to poetry rather than botany to represent the landscape.

He wrote an ecstatic account of ascending Mount Warning, the highest peak in the district. He described the mountain as charming for 'any admirer of scenery or botanist', its plants 'variegating the landscape with light and shade'. The prospect from the summit was 'appalling' in its vastness. In his heightened emotional state, Guilfoyle perceived the view to the west as a composition of 'far distant mountains suffused with a bluish vapour ... vying in grandeur with the mantle of

SCENERY ON THE TWEED—GREENWOOD, THE RESIDENCE OF MR. THOMAS CLARKE. (FROM A SKETCH BY MR. WILLIAM R. GUILFOYLE.)

verdure that sloped toward them from our feet'. The forest below became a symphony of foliage. The 'glossy leafage' of *Akania lucens* and *Grevillea hilliana* contrasted with the 'vivid green' of the Moreton Bay chestnut, while the leaves of *Eugenia melastomoides*, moving in the breeze, revealed 'the silvery white surface' on their undersides.

Enchanted by the scenery, William lost all sense of time and left it too late to descend. 'This, however, we scarcely regretted', he wrote. He was rewarded with a sunset 'like a beautiful dream'. In this scene of 'dusky grandeur', 'massive clouds rose above the horizon . . . diffused themselves and became tinted with every imaginable hue'. The sky was like 'a vast lake studded with islands of molten gold . . . embosomed in mountains of indescribable splendour'. The imagery of lake and islands recalled the picturesque elements he had encountered in the Sydney Botanic Gardens.[45] The sublime and the picturesque were fused.

Next day at dawn, Guilfoyle was transfixed as he watched 'the orb of day rise in splendour over the ocean which sparkled with golden light as it gently careered his way through the cloudless sky'. He looked on as 'mountain after mountain down the valley exchanged their dark shades' for the sun's 'glowing beams', until 'all Nature basked in the effulgence of the day'. The 'sublimity of the scenery' made an indelible impression. Even von Mueller, on reading this piece, remarked on its 'eloquent and almost poetic language'.[46]

Michael too wrote about the rainforest, using the same aesthetic language as his son. From the time he first sailed up the Tweed, Michael had responded to the subtropical landscape, which he described as 'beautiful, beyond imagination'. He was amazed at 'the botanical richness of the land, and the way in which nature has sheltered it'. He delighted in the 'bright green foliage' of the Moreton Bay chestnut clothed with 'gorgeous yellow and red flowers'. Another sight to 'dazzle one's eye' was the flame tree, with its 'mass of the brightest scarlet' blossoms 'backed up by the dark foliage of a huge Ficus'.[47] Michael also saw plants he had grown in his nursery

Scenery that 'might be mistaken for that of nature'

Sydney Botanic Gardens, albumen print, *c.* 1870, private collection

A 'rustic octagonal summerhouse' thatched with grass-tree leaves in the Sydney Botanic Gardens

John Sharkey (attrib.), *Rustic Summerhouse with Roof of Xanthorrhoea Leaves*, albumen print, *c.* 1879, Mitchell Library, State Library of New South Wales

'Models of pioneering enterprise': a farm on the Tweed River

W. R. Guilfoyle, *Scenery on the Tweed—Greenwood, the Residence of Mr Thomas Clarke*, from *Australasian Town and Country Journal*, 14 December 1872, p. 784, State Library of Victoria flourishing in the wild. Among these was the Queensland gold blossom tree, *Barklya syringifolia*, a 'splendid shrub' with 'heart shaped, lively green foliage' and 'spikes of golden yellow flowers'.[48]

When Michael took up his selection, Ferdinand von Mueller could scarcely contain his delight. The Tweed was a place where 'no plant of any kind will come amiss[;] even if not useful it will be geographically interesting'.[49] The move to the north opened 'the prospect of obtaining full insight into the vegetation of the whole Cape Byron District', which was 'very imprecisely known'.[50] When he heard that William was going to join his father, the famous botanist made a point of reminding him that 'a diligent search among the plants there' would reveal 'much novelty'.[51] Von Mueller also expressed concern for the vanishing natural world of the Tweed. He believed that 'a few square miles [of forest] ought to be preserved from encroachment of any kind for all time', and hoped that the Double Bay nurserymen-turned-pioneers would 'allow a good deal of the best and grandest native vegetation to remain in its pristine state'.[52]

The nurseryman and the scientist soon established a routine. Request followed request. William collected specimens, noting their localities and heights. Two sets were despatched by mail to Melbourne, both were named, and one set was sent back to the Tweed.

From 1870 to 1873, one was likely to find William Guilfoyle up a tree collecting seeds, flowers and leaves. At these dizzying heights, the future director of the Melbourne Botanic Gardens might cling to a liana and snatch the pale greenish-yellow flowers of the cow-itch bean (*Mucuna gigantea*), or take seed from the golden-yellow flowering belum wood (*Weinmannia biagiana*).[53] He ascertained the localities and heights of two native species of citrus, and the range of the fifty-foot evergreen Mount Dryander hardwood (*Amorphospermum antilogum*).[54] He sent von Mueller specimens of the thirty-foot Queensland olive (*Olea paniculata*), the rusty-leafed Australian tamarind (*Diploglottis cunninghamii*) and *Mappa fanarai*, a distinctive tree occurring on the edges of the brushlands. The 'great local knowledge' of the man in the field was indispensable to von Mueller.

At the same time, Guilfoyle was seeing, collecting and learning to name the forest beyond the clearing. Von Mueller's instruction was rigorous. Before leaving Sydney, Guilfoyle had been required to visit the herbarium and make a tracing of a dried *Strangea* so that he would be able to ascertain 'the precise spot of its growth' when he arrived in the north. In the following year, von Mueller suggested Guilfoyle go to Cape Byron to collect the plant in flower, reminding him: 'you have a rare claim yet to connect your name with the vegetation of Australia, if you would carefully gather all the plants on the Tweed'.[55]

In 1870, von Mueller agreed in principle to name an *Aspidium* after Guilfoyle's father, but his good intentions were thwarted when William's first specimen arrived so crushed that it could not be identified. Ever ready to draw a lesson from misadventure, von Mueller instructed William that in future specimens should be laid out on paper to dry.[56] Once learnt, the lesson would never be forgotten.

Von Mueller's botanical instruction bore fruit when Guilfoyle came to write for the public. For example, in his 'Vegetation and Scenery of the Tweed River', published in 1872, he could inform his readers that the *Strangea*, although plentiful at Cape Byron, rarely occurred on the coastal dunes of the Tweed.[57] A landscape that until recently had been known only to cedar-cutters and Aboriginal people was being brought into the domain of European scientific knowledge.

Like a good tutor, von Mueller unflaggingly encouraged his pupil's zeal. Soon after Guilfoyle arrived on the Tweed, von Mueller wrote to compliment him on having 'supplemented' Charles Moore's pioneering work in collecting 'rare plants from Mount Warning and the Tweed'. In August 1871, von Mueller informed William that the plants he had 'so attentively collected' included 'several northern species new to New South Wales', along with an 'extremely rare and as yet so imperfectly known' climber, *Petermannia cirrosa*.[58] Guilfoyle's

The view from Mount Warning: 'far distant mountains suffused with a bluish vapour . . . vying in grandeur with the mantle of verdure that sloped toward them from our feet'

W. R. Guilfoyle (attrib.), *Tweed River and District from Mount Warning*, from *Australasian Town and Country Journal*, 17 May 1873, p. 625, State Library of Victoria

Von Mueller's gardens

View of the Melbourne Gardens, albumen print, n.d., private collection

reward? In the sixth volume of the *Flora* in 1873, von Mueller named a new leafless orchid *Epipogium guilfoylei* after his frontier correspondent. Guilfoyle was now in celebrated company: von Mueller reminded him that his 'honoured name' would stand with that of I. G. Gmelin, the great eighteenth-century Siberian scientific traveller who had discovered *Epipogium gmelini*.[59]

Guilfoyle's rewards were dwarfed by the honours heaped upon von Mueller, a colossus among antipodean men. In 1871, William wrote to 'Baron von Mueller' congratulating him on his elevation, but von Mueller demurred. For all his 'baronial dignity', he was not entitled to use this form of address, although the honour was 'a very high and rare one and was not conferred on every man by the throne'.[60] Not every man, it seems, deserves a barony.

Although von Mueller would remain 'the Baron' for the rest of his life (in the colonies, after all, a title was a title), in 1873 he would prematurely lose his most coveted office when he was summarily dismissed as director of the Melbourne Botanic Gardens.[61] Guilfoyle was chosen in his place. There is a poignancy in von Mueller's anguished letter to his successor:

> I should be glad, my dear friend, if you will first of all look for me when you arrive. Meanwhile I can only say I am disgraced and degraded as Director and that I have been forced out of my creation suddenly after twenty one years without a single word of thanks for my honorary Directorship since 1857.[62]

Von Mueller would never enter the gardens again.

Guilfoyle's appointment has been portrayed as a consequence of short-sightedness and parochialism. In this version of the story, von Mueller features as the misunderstood genius brought undone by a bureaucratic state given to jobbery and patronage.[63] Certainly J. J. Casey, the minister responsible for appointing Guilfoyle, might be accused of patronage; after all, he knew the Guilfoyles and was a shareholder in the Tweed River sugar mill.[64] It is also indisputable that Guilfoyle was not of the same scientific calibre as von Mueller. On the

WILLIAM GUILFOYLE

BOTANIC GARDENS, 1873,

UPON THE RETIREMENT OF BARON VON MUELLER FROM THE DIRECTORSHIP, 1873.

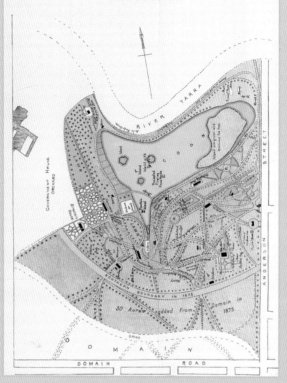

BOTANIC GARDENS, 1901,

SHOWING ALTERATIONS AND IMPROVEMENTS EFFECTED SINCE 1873,

BY W. R. GUILFOYLE, DIRECTOR.

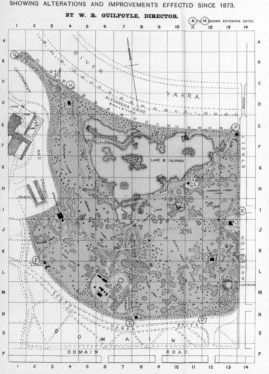

other hand, this romantic tale of fallen genius ignores several considerations.

Casey was at least encouraging colonial talent rather than following the advice of the Board of Inquiry into the gardens and opting for an overseas appointment.[65] Furthermore, as events would show, Guilfoyle had learnt something that had escaped von Mueller: how plants might be gardened into a poetic landscape. By changing from nurseryman to botanical collector and integrating his new knowledge with his understanding of landscape gardening, Guilfoyle in this regard had outdistanced his mentor.

In time, von Mueller's work in the gardens would vanish without a trace. Just as Guilfoyle had previously criticised the 'straight lines' of Charles Fraser's system garden in Sydney, in Melbourne he immediately targeted von Mueller's geometrical design, recommending that 'seven or eight parallel and therefore inappropriate walks' be removed from the experimental garden. Elsewhere, he looked to Charles Moore's example. The 'diversity and charm of the landscape' would be enhanced by a rustic bridge and a thatched summerhouse. Visitors would peer through tropical and subtropical plantings and glimpse a lake studded with islands. When a rock border was built at the end of the lagoon, Guilfoyle saw to it that 'every separate stone was lodged in its proper position' to create 'the appearance of nature'.[66]

During his three years on the Tweed, Guilfoyle had learnt that writing could make the primeval forest accessible. Language could not only be used to describe plants scientifically, but could also transform 'pristine nature' into the picturesque or the sublime. Now, he set out to introduce the citizens of Melbourne to the plants of the tropics. To support his case for remaking the Melbourne gardens, he forwarded his writings on the South Seas to his superior, Clement Hodgkinson, with a note asking him to take care of them, as Guilfoyle also wished to lend them to J. J. Casey. In the following years, he lectured and wrote widely about the wilderness that had inspired him, and kept the public in touch with his work through a series of

A plan of von Mueller's geometrical design for the Melbourne Botanic Gardens, 1873

Botanic Gardens, 1873, upon the retirement of Baron von Mueller from the Directorship, Guide to the Botanic Gardens, Melbourne, 1902, University of Melbourne Archives

Not a straight path in sight: Guilfoyle's gardens

Botanic Gardens, 1901 showing alterations and improvements effected since 1873, Guide to the Botanic Gardens, Melbourne, 1902, University of Melbourne Archives

The rockery around the lagoon: 'every separate stone . . . lodged in its proper position' to create 'the appearance of nature'

D. McDonald (attrib.), *The Foot Bridge in the Botanical Gardens, Melbourne*, albumen print, c. 1876–1880, Australian Reference Collection, Ballarat Regional Library

The thatched summerhouse, recalling Sydney Botanic Gardens

J. W. Lindt, *Rustic Summerhouse, Botanic Gardens, Melbourne*, albumen print, c. 1881–86, Archives of the Royal Botanic Gardens, Melbourne

One of the 'picturesque specimens' of *Eucalyptus rostrata* (red gum) in the central part of the Gardens retained on the insistence of Clement Hodgkinson

J. W. Lindt, *Princes' Lawn*, albumen print, n.d., Archives of the Royal Botanic Gardens, Melbourne

'Notes on the Botanic Gardens' in the *Australasian* and the *Weekly Times*.[67]

From the outset, Guilfoyle was confident that 'within very few years' his improvements to the Melbourne Gardens would 'in many points rival and in some even excel the famous Botanical Garden of Sydney'. If nature was prodigal in Sydney, it had 'also been very kind' to the Victorian capital. He was sure that a 'marvellously wide selection' of plants, 'from the grandest down to but the most frail', would grow outdoors in Melbourne. Yet, for all his confidence, his new plantings suffered from an 'insufficient supply of water' on days of 'excessive heat'. Melbourne and the tropics were still worlds apart.

To implement his vision of the gardens, Guilfoyle cleared the remaining indigenous vegetation. He had barely arrived in his new post when he decided that the 'wilderness' of melaleuca scrub on the eastern side of the lagoon should be 'destroyed' and replaced by 'a nook of genuine tropical beauty'. The soil levels would be raised to pave the way for plantings of palms, large *Dracaenas*, *Araucaria*, *Ficus* and *Laurus*, with 'a lawn or pleasure ground and gay ribbons of bedded out flowers'.[68] This plan incorporated a novel means of flood control. As Clement Hodgkinson (1818–1893), the Assistant Commissioner of Crown Lands, explained to J. J. Casey, planting a carpet of lawn with palms and other vegetation 'indigenous to the flooded lands in the northern part of New South Wales' would prevent the soil from being 'swept away by floods', as 'such vegetation was known to withstand the effects of much higher and more violent floods than those which occur in the Yarra'.[69]

Guilfoyle next targeted the gardens' remnant gum trees. Gums, he opined, 'should not be distributed at random'; rather, a plantation of all known eucalypts should be established outside the gardens to provide 'a good background for vegetation less characteristic of the climate'.[70] He therefore sought permission to remove all the offending trees, burning the wood to heat the conservatories and using the stumps to ornament the fern gullies and rockeries.[71] His application,

WILLIAM GUILFOYLE

View in the Botanical Gardens

however, had to be approved by Clement Hodgkinson, who was also a garden designer, having created Melbourne's Treasury Gardens in the 1860s.[72] Hodgkinson had his own views. He insisted that Guilfoyle retain 'a few of the picturesque specimens' in the central part of the gardens.[73] This left Guilfoyle free to remove fifty-five large eucalypts, which were occupying 'space where good plants should stand' and obstructing 'pleasant views of extended scenery'.[74] These trees produced enough firewood to pay private contractors to clear the lagoon. Guilfoyle had made his clearing.

Guilfoyle's vision for the Melbourne Botanic Gardens fused his South Seas recollections with European landscape theories. He was aware of the writings of the eighteenth-century philosopher Edmund Burke, having acquired his treatise *On the Sublime and the Beautiful* within months of taking up his position in Melbourne.[75] Burke's aesthetics contrasted the beauty of the man-made landscape with the sublimity of the elemental forces of nature, which inspired the kind of ecstasy Guilfoyle had experienced so intensely at the volcano on Tanna. Guilfoyle's ideas of beauty were also shared by 'Hortus', a local writer whose newspaper columns on 'The Formation of Parks and Gardens' so impressed Guilfoyle that in 1874 he recommended Hortus to design a lake for the city of Sandhurst (now Bendigo).[76]

Yet Guilfoyle went far beyond Hortus's pattern-book aesthetics. He favoured the subtropical vegetation of his frontier experience over the more conventional deciduous trees of European garden design. As early as 1873 he recommended avoiding grouping deciduous trees 'on account of the depressing effect upon the eye . . . of a continuous series of unclothed branches' during the winter months.[77] He found an ally in Clement Hodgkinson, who criticised the 'ungainly' winter appearance of the avenue of planes planted by Joseph Sayce along the newly formed South Yarra drive.[78]

Where a more conventional designer would have suggested planting the fashionable pine as a backdrop to the planes, Guilfoyle proposed the Moreton Bay fig (*Ficus macrophylla*).[79]

Sayce objected, arguing that figs were 'only beautiful when well clothed with branches and leaves to the ground', but Guilfoyle made nonsense of this. He reminded Sayce of 'the natural growth of the tree in its native clime', where it could be seen 'towering to an altitude of more than one hundred feet', its 'huge stem' producing buttresses that stood out 'on all sides'.[80] 'What can be more beautiful', Guilfoyle asked, 'than the dense glossy evergreen foliage of the Moreton Bay fig?'[81] He was so enamoured of the species that he not only sketched it in 1872, but also republished the sketch, *The Great Fig Tree of the Tweed*, as the frontispiece of his *Australian Botany for the Use of Schools* in 1880 and 1884.[82]

Having overturned Sayce's design of the avenue, in 1876 Guilfoyle began to redesign the grounds of Government House. Here he was following in the footsteps of Charles Moore, who had visited Melbourne from Sydney at the beginning of 1873 and had suggested changes to Sayce's landscape design.[83] Sayce had suggested lining the drive to Government House with 'high growing and thickly spreading' araucarias grouped on hillocks, but Guilfoyle foresaw that the trees would 'eventually obscure the view of the park scenery'. Instead, he recommended planting 'shrubs of good foliage and various heights in the foreground so as to slope gradually towards the drive', with lawns in the intervening spaces.[84]

What resulted was a stunning ensemble. Palms and tree ferns grew through a 'rich green mantle' and the horizontal lines of the lawns complemented the vertical walls of the building. From the drive, visitors could glimpse the expanse of lawn on the levelled summit of the Domain hill.[85] The garden gradually opened to view, and was seen *en tout* from the house, where Guilfoyle initially wanted to lay out the formal terraces as a gravel parterre around a fountain.[86] From the entrance to the house, a heavily planted curving centre bed dominated the lawn, like an island in a tropical sea. Beyond was a sequestered fernery and rockery where the governor, his family and their entourage could retreat from the heat of summer.[87]

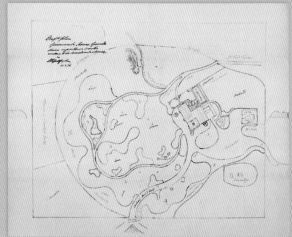

In the botanic gardens, the Fern Gully was more than a summer refuge. It was an essential part of Guilfoyle's understanding that visitors should be able 'to pass gradually from the sub-tropical into the more temperate zone'.[88] To this end, he initially planted the gully with thirty to forty specimens, ranging up to twelve feet, from the temperate forest at Macedon, in keeping with what Sayce had first proposed.[89]

Again Guilfoyle sought inspiration from nature. Soon after his appointment he travelled to the Black's Spur on the Great Dividing Range, some fifty miles from Melbourne. Here he sketched the temperate forest with its tall mountain ash above an understorey of tree-ferns. Two years later, ferns from this location were planted in the Fern Gully.[90]

In 1880, in order 'to render the fern gully still more interesting to the public', Guilfoyle raided the natural gullies of Macedon and Dandenong for shrubs and herbs, including the native musk tree (*Olearia argophylla*), native hazel, the native beech (*Nothofagus cunninghamii*), the broad-leaf flax lily (*Dianella tasmanica*) and the native clematis (*Clematis aristata*). He also introduced 'a number of choice New Zealand ferns'.[91] For visitors who wished to 'become acquainted with the names of the majority of our Australian hardy ferns', he laid a winding path almost a thousand feet long.[92]

Guilfoyle's *leitmotiv*, the Tweed River forest scenery, also provided inspiration. In 1875 two twenty-foot ficus were planted in the Fern Gully, along with lianas for extra verisimilitude.[93] The Fern Gully was changing from a temperate landscape to a subtropical wonderland with all the 'diversity of form and foliage' that contributed to the 'very picturesque effect in the lights and shadows of the Australian bush'.[94]

To heighten this illusion, Guilfoyle also planted *Wigandia caracasana* (Caracas big leaf), *Ricinus* (castor oil plant) and other subtropical shrubs.[95] He combined these with shade-loving species from temperate climates: hydrangeas, mimulus (monkey flower), forget-me-not and violets, as well as 'Mr Thomas Lang's splendid rhododendrons'.[96]

'What can be more beautiful than the dense glossy evergreen foliage of the Moreton Bay fig?'

W. R. Guilfoyle, *The Forest Monster*, from *Australian Botany: Specially Designed for the Use of Schools*, 1884, private collection

Guilfoyle's sketch plan for Government House, 1876

W. R. Guilfoyle, *Draft Plan Government House Grounds Showing Important Works Necessary to be Carried Out at Once*, 19 July 1876, Public Record Office Victoria

Guilfoyle's design for the drive of Government House

W. R. Guilfoyle, *Rough Sketch Showing Effect by Contrasting Foliage. Also the Order to be Preserved in Planting According to Height*, Public Record Office Victoria

An early view of the Fern Gully,
before it went wild

D. McDonald, *Fernery, Botanic
Gardens, Melbourne*, albumen print,
c. 1876–80, State Library of Victoria

The Fern Gully as a landscape 'where
all is left to nature'

J. W. Lindt, *Fernery, Botanic Gardens,
Melbourne*, albumen print, c. 1881–86,
Archives of the Royal Botanic
Gardens, Melbourne

Botanic Garden, Eastern Lawn,
looking from the Fern Gully to
the Volcano

W. R. Guilfoyle, *Catalogue of Plants
under Cultivation in the Melbourne
Botanic Gardens*, 1883

In time, however, the influence of Charles Moore's Sydney
Gardens with its medley of plant juxtapositions receded. By
1893, Guilfoyle was seeking to recreate a landscape 'where all
is left to nature'. To this end, he planted palms and dracaenas
of the Tweed and Pacific, along with the *Grevillea hilliana* that
he had seen from Mount Warning. In that year, John Gould
Veitch's son, James Herbert (1868–1907), visited the gardens
and was entranced by the 'tangled vegetation of the gully'. At
its margins, there were 'magnificent trailing masses of Tecoma
and Plumbago in full glory'. Veitch was struck by how 'Mr
Guilfoyle leaves everything to ramble at will—everything to be
as though it happened'.[97]

As Guilfoyle's plantings extended, he introduced more
plants from subtropical Australia. At the head of the temperate fern gully, he began to form a collection of palms. He
brought in seeds of *Livingstonia* and *Seaforthia elegans*, two
palms from the far north of Queensland that were also found
in the cooler clime of the Illawarra, south of Sydney. His activities popularised the palm in a city where 'this most interesting and charming tribe of plants' had previously been little
known.[98] At the same time, the transition from temperate fern
gully to sheltered palmatum realised his ambition to allow visitors to experience 'the changing character of the vegetation' in
various parts of the gardens.

Visitors emerged from the palmatum on to the Eastern
Lawn, where there were plantings of 'several useful and ornamental trees and shrubs indigenous to Queensland and
Northern New South Wales which for several years were considered too tender for cultivation here'. Among these was the
diamond-leaf laurel (*Pittosporum rhombifolium*), which
reached a height of eighty feet on the banks of the northern
rivers.[99] From the same region came *Eugenia jambolana*,
known as 'durible' ('hardwood') to Aboriginal people, who
used its wood to make spears and boomerangs.[100] In the wild,
where it grew to seventy feet, it was 'a marvellously beautiful
object'. It was best to catch it in flower. Imagine a tree with 'the
whole of its branches, great and small . . . covered with rich

WILLIAM GUILFOYLE

MELBOURNE VIEWS.

VIEW IN BOTANICAL GARDENS.

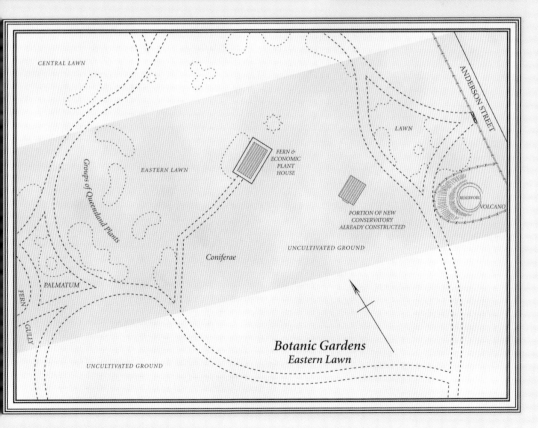

magenta coloured bloom', which from a distance gave the appearance of 'rich pile velvet'.

Almost as beautiful was the scarlet-berried scrub myrtle (*Nelitris ingens*) whose branches bent to the ground under the weight of their foliage. Guilfoyle also planted the Moreton Bay chestnut, which reached a height of 150 feet in the scrubs along the northern rivers. It was a 'very striking and beautiful' tree with 'bright green foliage' setting off 'large masses of orange and pea-shaped flowers'. Guilfoyle recounted how Aboriginal people roasted and ate the three or four seeds found in the pods.[101] Among the other northern plants in this part of the garden was *Tecoma jasminoides*, 'one of the most beautiful of Australian climbers'; at Moreton Bay and on the banks of the Tweed River, the tecoma encircled the tallest forest trees with stems eighteen inches in diameter.[102]

Having been introduced to plants from Queensland and New South Wales, visitors encountered the Pacific in the nearby conservatories. In the old palm house, there grew six hundred exotic ferns and a large collection of tropical economic plants, which Guilfoyle had introduced since his arrival in the gardens. Among these was a large-leafed breadfruit, which he had received from Fiji in 1879. This plant re-awakened a memory of the avenue of breadfruit in the French missionaries' garden on Apia in 1868. He described these as 'more picturesque' than anything else that 'could be imagined'; if they were still alive, they would have grown into 'magnificent objects'.[103]

The gardens were suffused with Guilfoyle's memory of plant-hunting in the wilds. When he planted the new conservatory, he was still harking back to the *Challenger*'s voyage twelve years before. Potted crotons and Fijian fire plants recalled the 'glorious sight' of brightly coloured foliage backed by the 'large unbroken leafage of the banana' on the islands. He recollected how crotons were 'esteemed by the natives for growing on the graves of deceased relatives'.[104] He described the 'very showy' *Hibiscus lambertii* as if seeing it for the first time: on the island of Tanna, its crimson flowers were 'so profuse' that some of the officers thought it 'could not possibly be a plant in flower but a red blanket or cloth spread out to dry'.[105]

Even so, he understood that it would take time to realise these tropical landscapes in Melbourne. To soothe his political masters and assuage a public impatient to see results, Guilfoyle turned to the cordyline. The usefulness of this 'arborescent species' could not be overestimated: by contrast with the slow-growing palm and the banana, which was 'seldom seen out of doors' in Melbourne, cordylines gave an 'instant' tropical effect.

In 1875 Guilfoyle addressed the Victorian Horticultural Society on 'The Dracaena and the Cordyline', illustrating his lecture with examples in pots and speaking with intense excitement about seeing these plants in the wild for the first time. He vividly described the forest surrounding an almost extinct volcano on Fiji, where crotons provided 'the most gorgeous of all leafage', their colour highlighted by the bright emerald-green fronds of tree ferns and feathery Kentias and Cocos palms with orchids covering their trunks. Soaring above all this were the lofty island chestnut trees and figs, 'bound together by climbers much thicker than one's arm'.

For his audience of armchair travellers, Guilfoyle acted out the perils of the plant-hunter in wild places. He questioned popular assumptions that the South Seas were inhabited by 'savages . . . with crude tastes'; on the contrary, he was pleased to report that the islanders were 'lovers of Cordylines'. With consummate stagecraft, he recounted how an old grey-headed chief stopped him when he went to take a piece of a magnificent dracaena that grew in the village. Whenever Guilfoyle went to touch the plant, the chief would catch his arm and say 'tabu', 'tabu'. No bribes could shake his resolve. Guilfoyle closed the tableau by informing his audience that the plants were grown in honour of deceased relatives, and if a native on Vate (Efaté) dared to touch one of them, 'the club is his fate'. The implication was that he had been lucky to escape.[106]

Nowhere did Guilfoyle conjure the South Seas more evocatively than in the Anderson Street corner of the gardens, where

Temple of the winds. Botanical Gardens. Melbourne.

he transformed an above-ground reservoir into the largest of 'a group of volcanic craters'. Rockery was used to mimic a lava flow, and the furnace that heated the adjacent palm house was strategically sited at the bottom of one of these craters to give visitors the impression that 'the volcano may become active at any time'.[107] Drawing on his sublime and terrible experiences on Tanna and Fiji, Guilfoyle turned part of the Victorian gardening repertoire into an imaginative exploration of the tension between nature and culture.

Guilfoyle's use of metaphor was even more explicit in his design and siting of the Temple of the Winds, erected during 1901 in memory of Charles La Trobe, Victoria's first governor, who was also a botanical collector and founder of the gardens.[108] The temple appears at first glance a European neo-classical folly, possibly based on the one at Kew Gardens, but there are some significant points of difference. The siting of the Melbourne temple recalls the dramatic view from Mount Warning. It was perched on top of a cliff, providing a view of the azure Dandenong Ranges to the east over a vivid carpet of pigface (*Mesembryanthemum*), planted to flower in succession for months.[109]

Furthermore, the temple's capitals are surmounted by stag-horn ferns. This detailing might be explained by the turn-of-the-century enthusiasm for Australian decorative motifs, except that Guilfoyle was using this motif much earlier. In 1875, staghorn ferns were reported to be 'one of the greatest novelties in the Gardens',[110] and in 1880, Guilfoyle had arranged 'stag horn, elk horn and bird's nest ferns . . . to form capitals to the upright supports to the roof' of the renovated palm house.[111] The idea may have germinated during his expedition to Mount Warning in 1872, when he had described the 'palms and tree ferns of extreme beauty . . . shaded the stag horn, the elk horn and bird nest Asplenium—like capitals decorating a colonnade'.[112]

By contrast with this evocation of the elemental, the Museum of Economic Botany was a temple to utility. In von Mueller's time the museum contained 'an extensive collection of dried

Guilfoyle looked to the cordyline to create tropical scenery in Victoria

J. W. Lindt, *Princes' Lawn*, albumen print, *c.* 1881–86, Archives of the Royal Botanic Gardens, Melbourne

The Temple of the Winds, Melbourne Botanic Gardens, *c.* 1920

Temple of the Winds, Botanic Gardens, Melbourne, postcard, *c.* 1920, Archives of the Royal Botanic Gardens, Melbourne

The staghorn fern, the inspiration for the capitals on the columns of the Temple of the Winds

The Stag's horn fern, from D. T. Fish, *Cassell's Popular Gardening*, vol. 3, n.d., private collection

plants indigenous to all parts of the globe', and possessed 'but few attractions to the public'.[113] Under Guilfoyle, it became a celebration of the clearing. The once-mighty giants of the Australian forest, felled by the axe of the settler and timber-getter, now rested against the Museum's walls as 'massive planks of Blackwood, Podocarpus and *Dacrydium cupressinum*', their economic value explained by labels. Here, the death of the forest heralded the advance of settler society.

This narrative of progress was counterpointed by 'a large, flat, oval shaped slab of stone with small pieces of rounded basalt', with which the ill-fated explorers Burke and Wills had attempted to grind seeds to sustain themselves. The presence of this relic reminded visitors of the disasters that could befall Europeans in Australia if they did not acquaint themselves with the nature of the country.

The imperial passion for acclimatisation was also represented in the museum's collections. There were examples of gums, essential oils, dyes, tobaccos, fibres, perfumes, medicinal products, cocoa, coffee, tea and sago, all accompanied by labels explaining their uses.[114] The exhibits indulged the imperial dream that Victoria might emulate the tea fields of India, Ceylon or China. The lessons of the museum were reinforced by an extensive medicinal garden 'not more than a few paces' away, with European, American and Australian plants.[115] By visiting the museum, visitors 'could gather more botanic knowledge in a week' than they could 'hope to learn by years of reading'.[116]

Guilfoyle seized every opportunity to find plants of economic value. When he visited Queensland in 1882 on a holiday occasioned by ill health, he collected upwards of nine species of jute on an expedition accompanied by 'some black trackers', who guided him from Cooktown toward the Dividing Range.[117] His knowledge of agriculture would see him appointed as a specialist adviser to the Victorian Royal Commission on Crops in 1885.[118]

As part of the imperial schema, Guilfoyle was adamant that 'all plants should be classified and arranged by one universally acknowledged authority', which he believed should be in London. Plants would then be known by an agreed name wherever they grew in the world.[119] To this end, he established beds in various parts of the gardens where plants were grouped according to their taxonomic orders. When James Herbert Veitch visited the gardens in 1893, he noted that some beds were devoted to natural orders, some reserved for the flora of various countries or continents, and others were 'arranged from the gardener's point of view'.[120] Guilfoyle had integrated the botanic and the scenic, the taxonomic and the poetic.

Guilfoyle's trip to Europe in 1890 sharpened his perception of colonial and European differences.[121] Recollecting this tour in an 1893 lecture entitled 'Glimpses of Some Botanical Gardens and Their Conservatories', Guilfoyle emphasised that what set Australia apart was its climate and soil, which were 'favourable for the cultivation of almost anything'.[122] With the opportunities for education and 'increasingly liberal land laws', 'our young men' would become not only 'owners of flourishing gardens, but horticulturalists in the truest sense, second to none in the world'.

Rather than creating a longing for Europe, the trip re-affirmed the colonial experience. If Britain was 'a garden from one end to another so beautiful in the simplicity of nature', the colonies had the potential for unlimited acclimatisation and for technology to transform nature and obliterate the wilder-ness. There was 'no doubt that as the facility of communi-cation with Europe and America' increased, the Australian colonies' 'vast resources' would bear fruit in 'the commercially valuable productions of its vegetable kingdoms'.[123]

Guilfoyle's reading of the colonial clearing as an intersection of cultivation, technology and nature also informed his tour of New Zealand in 1908. Leaving Auckland on the train and seeing the country for the first time, he gloried in the riot of colour: 'gorgeous crimson-flowered rata', white blossoms, scarlet berries and golden flowers 'all mingled in picturesque confusion'. Above this 'jungle' towered gigantic trees, which were 'fast becoming scarce' due to timber-getters. As the train

4320. FERNS & NIKAU. WAITAKEREI. AUCKLAND.
BURTON BROS. DUNEDIN

ascended to the Rotorua springs, nature became scenery: Guilfoyle's eye constructed 'charming views of broad fertile valleys studded with robust Cordylines, or cabbage trees'. He peeped into 'woody dells, beauty spots in fact', where he would have loved to roam. From the train, a rough-hewn clearing was transfigured into 'garden-like expanses of spacious lawns and streams'. The colonial garden was the aesthetic antithesis of the brute, technological force of the frontier.[124]

With time, Guilfoyle's gardens became essays in colour. He perceived the red-flowering Western Australian gum tree (*Eucalyptus ficifolia*) as 'one of the most gorgeous plants of the Australian continent', 'a blaze of fire in nature' that could 'dazzle the eye' when in flower.[125] In the Melbourne gardens, the colours of this eucalypt were carefully selected. As James Herbert Veitch observed, Guilfoyle had assembled nine shades ranging from white to red.[126] His colour schemes had little to do with the English sensibilities essayed by Gertrude Jekyll in her *Colour in the Flower Garden* (1908).[127] Rather, he drew his colours from the sky, the mountain and the vegetation that clothed the earth.

By re-creating the scenery of empire's frontier, Guilfoyle simultaneously created a wilderness and a clearing, an imperial space presided over by the adjacent Government House, where the Union Jack flew when the governor was in residence. Yet the great cosmos of empire that was the Melbourne gardens, with its beds dedicated to the flora of countries and continents—from South Africa to New Zealand —was almost undone by more ambitious imperial schemes. In 1900 he confessed to the grand old man of botany, Sir Joseph Hooker, that the cost of sending a Victorian contingent to the Boer War had led to 'unmerciful cuts' to his funding.[128]

Guilfoyle's aesthetic evocation of both sides of the frontier —the wild and the tame, the sublime and the beautiful—also informed his other landscapes. At Warrnambool Botanic Gardens in Western Victoria, he created a *tour de force* of sweeping lawns, palms and ficus that evoked the scenery of Mount Warning, while the ascent to Camperdown Botanic

New Zealand scenery near Auckland, about 1885

Burton Brothers, *Ferns & Nikau, Waitakerei, Auckland*, c. 1885, albumen print, private collection

Melbourne Botanic Gardens: an imperial space presided over by the adjacent Government House

Government House from the Botanic Gardens, albumen print, Archives of the Royal Botanic Gardens, Melbourne

Gardens, up an extinct volcano, is lined with *Eucalyptus fici-folia*.[129] The height of these imaginings was his plan (sadly, never executed) for the windy shores of Lake Colac, which he offered to metamorphose into a tropical lagoon fringed with palms.[130]

All this was a testimony to how a nurseryman's son transformed himself into a 'magician', an accolade bestowed on him by Melbourne's august newspaper, the *Argus*, after his death in 1912.[131] In the words of the European artist Morgenstern Rudinoff, who visited the Melbourne Botanic Gardens in 1903, Guilfoyle had conjured something 'like a Paradise', a garden 'the like of which I have seen nowhere else—no, not in Europe itself'.[132]

A garden 'the like of which I have seen nowhere else—no, not in Europe itself': Morgenstern Rudinoff paints Guilfoyle's botanic garden

E. S. Fysh, *M. Rudinoff in the Botanic Gardens, Garden Gazette*, May–June 1903, p. 240, State Library of Victoria

Photo by E M. Rudinoff in the Botanic Gardens.   *E S Fysh*

v. | Josiah Mitchell
The Man of the Soil

MR. JOSIAH MITCHELL.

The Man of the Soil

Josiah Mitchell (1822–1881) was 'to a very great extent, a self taught man'.[1] Born at Whitehaven, Cumberland, in 1822, he left school at a very early age with only 'the rudiments of education'. As chance would have it, he first went to work at Gillarrow in his native county on the farm of Captain J. R. Walker RN, a gentleman well known in the north of England as a pioneer of many modern improvements in agriculture. After learning the ordinary operations of farming, Mitchell was apprenticed as gardener to the same establishment. On finishing this apprenticeship, he found work in the gardens of the Earl of Lonsdale at Westmoreland and then under Charles McIntosh (1794–1864), the gardener responsible for planting the celebrated grounds and conservatories of the Duke of Buccleuch's Dalkeith estate outside Edinburgh.

Josiah Mitchell, from *Leader*, 23 April, 1881

McIntosh was a prolific writer who 'contributed largely to the literature, and to the scientific advancement of the profession'. He wrote for Paxton's *Magazine of Botany*, the *Gardener's Magazine* and the *Gardener's Chronicle*, and edited the horticultural pages of the *Scottish Farmer* in the last three years of his life.[2] He was also author of several books, including *The Practical Gardener and Modern Horticulturalist* (1829), *Greenhouse, Hothouse and Stove* (1838), *Flora and Pomona, or the British Fruit and Flower Garden* (1839), and *The Book of the Garden* (1853).[3] Writing for a newly literate class, he had little patience for Latin nomenclature, which precluded his readers from learning about plants. He wrote with barely concealed indignation:

> It cannot have escaped the observation of every reflecting mind, that the inculcation of the first principles of science in dead languages, which do not form a branch of education in minor schools, must necessarily act as a considerable drawback to those pleasures whose genius may lead them to the study and attainment of the science of botany.[4]

The professional gardener of the mid-nineteenth century conceived of himself as a vital participant in the continued advance of civilisation, not as a decorative appendage. In this

The Australian hakea: according to Charles McIntosh, scarcely worth the pot it grew in

Hakea obliqua, from *Loddiges Botanical Cabinet*, vol. 17, plate 1682, State Library of Victoria

Aquilegia glandulosa: Charles McIntosh's idea of a good flowering plant

Aquilegia glandulosa, from *The Botanist*, vol. 5, plate 219, State Library of Victoria

Glenara, near Bulla: a Mediterranean paradise with an Italianate terrace looking over orange groves and vineyards

Eugene von Guérard, *Mr Clark's Station, Deep Creek, near Keilor*, 1867, oil on canvas, 68.2 × 121.8 cm, purchased with the assistance of the National Gallery Society Victoria and Mr and Mrs Solomon Lew, 1986, National Gallery of Victoria, Melbourne

scheme of things, righteous gardeners would have no truck with the fashionable classes' enthusiasm for filling their glass-houses with the plants of New Holland. These exotic plants, according to McIntosh, were 'scarcely worth the pot in which they grow', and the 'mania for accumulating species' was a poor substitute for 'forming judicious selections of good flowering plants'.[5] Gardeners like McIntosh possessed a moral sense as certain as the coming of the seasons. Confident of their role, they chastised amateurs for caprices much as preachers warned congregations about the vanities of the world.

McIntosh's junior employee, Josiah Mitchell, would employ his writing skills to put forward similar views, but he would not do so in Britain. His opportunities there were limited to managing estates. After his time at Dalkeith, he moved from one post to another. He worked in Dorsetshire for a while, then took a position as gardener and steward to William Pinney, MP for East Somerset. From there he proceeded to the Royal Botanic Gardens in Kew. Before quitting England, he was gardener and steward to Mr T. G. Corbett of Elsham Hall, Lincolnshire. Finally, in 1853, at the age of thirty-one, Mitchell emigrated to the colony of Victoria, exchanging the English conservatory, with its 'ill suited *Hakea*, *Isopogon* and eucalypt', for the Australian wilderness.[6]

Victoria then was a byword for golden opportunity, but Mitchell initially resisted the lure of the goldfields. He found employment in the Melbourne Botanic Gardens under its superintendent, John Dallachy, a Scottish-trained gardener who had arrived in Melbourne from Ceylon in 1848. Yet gold unsettled even people of temperate and regular habits. Mitchell was soon to be found amid the hurly-burly of the Forest Creek diggings at Castlemaine, where desperate gold-seekers denuded the creek flat and hillsides of timber and upended the soil with spades and picks. Mitchell did not prosper on the diggings and retreated to Melbourne, where he found employment laying out the General Cemetery (to the plans of architect Albert Purchas). He stayed there for several years before he went into a nursery partnership with a man by the name of Elliot.[7]

JOSIAH MITCHELL

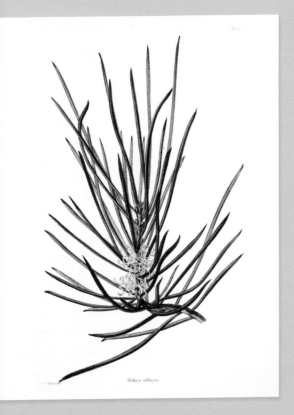

Hakea obliqua

Aquilegia glandulosa

Mitchell and Elliot became 'two of the most scientific, practical gardeners in the colony'.[8] In the heady days of gold, when the value of the pound was inflated and frugality was thrown to the winds, the two paid £335 annually to rent Fern Hill in Moonee Ponds. (In more sober times, this extravagant rent was reduced to £125.) Among their clients was Walter Clark of Glenara on the banks of Back Creek near Bulla. Laid out by Purchas and his partner Swyer in 1857, the garden at Glenara was a Mediterranean paradise with an Italianate terrace looking over orange groves and vineyards.[9] Mitchell supplied Glenara with numerous fruit trees, 198 grapevines and 100 Chilean pines. He also grew 'fine oranges and lemons from seedling trees' and had a market garden at Fern Hill until 1859, when he moved to a twelve-acre orchard on the banks of the Saltwater River at Maribyrnong.[10]

Mitchell's initial thoughts about the colony can only be guessed at, but in 1860 he began to emerge as a public figure. In that year, he was elected president of the Victorian Gardeners' Mutual Improvement Society, an early and influential horticultural self-help group. In a lecture entitled 'Suggestions in Reference to the Objects of the Society', Mitchell described his fellow gardeners as occupying a position in the colony 'analogous to that which the first Romans did when they settled in England'. There was one important difference: his audience had 'the benefit of all the light which Science and Art has thrown upon cultivation from that time to this, to guide us in our future progress'. The continent would offer 'ample room . . . for all our energies'.[11]

Mitchell spoke with a confidence bordering on hubris. The gardener as a modern-day Roman was 'a powerful moral agent'. He stood on the edge of a vast, largely untilled and uncultivated land mass, where 'enemies in the shape of beasts, birds, insects and mildew-fungi' were 'legion'. Yet Mitchell optimistically predicted that the Australian soil and climate would be 'suitable for the growth of any plant that will thrive between the equator and the latitude of John o'Groats' in Scotland. It was therefore incumbent upon the society's members to obtain 'all the information we can get' regarding the production of particular fruits and vegetables, and to ascertain the scientific facts about 'the nature of the soil, subsoil, manure, aspect, shelter and situation'. By increasing and disseminating knowledge, members of the horticultural self-improvement society could contribute to a larger theatre of knowledge than they ever would in Victorian England. 'Collecting well ascertained facts' would not only guide future cultivators but also render 'some service' to the state.

Victoria gave Mitchell the opportunity to speak and write about scientific and horticultural matters. After 'upwards of seven years practice and observation in this colony', he could speak with some authority on 'The Principles of Cultivation Applicable to the Climate of Victoria' (1860), and on the virtues of 'Healthy and High Cultivation' for preventing insect attacks (1861).[12] These lectures allow a glimpse of Mitchell, labouring in his orchard on the Saltwater, while simultaneously conducting practical experiments and thinking about larger agricultural issues.

In the Australian climate, Mitchell had observed that the stocks used for grafting in England were 'worse than useless'. To overcome this problem, he successfully grafted pears on quince stock and apricots on plums. Echoing his old master McIntosh, he railed against 'the chaotic mass of names of fruits' and advocated 'a simple intelligible form of nomenclature which would benefit everyone in any way connected with fruit trees in the colony'.

He believed that in the 'semi-tropical climate' of the Saltwater, 'the exposure of the soil to the sun, heat and rain . . . rapidly decomposes the organic and at the same time increases the inorganic food of plants'. In January 1863 he wrote to the Melbourne *Yeoman and Acclimatiser* suggesting it was the 'duty of every fruit-grower to supply the soil with vegetable matter', because 'trees want all the moisture they can get'. He criticised the practice of 'sowing down orchards with grass in this dry climate'. His preference was for 'green crops such as turnips, marigolds, rape, mustard and lupins which extract a greater portion of their bulk from the atmosphere'. These would maintain soil fertility and prevent trees from dying 'before their time'.[13]

A twelve-acre plot was a very small vantage point from which to ruminate on such large questions. In 1863 Mitchell successfully applied for the tenancy of the Model Farm, located in the north-west of Royal Park beside the Moonee Ponds Creek. It was near the zoological gardens, where the colony's acclimatisers were importing birds and beasts from as far afield as India and North Africa to populate the 'howling wilderness'.[14] In his application for the position, Mitchell declared that he had studied botany, vegetable physiology, chemistry and meteorology. He also claimed to have introduced Californian prairie grass into the colony and to have proved that mangolds and sugar beet grew in brackish soil where nothing else would.[15] After his successful application, he had 130 acres to experiment with for an annual rental of £165.

Appearances, however, can be deceptive. The model farm had proved of limited use for experimental agriculture because the acreage was too small for the successful rotation of crops. Moreover, Mitchell found the farm in a neglected state. Paddocks were grazed bare or covered with a 'rank and luxuriant crop of weeds', including thistles and 'a mass of cape weed'. (By 1870 the Board of Agriculture was reporting that cape weed 'appears to be overrunning the country and promises to become a greater pest than the thistle and burr'.[16]) The acacia hedges dividing the paddocks were in 'a wild state', and the fence on the northern boundary was falling to pieces. This neglect extended to the flower garden, lawn and vineyard, all of which were 'in a sorry plight with weeds and every description of rubbish'.

There was an added sense of urgency because spring was fast advancing. Mitchell informed his superiors he had 'little time . . . for writing'. He refused to foreshadow 'things that may never be realised'; instead, he settled down to work.[17]

One of his first projects was the digging of a manure pit to collect the drainage from the house and stables. For Mitchell

'rational agriculture' relied on manure to produce 'good crops
. . . without diminishing the original fertility of the soil'. He
also arranged for the delivery of waste from the nearby Brunswick abattoirs.[18] His critics were quick to point out that not
every farm in the colony had the benefit of being near an
abattoir, but Mitchell defended the Model Farm as a microcosm
of the larger issues facing colonial agriculture.

To prevent soil exhaustion, he rotated crops over a six-year
cycle. For the first crop, he recommended growing a naked-
stemmed cereal with farinaceous seeds. The next year, he
planted a crop with 'a branching stem and fleshy root'. In the
third year came a crop of oats, and in the fourth year green
crops, 'chiefly mangolds, heavily manured'. Finally, the soil was
rested for two years by sowing pasture.[19]

Mitchell also experimented with irrigation: potatoes one
year, deep-rooted crops the next. Even bad times were useful
to him. The 'extreme drought' of 1867–68 provided an opportunity to test 'the commonly received opinion that to cart out
and spread manure in dry weather results in the great loss of
the fertilising qualities of the manure'.[20] All these observations
helped establish 'important facts and principles in connection
with the cultivation of the soil'.[21]

Yet as the 1860s progressed, Mitchell's initial optimism
gave way to a realisation that the colony's arable land was
being permanently ruined by inappropriate agricultural
practices. He voiced these concerns in his 1866 lecture on
'The Rotation of Crops'. Ever since 'the first plough furrow
was turned beneath this country's azure sky', he observed
dismally, 'intelligent man has ignored the laws of nature';
in a few years, he predicted, this ignorance 'will undo the
work of ages'.

The colonial farmer could not depend on 'traditional history
handed down through generations'. His 'hallowed memories
of "*auld lang syne*", were irrelevant to the colonial landscape.
Emigration had broken 'nature's bond' to 'mountains blue and
melon skirted streams, since childhood loved and dreamt of in
his dreams'.[22] Mitchell viewed this problem as 'inseparable

The promise of manure

From *Nature*, 3 February 1870, p. 354,
State Library of Victoria

A 'picture of man as destroyer'
in the United States of America
Camp in a Pine Forest, from
H. W. Bates, *Illustrated Travels*, vol. 3,
n.d. but *c.* 1870, private collection

from the settlement of a new country'. Land in the colony was 'an investment and nothing more'.

Seeking to understand 'the history of colonial culture in our time', Mitchell turned his attention to America. As a self-educated man, he had read Johnson's *Chemistry of Common Life*,[23] which described the misadventure of contemporary American land settlement. For Mitchell, America presented a 'picture of man as destroyer'. The new settler in a virgin landscape was surrounded by 'fertility everywhere', but his 'exhaustive farming practices' gradually dimmed the 'smiling landscape'. Eventually, the settler forsook 'his long cultivated farm and hew[ed] out another from the native forest'. The result was a moving frontier of devastation, with 'a wall of green forests on the horizon' and 'a half desert and naked region behind'.[24]

Mitchell knew Victoria's situation was different. Unlike American farmers, Victorians were not under constant pressure to crop land to supply the European grain market. At the same time, Victoria had 'no far West to fall back upon', and therefore had to husband its arable soils. Victorians could not afford to clear the land and move on. To illustrate this point, Mitchell drew on the analogy of 'a farmer who commences to clear the timber off a field and cart it to Melbourne':

> The trees took a long time to grow; and they are quickly cut down. It would take a long time for other trees to attain to the same size. Now precisely the same thing happens to the mineral and vegetable substances which give fertility to the soil as happened in the case of the timber, when the cultivator begins to take crop after crop of the same sort of grain or hay, without intermission, without change, without manure.[25]

As a remedy, Mitchell championed 'collecting, decomposing and applying to the soil all refuse animal and vegetable matter, the occasional purchase of phosphates', combined with the rotation of crops. 'We have much to learn yet in this climate', he remarked. Yet he also believed 'we have a good foundation of grass to build upon if only we turn it to proper account'.

JOSIAH MITCHELL

thereon for the past twenty years, it has produced surprising results. Having established his propositions single-handed, and at his own cost, a portion of the imperial domain at Vincennes was allotted to him, as an experimental farm, and the crops he there produced, the *Conférences Agricoles* he there held among the crops, together with his numerous

Comparative size of wheatsheaf produced from soil completely manured.

published works, and the effect of his lectures, have made such an impression, that his method of cultivation has been adopted at more than five hundred places in France ; while from Spain, Portugal, Italy, Belgium, and Germany, and from the French colonies, farmers and cultivators have resorted to Paris and to the experimental farm at Vincennes, to acquaint themselves with the method which

under ordinary circumstances would more than double their harvest.

Prof. Ville's method of instruction is as simple and definite as his method of fertilisation, as if he had in view the large number of small peasant proprietors in France, and wrote and lectured for their especial benefit. You may sow wheat, he says, in soil wanting nitrogenised matter, phosphates, potash, and lime, and it will grow and bear grain, but the stalk will be very short, thin, and weak, and the vegetation precarious. Mix with the soil a substance composed of carbon, hydrogen, and oxygen, the result will be exactly the same. And why? Because plants take all the carbon they need from the carbonic acid of the atmosphere, and hydrogen and oxygen from water. Hence, to add these three elements to the soil is useless ; on the other hand, if some substance containing assimilable nitrogen be added, a salutary effect is at once produced, for plants derive nitrogen partly from the soil, partly from the air. But this effect is as nothing compared with that of manures affording certain mineral elements : mix these as well as the nitrogenised matter with calcined earth, and its fertility will equal that of the richest soil. The vegetation, no longer thin and starved, acquires vigour and activity, the plant grows straight and strong, is of a rich green colour, and produces a well-formed ear filled with large and heavy grain.

Comparative size of wheatsheaf produced from soil without manure.

Many of the mineral elements required by the plant already exist in the soil ; consequently, to render it productive the farmer has to discover which of the fertilising elements are wanting, and apply them to his field. To do this, it is not necessary that he should be an analytical chemist : the vegetation of his fields will do it for him. He has only to sow or plant a small experi-

For Mitchell, the problem of colonial agriculture was that 'we farm too little and plough too much'. He was particularly critical of the Selection Acts, which he believed impeded the adoption of better farming practices. Selectors on 'small patches of land' were 'driven to depend exclusively on the plough' because of 'the high price of labour and want of manure'. The solution was to encourage the creation of a new class, the 'farming grazier'. The size of selections should be increased to more than 640 acres of 'real good land, fifteen or twenty miles from a market'. In this way, sheep and dairy cows could be pastured in tandem with growing grain, and selectors would be able to afford 'the purchase of phosphatic manures and the occasional cropping of green manure'. This would render 'cultivation more profitable' without exhausting the soil. By contrast, the grazing practices of the squatters encouraged the growth of 'troublesome grasses' while 'the better sorts . . . died out'. In Mitchell's opinion, 'the cheapest method of restoring the fertility of such land would be to let it run to bush'.[26]

While the self-educated Mitchell was astute enough to sound the alarm over deteriorating soil fertility, his analysis was influenced by his interpretation of the Bible. He believed the colony's soils had been formed by the violent geological upheavals associated with a cataclysmic Creation. This had been followed by a time when 'she oaks rear their wiry forms, through which the wind sighs with melancholy sound and gum trees hang their flint coloured leaves to break and modify the force of the scorching blast'. This 'progressive development of vegetable life' was accompanied by 'amelioration of climatic conditions'; eventually, 'what was once a barren island of rocks and stones became fitted in climate and soil for the residence and sustenance of man'.[27]

Melbourne's scientific community shared Mitchell's concerns about soil exhaustion. John Macadam, a Victorian chemical analyst, had already observed that colonial soils became impoverished because of a phosphate deficiency.[28] To promote more sophisticated understanding of colonial agriculture, von Mueller corresponded with the pre-eminent German organic

JOSIAH MITCHELL

chemist Justus von Liebig, and proposed that the Victorian government appoint a professor of agriculture to the university.[29] Meanwhile, Edward Wilson, proprietor of the *Argus*, turned to Darwin rather than to biblical theories of a cataclysmic Creation to explain the compaction of the soil, the decline of indigenous grasses, and the death of trees arising from European pastoral occupation.[30] The condition of the land engaged the best minds in the colony.

Mitchell continued to develop his views about the relationship between agriculture and society. In 1870, he had an opportunity to address the Victorian Agriculture Society at Heidelberg, outside Melbourne. He rose to the occasion with an earnest lecture on 'What is Rational Agriculture?' Since his 1866 lecture, Mitchell had grown in cogency. In place of long-winded quotations from popular primers, he now drew on the German poet–philosopher Goethe. His audience heard (probably for the first time) that nature ordered 'the seizing and retaining of space, in the great or small scale'. In Goethe's scheme of things, patriotism was a universal feeling, founded on interest in the soil. In defining the nation in terms of attachment to land, Mitchell articulated a view that was to have a powerful resonance in the formation of an Australian national identity.

Mitchell was particularly concerned about the 'large and ever increasing number of Australian born youths fast growing up to manhood' in country districts. These young men, he argued, would 'learn, whether we take the trouble to teach them or not'. In the absence of formal instruction, they would imbibe knowledge 'from practices they see carried on around them, and in which they are engaged'. Mitchell feared that 'those coming men into whose hands the cultivation of land must fall . . . will become possessed of the erroneous notion that ploughing, sowing, reaping and mowing constitutes the sum total of cultivation'. This would lead to an 'insane desire to convert the fertility of the soil at all hazards into hard cash—to sell the birthright of mankind for a few pieces of glittering ore'. He again likened this to the American experience,

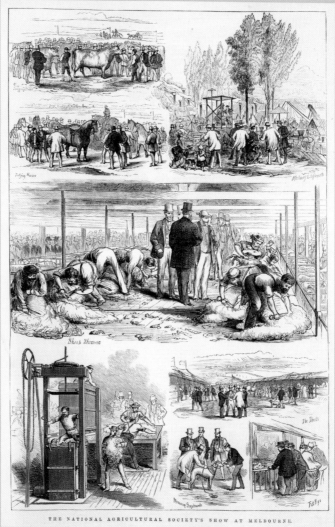

THE NATIONAL AGRICULTURAL SOCIETY'S SHOW AT MELBOURNE.

where 'the settler subdues a piece of land, flogs it to death, abandons the carcass, and repeats the operation on a new subject'. Already there had been a 'mass exodus of farmers from . . . exhausted districts of South Australia coming to Victoria to take benefit of our recent Land Bill'.[31] Mitchell blamed this problem on government policies of 'settling the people . . . on too small portions' in a colony that had a 'limited area of good agricultural land'. Unless measures were taken to counter the 'absurd notion of farming' that resulted, poor agricultural practices would become self-perpetuating.

To educate the populace in better farming practices, Mitchell looked to voluntary organisations. Foremost among these were the agricultural shows, which acted as 'schools for adults'.[32] Victorians, however, were still 'without any public body to represent our greatest and most important industry—agriculture'. He predicted that 'all interested in the progress of the colony' would soon join in 'fostering and promoting the development of its varied resources'.[33]

This prediction came to fruition in December 1870 with the founding of the National Agricultural Society of Victoria (later to become the Royal Agricultural Society of Victoria), which would establish the Melbourne Agricultural Show. At the public meeting held to establish the society, Mitchell spoke in support of a motion that 'this Society shall have no connection with the Government'; the society refused to ask for any subsidy 'beyond a grant of land and money to aid at the outset in erecting the necessary buildings'. Mitchell pronounced the voluntary principle superior to any other. Annual grants, he suggested, would 'paralyse energy of action on the part of committee members' and weaken public support.[34] He joined the inaugural committee of the society alongside several other supporters of voluntarism, including William Clarke, one of the largest landholders in Australasia.[35]

The society also decided not to include the word 'horticulture' in its title. It was considered 'undesirable' to 'bind the Society to a certain amount of funds for that purpose'. Doubtless this decision was influenced by Mitchell, who had retired

What does this painting depict? Agricultural abundance, or 'the erroneous notion that ploughing, sowing, reaping and mowing constitutes the sum total of cultivation'?

J. H. Carse, *Harvest Field*, 1870, oil on canvas, 76 x 114.2 cm Bendigo Art Gallery

A school for adults: the Melbourne Agricultural Show, 1874

The National Agricultural Society's Show at Melbourne, in *The Illustrated Australian News*, 2 December 1874 State Library of Victoria

from the presidency of the Victorian Horticultural Society a year earlier.[36] The gardener's horizons had broadened beyond his original calling.

Mitchell had also begun to write about the agricultural landscape. In September 1870, he went to see the New South Wales Agricultural Exhibition in Sydney and report on it for the Melbourne *Leader* newspaper. He expressed the hope that 'the example set by Sydney folks' would counter the Victorian disposition toward 'horse or foot racing, cricket and the like' and stir a 'sense of what our duty is' in 'promot[ing] the development of this new country'. As a self-improver, Mitchell spurned 'the frivolous and the entertaining' and celebrated 'popular, useful and instructive institutions'.

More than two thousand people visited the New South Wales Agricultural Exhibition. Mitchell was especially taken with the exhibits by Sir William Macarthur of Camden Park and Mr Walter Hill of the Brisbane Botanic Gardens for the 'truly admirable and practical manner in which they illustrated the capabilities of New South Wales and Queensland'. He was enraptured by Macarthur's assembled cornucopia of colonial produce: bags of plant seeds, jars of preserved raisins and prunes, wine and olive oil, and roots of turnips, mangolds and carrots. Macarthur had taken every opportunity to instruct his audience, even arranging dried plant specimens as 'industrial trophies' on the pillars of the exhibition hall.

To Mitchell, the austere Scot, Walter Hill's exhibits of Queensland produce were overwhelming in their abundance. Cotton, tobacco, allspice and coffee conjured up the fecundity of the tropics 'in the most forcible manner'. There were 'all the varieties of cotton', seventeen kinds of sugar cane, preserved pineapple, lime, lemon and Seville orange, Indian and West Indian ginger, cinnamon bark and oil, and Jamaican pepper. All had been 'introduced by Mr Hill during the past fifteen years'. As if these were not enough, Hill showed at least ten varieties of hemp—some native to Queensland, others drawn from places as diverse as Mexico, India, Ceylon and Guinea. Clearly, Queensland agriculture could thrive given 'the right application of intelligence, practical skill and untiring industry', together with 'a small monetary outlay', a prospect that appealed to Mitchell's faith in thrift, intellect and practical self-help.

Mitchell might have ended his exhibition epistle on this celebratory note if it had not been for the Victorian display, which he found embarrassing—'the shabbiest lot in the whole place', 'in the main of interest only to the botanical student'.[37] The Sydney growers laughed at the Victorians' dracaenas, taunting the colonists 'for having nothing better to send'.[38] It was 'decidedly unpleasant' to be led by the arm to a pot containing 'mere fragments' and sarcastically asked, 'Is this what you call a plant?' By contrast, Mr Hill's dracaenas were a feast of luxuriant colour.

The Victorian exhibit was the work of Ferdinand von Mueller. Mitchell was affronted to see von Mueller's name in large black letters on 'flaming yellow labels', which he saw as a sign of self-promotion and 'scientific meretriciousness'. By comparison, the achievements of Sir William Macarthur and 'plain Mr Hill' could only be identified by turning to the exhibition catalogue. To a self-made man, this proved that 'practical merit' was better than 'any number of medals' and 'a host of titles'.[39] In the colonies the fruits of the earth would be increased by honest, hard-working, practical, self-educated men rather than by a scientist of international renown.

When these criticisms appeared in print, von Mueller immediately began mustering support. He wrote to Michael Guilfoyle in New South Wales:

> In last week's *Leader* dear Mr Guilfoyle the enclosed article appeared. Do you think it just? I believe to send a reply to the *Leader* . . . would receive no admission unless changes there brought alterations towards me. Yet in the Sydney press something might be done for me perhaps, I leave the matter in your hands.[40]

In the event, it was Charles Moore, director of the Sydney Botanic Gardens, who rose to von Mueller's defence, claiming that Mitchell's column reflected 'severely and unjustly on his friend and colleague'. Moore characterised von Mueller as one of 'the most talented cultivators of the plants in this or any other part of the world'. It was no fault of his that he could not produce 'the same kinds of exhibits that Mr Hill did'. The Victorian climate was the culprit.[41]

Mitchell replied tartly that he was well aware of Victoria's capabilities. Surmising (correctly) that von Mueller had been orchestrating his defence behind the scenes, Mitchell suggested that 'Mr Moore might appear as the tool of his astute friend and professional colleague'. Moore's criticisms of Mitchell were 'unjust', 'impertinent' and uncharitable. It was the duty of an honest columnist to ask questions on behalf of the public (as 'one who pays the piper') when things went awry.[42]

Von Mueller's Sydney exhibition was only one sign of his inability to create a culture of display through which the self-improving class could take pleasure in the fruits of colonial horticulture. His critics claimed the Melbourne Botanic Gardens too reflected 'an absence of taste'.[43] As the *Argus* put it, 'the cry is the public want flowers'.[44] Von Mueller's position in Melbourne was under threat.

In December 1870, only weeks after the spat with Moore, Mitchell was appointed to the Board of Inquiry into the administration of the Melbourne Botanic Gardens. (He was not the only horticulturalist on the board; its other members included William Sangster, a nurseryman and landscape gardener who would write for the *Australasian* in the 1880s.) While the inquiry was running, Mitchell continued to contribute to the agricultural pages of the *Leader*. Von Mueller, smarting under Mitchell's criticisms, complained to the Minister of Lands, J. J. Casey:

> Mr Mitchell wrote most bitterly against me in the *Leader*. He has continually written against me; and therefore cannot be considered an impartial member of the board, and his connection with the Press gives him undue influence publicly against me.[45]

Casey replied that Mitchell had only accepted the position on the Board of Inquiry 'on condition that he was permitted to continue his connection with one of the agricultural journals'.[46] In any event, Mitchell was far from being von Mueller's only public critic. The *Australasian*'s January 1872 horticultural editorial on the Melbourne Gardens pointed out that as a result of von Mueller's shortcomings, Victoria was losing face among the principal members of the English nursery trade, who 'ridicule our attempts at horticulture'.[47]

Even von Mueller's plant introductions were to draw criticism. In October 1872, the *Geelong Advertiser* reported a call by a local nurseryman for legislation to control the spread of cape weed, which von Mueller had allegedly introduced from South Africa. Charles Wyatt of Frogmore Nursery near Geelong claimed that the weed's prevalence in the Western District was 'a matter of notoriety', and it was spreading with 'alarming rapidity'. Without legislative intervention, Wyatt predicted that 'half the farmers of the country will be ruined'.[48]

When the Board of Inquiry reported, it recommended that the gardens 'should have more than a scientific object': they 'should also be the place where the whole colony could study horticulture, arboriculture, floriculture and landscape gardening in their most perfect forms'. Victorians were looking to professional gardeners to champion 'cultivated and refined taste' and simultaneously to create an accessible representation of science.

Meanwhile, at the Model Farm, Mitchell's lease had been renewed, even though the Board of Agriculture had been abolished in December 1870.[49] At this time, he became agricultural editor of the Melbourne *Leader*, a position he held from 1871 to 1874. In this new role, he campaigned relentlessly for improvements in Victorian agricultural practices.[50]

Mitchell envisaged the press as both a universal educator, instructing farmers about new farming practices, and as a vehicle by which farmers could share their practical knowledge. He was conscious that a great deal of practical information was currently being 'lost through not being analysed and submitted . . . to the printing press'; he therefore asked 'practical men scattered over the country' to contribute their

Ferdinand von Mueller: a man
with 'any number of medals' and
'a host of titles'

Ferdinand von Mueller, La Trobe
Picture Collection, State Library
of Victoria

Land for farmers, not 'mere
cockatoo destroyers of little
patches of soil here and there'

Algernon Hall, *Farm Homestead,
Wooragee, G. Graham Esq.*, 1866,
albumen print, La Trobe Picture
Collection, State Library of Victoria

A twenty-acre selection at Mount
Warrenheip, close to where Thomas
Lang established his nursery

Saul Solomon, *Mount Warrenheip
from the South, Melbourne Road*,
1866, albumen print, La Trobe Picture
Collection, State Library of Victoria

knowledge of local circumstances to his newspaper. He also sought to create common ground between farmers' clubs and the press, and so build his readership.

One can glimpse Mitchell's concerns in a lengthy piece entitled 'The Future of Farming in Victoria', written in May 1873. Again he reminded readers that, unlike America, Victoria did not have a limitless frontier. As a result, 'long tilled land must be so managed as to continue to supply our own people at least with food'. The existing land legislation had created a class of small farmers who were 'mere cockatoo destroyers of little patches of soil here and there'. To foster a more rational agriculture, he proposed that farms should be 'no less than three or four hundred acres' in area. Each would be subdivided into six paddocks of roughly equal size, half of which would 'remain under grass for three years while the other half was to be tilled under a succession of crops'. This regime would need to be modified in the 'lighter soils' of the Wimmera and other parts of north-western Victoria, where the land might only bear two successive crops, then be replaced by grass for four years. This 'new system' of farming would produce an independent class of farmers, freed from crushing rural poverty, who would form a permanent attachment to the land and contribute to a distinctive national ethos.[51]

Mitchell's gritty assessment can be contrasted with the romantic portrayal of small-scale selection by the government surveyor, Henry Byron Moore. In *A Brief Report on the Land System of Victoria*, Moore praised the 1865 Amending Land Act for increasing the minimum size of selections adjacent to the goldfields from twenty to eighty acres, thereby 'decidedly improving the moral and social condition of a large section of the population'. In Victoria, Moore wrote, 'a scarcity of food is almost impossible at least for many generations'. He rhapsodised about little homesteads in forest clearings where 'the wheat field and potato patch bear proof of the industry (rather than greed) of the occupants'.[52] This sentimentality was far removed from Mitchell's stark assessments of the relationship between poverty and ever-diminishing soil fertility.

Mitchell's concerns were shared by Alexander Wallis, who became agricultural writer for the *Australasian* in 1871 and secretary to the newly established Department of Agriculture in June 1872.[53] Wallis had learnt agriculture at the Royal Agricultural College in England, then studied forestry at the Stuttgart Polytechnic in Germany, where he had come under the influence of the Hohenheim Agricultural College, renowned for its contribution to agricultural experimentation and education.

Mitchell welcomed Wallis's arrival. Here was a new colonist who was up to the minute with the latest European understandings, and the two men found much in common. Wallis's first columns took up one of Mitchell's perennial themes, the relationship between science, education and agriculture.[54] In 1872, the two were both members of the Commission of Inquiry investigating the first outbreak of foot and mouth disease in the colony.[55]

Nevertheless, Mitchell and Wallis had different views of how long it would take the Department of Agriculture to implement scientific principles in colonial agriculture. Taking the long-term perspective, Wallis wrote, 'We do not omit to plant an acorn because it requires many years to become an oak'.[56] Mitchell disagreed in an editorial entitled 'A Department of Agriculture: What it Ought to Do'.[57] He suggested a 'faster growing tree would have afforded a more hopeful simile'. There was an urgent need for change. 'We shall have to pluck up that slow growing acorn and infuse more vitality into the department—more intellectual power of an appreciative or creative kind'. As a result of poverty, small farmers were being 'driven back . . . on nature and the rudest practice of an old art', and the social fabric was in danger. Mitchell again emphasised that 'the social position of the selector would be markedly improved through attachment to property, home and children'. Without a significant shift in government policy, he predicted, farmers would 'soon begin to denounce the new department as a sham and a delusion, even worse than the

JOSIAH MITCHELL

abolished Board of Agriculture'. Having sat on the Botanic Gardens Board of Inquiry, Mitchell was all too well aware that the 'present race, the men who pay, would like to see some prospect of return for the money'.

In the colony, science would be judged 'a sham and delusion' if it did not produce practical results in a form the public could understand. Farmers were especially interested in scientific investigations that shed immediate light on 'the causes of novel phenomena'. This kind of information 'could not be too abundantly supplied' to those engaged in agriculture.[58]

Through his journalism, Mitchell kept his readers informed of local agricultural experiments. He published a paper by one Mr Martin on 'Sheep Breeding on Tillage Farms', delivered to the Ballarat Farmers Club, reporting that the planting of shelter trees had doubled 'grass producing capabilities' on squatter John Cumming's Terrinallum station in the Western District, and had achieved the same result for the Anderson brothers of Smeaton Mill and Bullarook. Despite the success of these practical experiments, Victorian farmers were slow to respond to more advanced scientific analysis. Mitchell was critical of their lack of modernity; he believed they were no better than 'our forefathers who had never heard of agricultural chemistry or dreamt of science in connection with their business'. It was the Department of Agriculture's business to rectify this. Mitchell pointedly asked: 'when will our department enter upon the task of investigation and observation with reference to Australian specialities as to soil and climate?'[59]

In fact, this gap was filled by the wealthy private philanthropist William Clarke, who paid for the agricultural chemist R. E. W. McIvor to come to the colony. In his first address to the Ballarat Farmers Club in 1876, McIvor spoke on 'the nutrition of plants, the general nature of soils, the chemical principles involved in the exhaustion of land, the means of preventing exhaustion and the necessity of adopting a system of rotation of crops'.[60] He had become aware of this from his inspection of tenant farms in Clarke's Dowling Forest estate,

The Royal Academy of Agriculture
and Forestry in Hohenheim,
Germany: A. R. Wallis's vision
for colonial agriculture?

*Royal Academy of Agriculture and
Forestry, Hohenheim, Würtemberg,*
from Victorian Department of
Agriculture, *Annual Report,* 1874,
private collection

J. Cumming's Terrinallum station,
showing belts of shelter trees
(middle distance and on the horizon),
which doubled the property's 'grass
producing capabilities'

Louis Buvelot, *Terrinallum homestead,*
1869, oil on canvas, 83 × 149 cm,
La Trobe Picture Collection,
State Library of Victoria

located not far from Ballarat, which had a long history of overcropping with wheat and barley. His message was simple: oats, barley and wheat removed large quantities of nitrogen, phosphoric acid and potash from the soil; potatoes and mangles used up these chemical elements even faster. Furthermore, running sheep on cropping paddocks removed forty pounds of potash for every thousand pounds of unwashed wool. But there was a solution: these lost elements could be replaced by the application of bone dust.[61]

Clarke and McIvor persuaded the tenant farmers to reform their practices. This was affirmation of Mitchell's belief that once information was made available to farmers, they would 'work out for themselves the ideas they would find advantage in'. In America, this was achieved through the federal government's regular agricultural publications. In 1873, Wallis instituted a similar program in Victoria, using his annual reports to publicise agricultural discoveries by colonial bureaucrats and practical farmers, including Mitchell.

Wallis's second annual report, published in 1874, contained Mitchell's assessment of farms in the Smeaton, Spring Hill and Bullarook agricultural district, north and east of Ballarat.[62] These farms too had been continually cropped to supply the nearby goldfields. On visiting Green Hill farm, not far from the Anderson brothers' grain mill at Smeaton, Mitchell noted how 'until recently grain growing, not only on this farm but throughout the district, was the staple industry and under constant grain growing the land became considerably worked out'. The effects were apparent to the itinerant Welsh swagman; returning in 1871 after a two-year absence, he wrote that the 'Smeaton district, once considered the garden of Victoria, is now a ruinous area from continued exhaustion of the land'.[63]

By contrast, Green Hill now characterised 'the new system of farm management' Mitchell espoused. It was a single property of 590 acres, formed by amalgamating four separate farms. Sheep grazed on what had previously been overworked holdings: 'with the aid of these invaluable animals a change was taking place, from spoliation which leads to ruin, in the

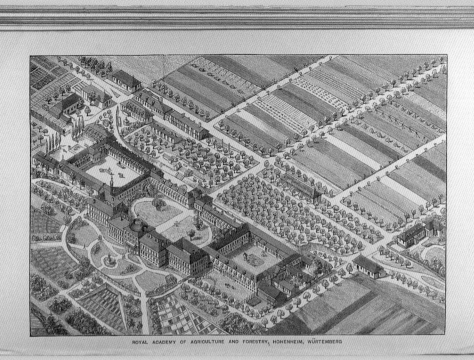

ROYAL ACADEMY OF AGRICULTURE AND FORESTRY, HOHENHEIM, WÜRTEMBERG

direction of a rational, enduring and profitable system of husbandry'. Similarly, Wattle Grove farm, at the foot of a denuded Scrub Hill between Kingston and Dean and adjacent to the Bullarook forest, afforded 'no evidence of poverty or wearing out', although it had been farmed for sixteen years. From these site inspections Mitchell believed 'the larger the area of pasture land in proportion to the arable land, and the greater number of stock which are kept, and kept well; the safer the system of farming will be and more likely to prove lastingly remunerative'.[64]

Another of Mitchell's contributions to the annual reports was an article on 'Orange Culture', also published in 1874.[65] Here, he drew on his 1870 visit to the Parramatta orange grove of James Pye, the father of orange growing in New South Wales. Mitchell found the grove 'a maze of beauty . . . with walls of golden fruit . . . intermixed and relieved by the dark green foliage . . . forming one of the most gorgeous and pleasing sights the eye can rest upon'. On a more prosaic note, he reported that Pye's grove was valued at £2000. In Victoria, by contrast, the cultivation of the orange had been given 'much less attention than it deserves'. Mitchell set out to rectify this by acquainting would-be Victorian growers with the requirements of oranges in relation to site, aspect and soil, plants and planting, pruning, and general management.[66]

Mitchell also believed that domesticated animals, like cultivated plants, were 'capable of being moulded and fashioned to serve the requirement or please the fancy of man'. Among cattle, 'the improved shorthorn' was 'a marvellous instance of the power of man to avail himself of the laws of nature for the benefit of his race'. Better breeding led to 'generous feeding and . . . improved cultivation'. He was therefore persuaded that 'every farmer should aim at keeping well bred stock'.[67]

In 1875 Mitchell put his words into action, taking charge of the Mount Derrimut herd of shorthorns for Robert Morton, a wealthy landowner who had spent considerable sums importing the breed. In the colony, where breeding was all-important, Morton named his cattle after European aristocrats: there were Dukes of Brunswick and Geneva—and, in a nod to local claims, the thirteenth Duke of Derrimut and his Duchess. So attached was the owner to these beasts that he had their likenesses painted by the colonial artist Frederick Woodhouse.[68] When Morton was to return to England, he decided that 'no other person in the colony was so well qualified' as Josiah Mitchell to superintend his herd.[69] Mitchell soon accompanied some of the cattle to another of Morton's holdings, Skelsmergh Hall near Kyneton,[70] where he believed the climate would better suit these aristocrats of the bovine world.

From Skelsmergh Hall, Mitchell made sorties into the surrounding countryside. In 1875, he judged an agricultural competition run by the West Bourke Agricultural Society.[71] The agricultural prizes and shows in the longer-settled districts advertised the new system of agriculture to the whole colony. Awarding prizes for sound farm management rewarded 'men of small means . . . but stouter hearts' who were 'intelligent cultivators'.

In the West Bourke competition, Mitchell was looking for an example of what could be accomplished by 'persevering well directed industry and . . . the judicious combination of grazing and grain growing, of pasture and tillage in such a way as is calculated to sustain the fertility of the soil and prove permanently remunerative'.[72] On this basis, first prize was awarded to the 131-acre Hay Hill Farm between Riddell's Creek and New Gisborne. Over nine years, this farm had been transformed from 'a plentiful crop of stones' studded with gum trees into a securely fenced, judiciously subdivided and skilfully managed farm, with pasture well laid down and providing abundant feed for stock.

The second prize-winner, Macedon Farm, three miles northwest of the township of Lancefield, was another example of the new farming regime championed by Mitchell. The judges appreciated its subdivision into fields of twelve to twenty acres with sheep-proof fences. They approved of the use of manure, which was carted out from the cow shed and piggeries in autumn and ploughed under on land intended for potatoes.

PYE'S ORANGE GROVE, PARRAMATTA.

The farm's rotation of crops did not go unnoticed, and the proportion of cropped land to pasture was seen as further testimony to the owner's 'skilful management' and determination to improve the fertility of his farm.

The transformative power of rational agricultural practices was also in evidence at Grange Farm, two miles from Lancefield, where the owner had cleared and fenced a heavily timbered property.[73] Before coming into his possession, 'the land had undergone the usual course of exhaustive cropping and was reckoned worn out'. This had been rectified by 'careful and systematic management' over six years, for which he was commended by the judges. They did, however, suggest changing the proportion of cropped land to pasture to reduce seasonal risk and dependence on expensive labour.[74]

Mitchell developed this thinking further in an 1876 address to the West Bourke Agricultural Society on the subject of 'Pasturelands'. As grain growing shifted from the older agricultural areas to the northern areas of the colony, where soil and climate suited wheat growing, 'the momentous question' became 'how can we best restore the fertility of worn out land?' Pastureland was not only 'the best medium by which to restore and maintain the fertility of soil' but was also 'the basis of our system of agriculture in the future'. Mitchell had been developing this understanding since at least 1869; he had now come to realise that soil exhaustion was an inseparable part of colonisation, 'caused mainly by the scarcity of capital on the part of first settlers'. Even if they are 'intelligent cultivators', those 'of small means but . . . indomitable courage and preserving industry' who 'go forth from the old countries to subdue the wilderness in the new one and win homes from the shadowy forest' are 'forced to bow to circumstances'.

This insight forced Mitchell to develop a different model, better suited to colonial conditions. At the Model Farm, he had followed the English practice of sowing pasture with a mixture of grass seeds and clovers; now he abandoned this as being too 'costly to be followed as a rule in this colony with labour and manure both scarce and dear'.[75] In its place,

Pye's Orange Grove, Parramatta

From *Picturesque Atlas of Australasia*, vol. 1, 1886, private collection

One of Robert Morton's shorthorn bulls: the Fifth Duke of Brunswick at 11 months

Shorthorn Bull, Fifth Duke of Brunswick at 11 months bred by Mr R. Morton, Mount Derrimut, Victoria, from Victorian Department of Agriculture, *Annual Report,* 1874, private collection

he recommended sowing rye and red clovers. He also encouraged farmers to gain an understanding of their district's particular needs by trying out new grasses in experimental plots. By sowing pasture with grass seeds appropriate to the soil and climate, they could render the 'grain sick land' of the older agricultural districts 'permanently profitable'.

Newspapers continued to play a large role in disseminating these new ideas. When William Clarke (in his capacity as president of the West Bourke Agricultural Society[76]) donated a £10 prize for the best essay on the topic of 'The West Bourke Agriculture Society's Third Annual Show', it was won by A. S. Beavan, editor of the *Lancefield Mercury*. Like Mitchell, Beavan extolled the benefits of tillage, stock and pasture as a solution to the impoverishment of Victorian agricultural soils. With an eye to his audience, he praised farmers as 'the most important and useful' contributors to 'the economy of the world'. He suggested that agricultural societies were 'well calculated to confer lasting benefit on the class for whose requirements and advantage they have been called into existence'. They could be 'a power in the land—socially, politically and educationally'. Victorian farmers could no longer afford to be a 'state milch cow', 'persistently milked' by those who 'do not bear their fair share of the public burden'.[77]

The resentment that underlay Beavan's essay was to find political expression three years later, when the Berry government imposed taxes on agricultural machinery, corn and wool sacks, and threatened to cut grants to agricultural societies if they encouraged political discussion about these measures. In response, a Farmers' Union was established in the northern frontier district of Rochester in June 1879 and rapidly spread throughout the farming areas of Victoria.[78] It drew up a populist platform to improve the position of disadvantaged and isolated rural communities. Its demands included the removal of duties on agricultural machinery, implements and salt (which was used in butter making and for improving the soil); the extension of railway communications into country districts; a more equitable distribution of public monies in country districts; the retrenchment of public expenditure and reduction of taxation; and the provision of irrigation channels in the new northern wheat districts of the colony.[79]

This platform was ratified in Melbourne in October, at a monster meeting held to establish the Victorian Farmers' Union. Mitchell took the opportunity to address the meeting on the need for 'some suitable and efficient means for imparting a sound agricultural education to young men intending to follow the business of farming', but his lobbying fell on stony ground. Victoria's long-neglected political constituency of 90 000 farmers believed that Melbourne was robbing the country of 'enormous sums of money' created by the farmers' 'bone and sinew'. At a time when farmers felt they 'could scarcely get a penny from the state', money was being wasted on unproductive public works in the cities. More than half a million pounds was being spent to build the Exhibition Building, the new Law Courts and Parliament House in Melbourne. To the impecunious small selector who felt 'a want of water supply, railways and other necessary things', these public works were profligate. There was 'too much centralisation'.[80]

Mitchell also believed small farmers were robbed of a voice in their own country. He had been elected to the organising committee of the Kyneton Farmers' Union, and at the inaugural meeting in August 1879 he argued that farmers, though they were 'the mainstay of the state . . . had gradually come to be looked upon as cyphers—people who did not understand politics or finance, and who were only fit to be used as taxpayers'. Taxes imposed 'on everything the farmer used' impeded his ability 'to compete on the world market'. In effect, farmers were subsidising high urban wages and protected colonial manufacturing. To change this, farmers must 'unite in a solid body'. 'So long as they were disunited', their lack of representation would continue. The Farmers' Union should 'support only those candidates for parliament who will thoroughly identify with and advocate the farming interests'.[81]

In 1880 Mitchell decided to put his ideas into practice and stand for the Victorian parliamentary seat of South Gippsland as a representative of the Victorian Farmers' Union. He stood with the blessing of the Kyneton branch, who sent a circular to the South Gippsland farmers soliciting their support for him.[82] The Gippsland seat was centred on Brandy Creek (present-day Warragul), in the midst of an impenetrable forest. Clearing had made little headway. Four years earlier, Henry Byron Moore had reported that although about 20 000 acres had been selected in the parishes around Brandy Creek, 'not one hundred acres have been cultivated for cereal or other crops'.[83] Surprisingly, there was already a nursery at Brandy Creek, where Mr Levien of Law-Somner, a Melbourne nursery and seed company, had planted 'fruit trees of all kinds'. Yet to journey fourteen miles from Brandy Creek was like 'entering the underworld'; the 'tree ferns and sassafras was so thick overhead' that the path was 'completely darkened'.[84]

These were the paths that Mitchell travelled to address political meetings in clearings with names such as Buln Buln, Jindivick and Drouin. Having spent his entire colonial life in the settled districts, he now found himself on the frontier. It would have come as something of a shock; as the *Australasian*'s agricultural reporter commented about Gippsland in 1880, 'people living on the plains had no conception of the hardships which the early pioneers of thick forest country have to put up with'.[85]

To these people of the forest clearings, Mitchell spoke as 'a practical farmer not unacquainted with science in all its bearing upon agriculture'. He told them something of his life—of how he had he had begun farming at the age of eleven, and of his experiences since then. He won support when he said he was 'vitally impressed with the excellence of the country' and pressed the need for roads and tramways. (Cannily, he made no mention of the Farmers' Union's demand for irrigation channels to be built in dry country.)[86]

Mitchell also suggested that a state nursery be established in Gippsland. It is not recorded how his listeners responded to

The 1880 Melbourne exhibition building, decried by Victorian farmers as a waste of public money

Charles Nettleton, *Exhibition Building, Melbourne*, 1880, albumen print, La Trobe Picture Collection, State Library of Victoria

'People living on the plains had no conception of the hardships which the early pioneers of thick forest country have to put up with': making do in Gippsland

Another forest giant at Calignee South, Gippsland, n.d., albumen print, La Trobe Picture Collection, State Library of Victoria

'Agriculture never throve in revolutionary soil': Buln Buln, Brandy Creek

Fred Kruger, *Buln Buln Brandy Creek*, albumen print, *c.* 1880, La Trobe Picture Collection, State Library of Victoria

the idea of raising trees in an impenetrable wilderness where the forest was seen as a curse.[87] Mitchell had a better chance of gaining support by focusing on his own standing as 'primarily an agriculturalist desirous of securing justice and fair representation to the class to which he belongs'.[88] He accordingly opposed the Berry ministry and its wasteful expenditure on urban public works. To Gippsland folk who inhabited the rudest of dwellings, the mighty dome of the Melbourne Exhibition Building was a symbol of metropolitan extravagance.

Mitchell took the conservative view that 'agriculture never throve in revolutionary soil'. He was therefore opposed 'to setting class against class and labour against capital', believing they should go hand in hand.[89] He stood 'for all those who prefer political honesty and independence and intelligence in a member'.[90] In the quicksand of politics, Mitchell portrayed himself as 'plain honest and straightforward'. He 'appeared before the electors from a sense of duty, having the welfare of the district at heart'. His 'sincerity of expression' was lightened by humour and unfailing courtesy, which he used to good effect during the campaign.[91] He refused to say a word against his opponent, and at a meeting in Brandy Creek, he disarmed hecklers by thanking them for giving him 'time to catch his breath'.[92] When the ballot was counted, however, Mitchell had lost, with 643 votes to the sitting member's 787.[93]

Defeated, he returned to Kyneton and continued to write. Until his death in 1881, he was Hodden Gray, agricultural writer for the *Australasian*.[94] In this guise he continued to voice the resentments of rural people. Although Mitchell was a commissioner for the Melbourne Exhibition of 1880 and adjudicated the awards for agricultural produce and implements, as Hodden Gray he criticised the Exhibition authorities for their 'comparative neglect . . . of the great industries that should be represented within the building by Vegetable Products'.[95] He did, however, concede that 'the grain grower will find no more interesting exhibits in the great Exhibition than the automatic reapers and binders'.

JOSIAH MITCHELL

Mitchell thought it 'deplorable' that although 'money enough . . . has been lavishly spent on botanical gardens and botanical science', there was no display of Victorian indigenous grasses and fodder plants in the Exhibition.[96] He was therefore not beguiled by the gardens surrounding the Exhibition, though they had been designed by nurseryman William Sangster, his former colleague on the Board of Inquiry into the Melbourne Botanic Gardens.[97]

For his part, Mitchell had long stopped gardening to pursue colonial agriculture. At a time when many Australian farmers had 'neither spare time to read newspapers nor [to] improve each other by exchanging views upon questions of interest to them', he left no field unturned in his efforts to educate people on the land. 'Clods', the title of his column in the *Australasian*, aptly described his ground-breaking efforts to write the colonial clearing and enlighten an audience that was too busy 'grubbing trees and clearing their farms' to read the lie of the land.[98]

William Ferguson

The Man Who Couldn't See

Wᵐ Richardson, Delt.   Printed by Fr. Schenck, Edinburgh

ABIES DOUGLASII, Lindley.

The Man Who Couldn't See

If wealthy colonists needed knowledgeable gardeners, ambitious gardeners required men of means and taste who could afford to acquire the rare and fashionable plant. William Ferguson (c. 1827–1887) was unusually fortunate in this regard. Ferguson had 'English and Scottish experience as a forester' before coming to Australia, and had worked 'for many years in some of the best establishments in England'.[1] His experience caught the eye of J. H. Brooke, owner of Mount Eagle estate at Heidelberg. Brooke was a democrat and land reformer who was elected to the Victorian Legislative Assembly for Geelong in 1856, but he was also a wealthy man who desired a grand garden; and no grand garden was complete without a collection of pines, which were all the rage in Europe at the time.

In the first half of the nineteenth century, plant collectors had combed every continent in search of new pines. 'The noble and lamented' David Douglas, remembered by the fir *Abies douglasii*, explored much of California only to lose his life in the Hawaiian Islands in 1834. He was followed by Carl Hartweg, who collected pines in Mexico, Guatemala, Ecuador and California during 1836 and 1846. In California, plant-hunters were so enamoured of pines that they eschewed the gold rush in favour of collecting. In 1850, John Jeffrey (remembered by *Pinus jeffreyi*) made an expedition to California, Oregon and Vancouver, backed by a syndicate of Edinburgh horticulturalists. William Lobb discovered the Western red cedar (initially named *Thuja lobbii* in his honour), as well as the Californian redwood, named *Wellingtonia gigantea* in memory of the Duke of Wellington.[2]

As pines from the new world made their way to Europe, pinetums—as collections of coniferous trees were known—became the essence of horticultural fashion. In the words of J. C. Loudon, an indefatigable garden writer and exemplar of horticultural taste, in England there was 'hardly a first rate residence, and not many second rate estates' without one.[3] Immigrant gardeners and horticultural publications soon imported this craze to Australia.[4] As English nurseryman-on-tour John Gould Veitch observed in 1865, there had grown up

The Douglas fir, named after David Douglas, a famous plant-hunter

Abies douglasii, from *Pinetum Britannicum*, vol. 2, plate 17, Edinburgh, 1884, State Library of Victoria

A Californian redwood

Wellingtonia gigantea, from *Pinetum Britannicum*, Edinburgh, 1884, vol. 3, plate 39, State Library of Victoria

Hugh Glass's Flemington House

Johnstone and O'Shannessy, *Flemington House*, albumen print, 1891, private collection

The garden at Flemington House: an area of twenty-five acres on the banks of the Moonee Ponds Creek

Johnstone and O'Shannessy, *Flemington House*, albumen print, 1891, private collection

in Victoria 'a very decided spirit for the introduction of any novelty which may be likely to prove of use or ornament to the gardens of the colony'.[5]

This lust for novelty seized Brooke of Mount Eagle, who acquired pines at extraordinary speed. When Daniel Bunce visited the garden in 1861, he recorded that 'under the skilful management of his gardener Mr Ferguson', Brooke had accumulated 'the largest number of conifers of any establishment in the colony'.[6] By that time, Ferguson had collected eighty-one conifers, including many 'only recently known in England'.[7]

The Mount Eagle pinetum had prized conifers from every reach of the globe. Its novelties included the Japanese yew (*Taxus japonica*), introduced to England the same year, and the plum-fruited yew (*Podocarpus andina*) collected from the Andes by Richard Pearch for the Veitches in 1860.[8] From the land between the Chilean temperate rainforest and the Patagonian steppe came *Libocedrus chiliensis*, and five araucarias including the Chilean monkey puzzle (*Araucaria imbricata*). The white cedar from eastern America (*Thuja occidentalis*) appeared with cedars from Lebanon, Mount Atlas and India. There were cypresses from the Himalayas and China (the funeral cypress, *Cupressus funebris*) as well as the Monterey and Lawson's cypresses from California. Junipers came from Europe, the Balkans, the Himalayas and Japan. Garden cultivars were represented by *Thuja warrenga* and *T. variegata* and *Biota meldensis*.[9] A Californian redwood also soon graced Mount Eagle; no pinetum was complete without this mighty monarch of the Sierra Nevada.

Yet both gardener and owner abandoned their pinetum in its infancy. Ferguson moved on by early 1863, and four years later Brooke left Victoria for Japan. Ferguson's next employer was Victoria's richest man, Hugh Glass, nabob of Flemington House.[10] Glass's suburban estate, about three miles from central Melbourne, had twenty-five acres of garden overlooking 'a picturesque sheet of water', part of the Moonee Ponds Creek.

In the mid-1850s, the *Gardener's Magazine and Journal of Rural Economy* published a series of brief comments on the

Drawn to Photograph

J. Colwell & D.H. Lizars Edinr

SEQUOIA WELLINGTONIA.

MARIPOSA GROVE, SOUTH CALIFORNIA.

villa gardens of various Melbourne grandees-in-the-making. Among these snippets was a diplomatic appraisal of Glass's garden by James Sinclair, a former landscaper to Russian aristocrats and designer of Melbourne's Fitzroy Gardens. Sinclair tactfully directed his readers' attention to the garden's future: it possessed 'healthy trees and thriving gardens' which 'when completed will be an ornament to Flemington'.[11] This absolved him from commenting on its present state—a wise decision, as the house was barely finished and the design for the garden incomplete. (In fact, the design, prepared by Edward La Trobe Bateman after 'much reading and reference to books on landscape gardening', would continue to evolve until 1865.[12])

The variety of aspect and soil at Flemington allowed a great diversity of plants to be grown. There were also two conservatories, an aquarium and a propagating and orchid house. Here, Ferguson could raise any plant his master desired. John Gould Veitch observed that at Flemington House, 'Mr Ferguson succeeds admirably in the growth of almost all classes of plants, both tropical and hardy'.

Hugh Glass was a man of extravagant horticultural ambition. In 1862, he had imported 600 Cedar of Lebanon of different sizes from England, but only one six-inch tree survived. After this calamity, a lesser person might have abandoned importing conifers, but nothing would deter Hugh Glass. He simply re-ordered the seeds and plants from England, tempting fate and the elements again.

With Ferguson in charge, conifers arrived at Flemington in huge numbers. By 1865, the estate had 'one of the most complete collections of coniferae . . . in the colony'.[13] Name any continent, and its conifers would appear in the Flemington pinetum. From California came *Pinus muricata*, which Ferguson raised from seed in 1864, and a Californian fir named after Hooker, the great taxonomist of Kew Gardens. *Pinus rigida* arrived from eastern North America, the Montezuma pine (*Pinus filifolia*) from central America, *Cedrus atlantica* from the Atlas Mountains in north Africa, and the Aleppo pine

WILLIAM FERGUSON

(*Pinus halepensis*) from the Levant. These were joined by several conifers from Asia: the stinking cedar from Japan (*Torreya grandis*), the prized Himalayan spruce (*Picea pindrow*), a Cashmerian cypress, and 'one of the most elegant and graceful' cedars, the Indian *Cedrus deodara*.[14]

Ferguson was not a gardener to disappoint his master's ambitions, or his own. In 1865 'a few packets of choice species of pinus seeds' arrived from England. The next year, hundreds were planted out in the hope that they would become 'a veritable forest'. Such was their abundance that Glass could afford to give them away to colonial public gardens.[15]

Ferguson's knowledge of the 'many new species hitherto unknown to the colony, more especially of the noble order of coniferae' was put to good effect when he addressed the Victorian Gardeners' Mutual Improvement Society on 'Ornamental Planting' in 1863. He suggested that there was 'no other country in the world' where there was 'such a scope for ornamental planting' as Victoria. The importation of 'the noblest of trees' from across the globe had given colonial gardeners command of a vast range of plants that would survive the exigencies of the climate. Conifers were especially 'well adapted for ornamental planting' in Victoria, being 'most capable of resisting drought and parching hot winds'.

Ferguson had strong ideas about what a garden should be. He criticised the planting of blue gums and other indigenous plants in private gardens and public parks. In his eyes, it was wasteful to plant native trees in a colony where one could grow 'trees which cannot be employed in the English landscape'. He also attacked 'the practice of indiscriminate planting adopted by the modern gardener'. The planting of evergreens 'properly grouped in large masses' produced 'a grand effect which nothing else could surpass'.[16]

At Flemington House, Ferguson produced an extraordinarily diverse composition in the 'gardenesque manner'. The most valuable trees and shrubs were planted near the house, 'each plant perfectly distant from those around it', so that the potentate could survey his botanical riches. Further afield,

CEDRUS LIBANI.

CEDRUS DEODARA.
AT SACHAR.

trees and shrubs were grouped according to their 'various forms, colours and habits' so as to simulate the effects of natural light and shade. This effect was heightened in the more distant part of the grounds. Here, 'the picturesque mode of throwing the plantation into groups' not only produced 'beauty, shelter and shade' but also helped the garden to harmonise with the 'external scenery'.[17] The whole arrangement was an 'indispensable accomplishment to the ornamental scenery of this country'.

Believing that 'a gardener commands a wider scope for acclimatising than any farmer',[18] Ferguson looked on his gardens as experimental grounds in which to discover what might be successfully grown in different parts of the colony. Guided by the plants' country of origin, Ferguson grouped them by aspect, soil and climate, gardening each part of the Flemington estate as if it were a different part of the globe.[19]

Many colonists were taken with the idea that Victoria had a Mediterranean climate and would grow the fruits of that region. The orange, in particular, evoked the allure of the eastern Mediterranean. Its appeal was so strong that in 1862 the squatter Suetonius Officer and his bride went orange-gathering on their Mediterranean honeymoon. At Jaffa, the newlyweds carefully chose orange trees to ship to their Murray Downs station, on the banks of the Murray River near Swan Hill.[20]

Ferguson too believed that 'wherever the vine is found to flourish in Victoria so too will the orange'. He put this principle into practice at Flemington House, planting an orangery in a walled garden.[21] In 1862, he addressed the Victorian Gardeners' Mutual Improvement Society on 'The Aptitude of Orange Cultivation for Profitable Cultivation in Victoria', a subject he felt was of 'considerable importance' to the colony.[22] It was 'the duty of everyone of us who has made this country his home to disseminate information about this fruit', he observed. The present generation of colonists had a moral responsibility to attend to the land so that the next generation could not 'accus[e] us of having being careless of the ground'.

The Cedar of Lebanon, which Hugh Glass imported by the hundreds

Cedrus libani, from *Pinetum Britannicum*, Edinburgh, 1884, vol. 3, plate 44, State Library of Victoria

'One of the most elegant and graceful' cedars: the Indian *Cedrus deodara*, which arrived at Flemington House in 1863

Cedrus deodara at Nachar, from *Pinetum Britannicum*, Edinburgh, 1884, vol. 3, plate 43, State Library of Victoria

Pines 'properly grouped in large masses' gave the grounds of Flemington House 'a grand effect which nothing else could surpass'

Johnstone and O'Shannessy, *Flemington House*, albumen print, 1891, private collection

Near the house, the most valuable trees and shrubs were planted in the gardenesque manner

Johnstone and O'Shannessy, *Flemington House*, albumen print, 1891, private collection

Trees and shrubs at Flemington House grouped according to their 'various forms, colours and habits'

Johnstone and O'Shannessy, *Flemington House*, albumen print, 1891, private collection

In Melbourne, Ferguson observed, it took time to produce the perfect orange. The fruit tasted acid in July and August, but it ripened in the months to December.[23] John Gould Veitch did not share this opinion. After tasting a Flemington orange in November (a month Ferguson judged kind to oranges in Melbourne), Veitch suggested that 'the Victorian winters are almost too cold' to produce sweet fruit.[24] Undeterred, Ferguson continued to give a glowing account of the orange's adaptability to the colony; only later would he turn his attention to the pests that blighted its golden promise.[25]

As a result of his experiments at Flemington, Ferguson gained a reputation as one of the 'very few people' in the colony who could advise on which imported plants might be acclimatised. By 1866, he was applying his knowledge to forest planting, imagining the colonial forests as vast pinetums. He exhibited the colony's first examples of Douglas fir cones at a meeting of the Victorian Horticultural Improvement Society, and spoke of his conviction that 'the magnificent timber trees of California and British Colombia' would flourish on the Snowy Mountains and Victoria's Western Alps as they did on the Sierra Nevada and McKenzie River. The same trees could 'profitably be planted' on 'many of our barren ranges', which had been denuded by gold miners. The Indian cedar would 'grow as vigorously on the plains and on the highest mountain ranges as it does on the Himalayas' and would be of 'immense value to succeeding generations', while the Mount Atlas cedar would also provide 'valuable timber'.[26]

What was Ferguson's understanding of forests? Some idea can be gained from his 1863 'Notes on Ornamental Planting', where he argued that 'it behoved man to imitate nature in arranging forests'. He saw 'a natural forest' as being made up of 'comparatively few' species of 'trees, shrubs and other plants present in any one place'. In this European understanding, there would be

> a prevailing kind of tree with perhaps one, two, three in a hundred
> of some other kind of tree, a prevailing sort of shrub with some

WILLIAM FERGUSON

subordinate undergrowths; and a generally prevailing kind of flowering herbaceous plant, fern, grass, moss or even fungi or lichen.

Influenced by notions of natural selection, he suggested that the stronger species 'in a state of nature' soon weaken and destroy others, even in 'the most favoured situations'.[27]

For Ferguson, re-planting forests along European lines was essential to avert the man-made threat to the colony's land and soil. In 1863, in a lecture on 'The Importance of Chemistry as Applicable to Horticulture and Agriculture', he had spoken of the risks of soil depletion. He damned unscientific agricultural practices, as a result of which 'lands . . . which a few years ago produced immense crops . . . were now barren'.[28] He returned to these concerns three years later in a talk on the 'Influence of Forests on Climate'. Ferguson observed that 'as man advances into the interior of this country, his first business is to get rid of vegetable mould, by burning and destroying the forest', in the process 'destroying that upon which his own existence depends and rendering the climate unsuitable for future generations'. He prophesied that the colonists faced ruin if they mismanaged their timber resources:

Unless a stop is put to the wholesale destruction of native forests, and new forests are erected on many of our ranges, man will have much cause for regret for having laid waste the true source of his prosperity and destroyed their blessings stored up in the soil for future generations by exhausting its vegetable mould.[29]

He implored the 'destroyers of the forest' to reconsider their wanton actions and pause 'before it is too late', and bluntly warned his listeners that unless colonial attitudes changed, 'future generations will look upon us as we do now our barbarous ancestors'.[30]

In 1867 a Board of Inquiry was appointed to report on 'the best means of securing the permanency of the state forests'. It recommended 'the extensive introduction of coniferous trees into the state forest of Victoria'.[31] There was a remarkable similarity between the pines recommended by the board and those Ferguson listed as growing at Flemington in his *Report on the Growth of Several Non-indigenous Trees Planted within the Vicinity of Melbourne*, which was furnished to the board in 1868. Ferguson's list included the Californian *Pinus insignis, P. ponderosa, P. radiata* and *Cupressus macrocarpa*, the American pitch pine, the Canary Island pine and the Himalayan *Pinus longifolia*, together with the Indian cedar, the Mount Atlas cedar and the Cedar of Lebanon.

Ferguson later claimed that his list had induced the board to recommend 'a number of species of exotic timber trees which they considered desirable for the introduction on a large scale into the State forests of Victoria'.[32] Ferguson's self-promotion, however, needs to be treated with some scepticism. The board's choice of trees was just as likely to have been influenced by Ferdinand von Mueller, who had grown many of these pines at the Melbourne Botanic Gardens and had liberally distributed them to botanic gardens, cemeteries and churchyards in country towns such as Kyneton, north-west of Melbourne.[33]

In 1869, the Victorian parliament passed a Land Act providing for the reservation of land specifically for timber production, and Ferguson was appointed Inspector of Forests.[34] This role gave him an opportunity to shape the future of the colonial landscape; in the process, he witnessed the destruction of the colony's forests at first hand and recorded it for posterity in his reports.

The new Inspector of Forests travelled around the colony, encountering 'wanton devastation' at every turn. In 1870 he went to the Castlemaine district, where he observed that Mount Alexander and its adjoining ranges were 'entirely denuded of timber'. He urged the colonists to take steps 'to protect and foster the growth of indigenous trees near the gold fields'. If this proved impossible, he recommended that they 're-plant non-indigenous trees in order that a constant supply of timber . . . be readily obtainable'.

The Macedon and Bullarook forests too were suffering 'severely from the . . . reckless manner in which the timber had

PINUS INSIGNIS.
MENDOCINO CALIFORNIA.

HAULING TIMBER.—MOUNT MACEDON.—see page 50.

been obtained'. In the Bullarook forest, he saw trees up to fifty feet in height being felled simply to obtain nine- or twelve-foot props for the Ballarat gold mines. He warned that it was 'only a question of time' before the whole of the Macedon range was denuded 'unless more stringent regulations were adopted for the preservation of the timber remaining in the state forest'. He also proposed establishing a nursery at Macedon, a locality he assessed as being 'peculiarly favourable for the growth of non-indigenous trees'.[35]

At Dean, Ferguson met the Anderson brothers, who had built a thirteen-mile tramway to haul timber from the Bullarook forest to their mill. The brothers had also established a nursery, where Ferguson saw thousands of exotic trees being raised to replant the forest. Their gardener, James Rodger, was successfully raising large numbers of *Pinus radiata*, *P. sylvestris*, *P. laricio*, *P. austriaca*, *P. pinaster* and *P. halepensis*, as well as the bastard cedar of north-west America (*Taxodium sempervirens*), elms (Huntington variety), Spanish chestnuts, willows, sycamore and oriental plane. In 1873 alone, 20 000 of these trees were planted out in the forest, and another 25 000 were given away to farmers and owners of freehold land. More than a dozen farms within a thirty-mile radius of the Andersons' nursery had groups and lines of the Andersons' trees, and a large plantation was formed near Smeaton.[36]

Ferguson was impressed with the brothers' reafforestation programme, but others were more sceptical. A sawmiller wrote to Clement Hodgkinson to say that the forest where he was working, between Whim Holes and Mount Mercer, south of Ballarat, was 'now denuded of all but saplings'. It was 'nonsense' to make a fuss about the Anderson brothers' planting ten acres when 'the next land board will alienate many hundreds of forest lands' for selection.[37]

Ferguson's travels took him to the Barmah forest on the Murray River, where red gum was being cut and shipped to India to be used as piles and railway sleepers. The red-gum forest was upwards of 50 000 acres, 'heavily timbered with

Pinus insignis (later *Pinus radiata*), which Ferguson recommended for Victorian conditions

Pinus insignis, Mendecino, California, from *Pinus Britannicum,* Edinburgh, 1884, vol. 1, plate 5, State Library of Victoria

The Macedon forest, which Ferguson found suffering 'severely from the . . . reckless manner in which the timber had been obtained'

Hauling Timber—Mount Macedon, from *Illustrated Australasian News,* 27 February 1871, p. 48, State Library of Victoria

The Anderson brothers' homestead at Dean, surrounded by ringbarked trees

William Tibbits, *Anderson Homestead, Dean*, c. 1872, University of Melbourne Archives

The Hamilton Gardens, laid out by Ferguson in 1870 and later redesigned by William Guilfoyle; Guilfoyle appears to have drawn over Ferguson's 1870 design

W. R. Guilfoyle, *Borough of Hamilton Public Garden*, 1881, Hamilton Art Gallery

magnificent trees not surpassed by any other forest in Victoria', averaging eighty to one hundred trees per acre in many places. Yet in 1870 Ferguson reported that the destruction of timber in this forest was 'very great'.

Around Hamilton and nearby Mount Rouse in Victoria's Western District, Ferguson found nearly all the timber dead over 'a very large tract of country', especially the box and white gum forest. The 'only living timber' were a few stunted specimens of lightwood and banksia. Again he warned that 'unless some measures are speedily adopted to replant this dismal tract, their loss would be felt at no distant date'. In the midst of this devastation, Ferguson laid out the Hamilton public gardens with trees from the world's forests in 1870, only to see them redesigned by William Guilfoyle in 1881.[38]

The colonial forests were not Ferguson's only responsibility. In 1867 he had been offered a position as curator of the Melbourne Botanic Gardens, but he had refused, saying he was concerned that he would not have 'complete control over the whole of the employees engaged on works placed under my superintendence'.[39] Two years later, however, the offer was repeated, and this time Ferguson accepted the appointment.[40]

He was soon embroiled in the controversy surrounding von Mueller's management of the gardens. In May 1870, William Lockhart Morton, a scientific savant and ally of von Mueller, publicly ridiculed Ferguson in the *Argus* as 'a mere landscape gardener', whose appointment insulted von Mueller as 'a man of science'. Morton suggested that Ferguson's appointment was calculated to drive von Mueller to 'resign his position'. In Morton's view, a botanic garden should 'bring together from the whole world every form of vegetable life' so that 'the thoughtful may study and admire their wondrous beauty'. It was also essential that 'the enterprising may learn what trees … may be profitably and successfully cultivated' in the colony. Ferguson only had a place in this grand scheme if 'colonial insipidity' demanded 'hybrid roses and other monstrous forms of vegetation'.

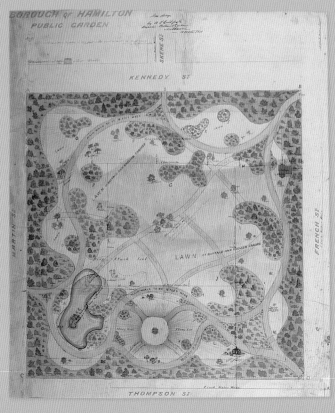

Ferguson's efficiency as Inspector of Forests also came under attack. In the same issue of the *Argus*, a correspondent writing under the *nom de plume* of 'Redgum' raised concerns about the cutting down of 'some of the finest red gum' in the Melbourne Botanic Reserve. The implication was clear. Ferguson might lament the destruction of rural forests, but he could not protect a 'few fine old giants of the primeval forest' in the botanical reserve against the timber-getters' 'war of extermination'.

Although Ferguson made it clear that he had not employed the men involved in 'destroying such valuable and ornamental trees', the incident cast doubt on his effectiveness. If such a thing could happen right under his nose in Melbourne, what was happening to the forests in country Victoria? Redgum asked rhetorically, 'What became of the firewood?'[41] The question was full of innuendo directed at destabilising Ferguson's position.

At the same time, the controversy about the taking of the red gums reflected a change in the political wind. In the late 1860s Clement Hodgkinson had dynamited red gums to implement his design for the Treasury Gardens. His reputation had not suffered, even though he was a member of the Forest Board at the time.[42] But then, Hodgkinson was von Mueller's superior.

The conflict between von Mueller and Ferguson was fundamentally about the director's power to impose his will in the gardens. Von Mueller complained that his authority was 'seriously impaired by the Inspector of Forests who utterly disregards my position of Director, who withdraws himself utterly from my control, who usurps largely my directorial power'.

Von Mueller took every opportunity to undermine Ferguson. In May 1871, he seized upon a request from the Shire of Creswick that Ferguson inspect Smeaton Park Reserve and 'advise the Council how best to proceed in the matter of planting the reserve with Forest Trees'.[43] Von Mueller played the ingénue, writing to the Chief Secretary to 'respectfully beg . . . instructions' as to 'whether the Forest Inspector is to proceed immediately to Creswick'.[44]

This seemingly innocuous question triggered the hoped-for reaction: Ferguson was directed 'not to make any more inspections of the State Forests and timber reserves'. The Board of Land and Works took the view that Ferguson's reports had not justified 'the heavy charges for travelling incurred during these inspections'. Instead of 'the occasional visit . . . by a scientific aboriculturalist', Crown land bailiffs were to 'stringently' enforce the forestry regulations, preventing the 'reckless destruction of full grown trees', and promoting the conservation of saplings. Ferguson's energies would be confined to 'unwooded reserves' in western and northern Victoria, where he could use his expertise 'much more advantageously' to create 'groves of useful non-indigenous timber trees', following the forestry practices of Prussia, France and Denmark.[45]

Von Mueller next sought to diminish even this area of Ferguson's influence. Conditions in the colony, he suggested, were not suited to 'the systems of forest culture' of Germany, France and Scandinavia. Von Mueller, as Government botanist, would be 'best able to advise the Government on special requirements for forest culture in this country'. This claim met an unsympathetic reception.

Von Mueller also challenged the government's proposal to plant reserves with groves of exotic trees, which he suggested would only grow in such spots 'after shelter has been created by quick growing native trees'. He preferred to see pines planted in 'the most sheltered and best irrigated places within the indigenous forests'.[46] This advice was given short shrift by Hodgkinson, who believed such plantings would be destroyed by bushfires and feral goats. To support the government's position, Hodgkinson cited the Chirnsides' success with their 'extensive plantations of non-indigenous trees in the exposed bleak Werribee plain'.[47]

In spite of all this manoeuvring, it was Ferguson, not von Mueller, who accompanied Hodgkinson and Alexander Wallis, the Secretary of Agriculture, when they set out to inspect the mountain ash forest on the Black's Spur, some sixty miles east of Melbourne, in February 1872.[48] Between Mount Monda

and Mount Julia, Ferguson saw trees 250 to 300 feet high, most 'as straight as an arrow'. He found an even larger specimen lying across a creek on the alluvial flats near the Watts River; it measured 435 feet 'from its roots to the top of the trunk'.

Following in the footsteps of the timber-splitters who had cleared tracks by firing the impenetrable scrub, Ferguson took every opportunity to go deeper into the forest, where he found other timbers growing in abundance. There were 'great quantities of blackwood' (*Acacia melanoxylon*) interspersed through the forests, mixed with sassafras and dogwoods, while splendid specimens of native beech (*Nothofagus cunninghamii*) grew to 150 feet in the deep ravines. It was 'rare to find such forests of sound timber in any other part of Victoria'.

Ferguson recommended 'the reservation of every acre wherever it would not interfere with settlement' in the district. The timber around the Watts and adjacent ranges was 'far more valuable than the land'. Yet the terrain was so steep that timber-getters had to split the tall trees into palings and shingles, and even then experienced great difficulty taking them out. For this reason, 'the number of splitters at present working in these forests is very limited and is likely to continue so'; in large areas, 'the axe of the splitter is as yet unknown'.[49]

Von Mueller agreed with Ferguson on the need for forest conservation, but he insisted that Ferguson should not be both forest inspector and curator of the botanic gardens. At the same time, von Mueller was under growing pressure. The Board of Inquiry into the Botanic Gardens had recommended that a clear distinction be made between the positions of Government Botanist and director of the gardens so as to address the growing public demand for a landscape garden rather than a scientific repository.

In July 1872, the Minister of Lands, J. J. Casey, summoned von Mueller and his arch-rival to his office to discuss the board's recommendations. At the meeting, Casey raised the issue of 'some difference existing between Mr Ferguson and Dr Mueller'. The minister was well briefed. He asked von Mueller to explain why he had ignored the government's

Clearing 'a few fine old giants of the primeval forest': red gum corpse with axe close by in the Melbourne Domain

Henry Burn, *Botanical Gardens and Government House Melbourne*, 1876, oil on canvas, La Trobe Picture Collection, State Library of Victoria

Chirnside's plantations at Werribee Park, on 'the exposed bleak Werribee plain'

Fred Kruger, *Bird's-eye View of Old Homestead, Werribee Park (As seen from the Mansion Tower)*, albumen print, *c.* 1880, La Trobe Picture Collection, State Library of Victoria

Tall timber and fern gullies on the Black's Spur about 1866

Charles Walter, *Blacks' Spur*, albumen print, *c.* 1866, private collection

directive that Ferguson 'should have quarters in the gardens', a refusal that had cost the government £147 for Ferguson's accommodation.

Von Mueller replied as an enlightened employer interested in the welfare of his staff. He explained that the quarters in question were occupied by 'a man who had charge of the forcing pits who was obliged by the nature of his duty to be constantly on the spot'. He had been there ten years, and 'his children were almost all born there'; besides, 'his wages were only eight shillings a day'.

The minister was unmoved. 'It was a peculiar thing', he mused, that 'the Prime Minister of the colony should make an order and that it should be disobeyed'. Having reminded von Mueller of the government's authority, he then addressed the central issue: was there 'any objection to allow Mr Ferguson to utilise his services in the gardens?'

Von Mueller chose his words with consummate skill. 'It would be a pity for the services of the forest inspector to be destroyed in any way', he replied, sidestepping Ferguson's duty to oversee the practical management of the gardens.

Casey pressed the point. 'Supposing Mr Ferguson has any time spare, is there any objection to allow him to utilise his services in the gardens?'

Cornered, von Mueller was forced to declare his long-held view that there should be separate horticultural gardens. This reply confirmed the inquiry's view: as long as von Mueller continued as director, there would be no place for ornamental horticulture in the botanic gardens.

Next, Casey turned his attention to Ferguson. This was Ferguson's opportunity to confront the eminent botanist in his minister's presence. He catalogued the tactics von Mueller had used to preserve his scientific domain from the ignorance of a 'mere landscape gardener'. After Ferguson had taken up his position in the gardens, von Mueller had refused to see him not once but 'several times'. Only after 'several written communications' from the minister did he agree to meet the new arrival and make arrangements for 'the practical superintendence of the gardens' to make them 'more ornamental than they had been'.

One of von Mueller's officers had then accompanied Ferguson around the gardens and directed all the employees that in future they were to 'receive all instruction from Mr Ferguson'. All appeared to be resolved. Ferguson had believed that 'the men all understood perfectly the arrangement, and every person was willing to act and assist me in everything'.

Appearances, however, were deceptive. Von Mueller had clung to his right to control who would raise new plants from seed. Ferguson was not given a single seed, even though at Flemington he had raised thousands.[50] This crucial work was given to von Mueller's trusted retainers, Henry Moreau and Gottlieb Schneider. Moreau went on raising pines, oaks, ashes and maples. Schneider, 'a practical gardener' who had worked in the Dresden Botanic Gardens before coming to Melbourne, continued as he always had; since 1858 he had raised from seed 'a great number of orchids' and 15 000 trees annually, as well as the sought-after Amazon water lily *Victoria regia* from South America. It was as if Ferguson had never entered the gardens.[51]

Matters had reached a crisis during 1870, when Ferguson went to Hamilton to lay out the botanic gardens, as the minister had instructed him. In his absence, von Mueller had ordered the men to stop work on Ferguson's alterations and improvements. The baron had reasserted his authority.

On returning, Ferguson had realised that that von Mueller would never willingly surrender power over his domain. As Ferguson put it to the minister: 'Such interference if continued will render it impossible for me to use the means at my disposal in an efficient and economic manner and will prevent proper discipline among the employees'. He appealed to Casey's political judgement about the need to improve the gardens: the sooner changes were made, 'the better for the gardens and the colony'.

Von Mueller witheringly replied that he had not been pre-pared to see 'whole lines of permanent trees . . . removed with-out his consent and scarlet geraniums put in their place'. Ferguson was unmoved by this sneer. He simply stated the facts: the trees in question had been transplanted and were thriving. But von Mueller conceded nothing.

Von Mueller's needling provoked Ferguson to lose his equi-librium in the minister's presence. He made a personal attack on von Mueller and his staff, charging that a large quantity of seeds had been lost to the state because they had been distri-buted among 'unskilled men and boys'. (If Ferguson had stopped to consider, he could have cited more telling evidence against von Mueller's practices. It was left to Alexander Wallis, the Secretary of Agriculture, in his March 1873 report on the gardens, to point out that 'propagating the seed in small boxes and then transferring each plant to a three inch pot' was exces-sively costly.[52])

Ferguson's slur against the gardens' staff offended Gottlieb Schneider, who took umbrage at being described as 'inexperi-enced'. Henry Moreau too complained that he had been 'subjected to a most unwarranted attack by the Inspector of Forests'; he asked that 'whatever difference exists between Mr Ferguson and the Director should be settled without refer-ence to the employees'.[53] Von Mueller forwarded their com-plaints to the minister.

Barely a week later, Ferguson compounded his error by again attacking his subordinates. In a letter to Hodgkinson, he admitted that he had 'very frequently' remonstrated with the messenger boy, Fred Pitcher, who had trampled the shrubbery borders in a 'slovenly manner' when directed to cut flowers by von Mueller.[54] Ferguson's irascibility lost him the battle to improve the horticultural appearance of the scientist's domain. Without the loyalty of his men, Ferguson was a landscape gardener in need of a change of scenery.

Two months after the fateful interview with Casey, Clement Hodgkinson put an end to the acrimony by physically sepa-rating the parties. He suggested that Ferguson could 'most advantageously' apply his skills to 'rearing large quantities of useful timber trees of kinds that have been found to thrive well in Victoria', using efficient European forestry practices.[55] Hodgkinson also recommended that Ferguson visit the forest reserves to identify areas denuded of indigenous timber and advise local managers where plantations could be established.

In December 1872 Ferguson's new appointment was confirmed, and he took up his position immediately. His first task was to establish a State Nursery at Mount Macedon, on a site he had inspected in April—an area of regrowth where the large timber had been cut out for the sawmills on the mount. This site had everything he needed. It was adjacent to a reservoir, and its aspect was 'admirably adapted to Nursery purposes', affording 'the necessary shelter required for rearing young trees'.[56] The soil and 'the undulating contours' of the site presented 'various aspects' that could be used to grow 'trees from different countries', a trick Ferguson had learnt from his experience at Flemington.[57] So that these trees would have a clean water supply, Ferguson recommended that the government extend the reserve by thirty acres to protect the reservoir from 'pollution by selectors'.

He began by making a clearing in the forest. First he cleared six 'heavily timbered' acres of regrowth stringybark, gum and messmate saplings; this revealed 'heavy stumps interspersed throughout the whole area', which were 'evidence of it having been heavily timbered at some former period'.[58] He had the stumps grubbed and removed, then burnt the lot by piling the saplings around the larger stumps and setting fire to them. This proved to be 'the most effectual way of clearing the land'.[59]

Yet the work of establishing the nursery had only begun. Next, a small patch—about half an acre—was cleared of all tree-roots by hand-trenching, then a portion was sown with seeds of *Pinus insignis*, *Wellingtonia gigantia* and other forest trees. This direct planting succeeded beyond Ferguson's most 'sanguine expectations'. He then had the future nursery site measured and subdivided into quarters, each one chain (about

twenty metres) in width by two in length. To protect his plantings from the wind, each quadrant was hedged with whitethorn mixed with small numbers of evergreen privet, pittosporum, olive, lilly-pilly and cypress. Oriental planes were planted to shade the main walks, which were designed so that a horse and cart could load nursery stock and carry soil and manure to any part of the nursery. Ferguson's plans received a setback, however, when heavy winter rains sent water rushing with 'irresistible force down the gullies', threatening to wash away the topsoil. To repair the consequent damage, he had the gullies and 'broken ground' filled with 300 cubic yards of soil.

By the end of June 1873, Ferguson had successfully planted three acres with more than ten thousand of the 'choicest and best kinds of Himalayan and Californian timber trees'.[60] Among these were 1500 of the more common conifers (*Pinus insignis*, *Abies webbiana*, *Cupressus macrocarpa* and *Cedrus deodara*) together with rarer species from the botanic gardens, which von Mueller reluctantly transferred when the minister directed him to. After another ministerial intercession, von Mueller sent Ferguson some seeds of unnamed Mexican forest trees and 'twenty-seven species and varieties of *Coniferae*'.[61]

Ferguson also collected seeds from Glass's Flemington pinetum. In 1872, he had already collected two large cones of the Queensland bunya pine from Flemington and exhibited them to the Victorian Horticultural Improvement Society.[62] In 1874–75 he returned to Flemington to review the progress of the plantings in order to prepare a report on the suitability of exotic timber trees for other parts of the colony. He was to grow many of these successfully at Macedon, where the avenue leading to his residence was planted with firs, pines and cypresses, Queensland and Chilean araucarias, and cedars from India, Mount Atlas and Lebanon.[63] These flourished from the outset; some grew three feet in one season.[64] On the nursery's steep southern slope, which was believed to be unsuitable for cultivation, he planted a thousand *Cupressus lambertiana* to investigate 'what could be done with similar situations and soils' elsewhere.

A gigantic Amazon lily, named after Queen Victoria, raised from seed in the Melbourne Botanic Gardens in 1858

Charles Walter, *Victoria regia*, *Botanical Gardens, Melbourne*, albumen print, *c.* 1866, private collection

'Admirably adapted to Nursery purposes': the State Nursery in Macedon

The State Nursery, Macedon, postcard, La Trobe Picture Collection, State Library of Victoria

Macedon offered 'a good opportunity' for testing the suitability of European trees to the colony's higher-altitude districts. Within ten years, a Californian redwood grew to thirty-five feet, proving that it would readily adapt to the 'mountain ranges and sheltered valleys in the cool districts of the colony'. An Oregon pine reached the same height in nine years. In the case of the Indian cedar (*Cedrus deodara*), the colonial climate was thought to be better than that of England, where thousands of acres of these trees had been planted by the Duke of Devonshire.[65] It also became apparent that Victoria's terrain and climate suited 'the best kinds' of English and American deciduous trees: the walnut, hickory, chestnut, elm, oak, ash, plane, lime and birch.[66]

This early success spurred Ferguson to experiment further. He set out to find an alternative source of tannin for the colony's tanning industry, to reduce its dependence on wattle bark. In June 1879, two Wardian cases arrived from London with twenty young Vallonea oaks and 'a lot of acorns covered with earth'. The cargo was judged to be so precious that the plants were left in their case undisturbed for a week. Then, under Ferguson's direction, the cases were gradually opened, a few inches at a time; the glass was not removed completely for several days.[67] This care was rewarded when two hundred acorns sprouted. They were planted out three years later.

The altitude of Macedon also encouraged tea growing. After five years of observation, Ferguson concluded that 'as far as soil and climate are concerned tea could be easily cultivated in Victoria'; he sent some tea plants to Creswick forester John La Gerche, instructing him to establish a trial plot there.[68] Another 'novel industry' was the growing of cork oaks (*Quercus suber*), a plantation of which was established in the Macedon nursery during 1880.

Ferguson's larger purpose, however, was still to replace the colony's forests. His forestry experiments soon extended beyond the original nursery. Six months after establishing the Macedon nursery, he chose fifty acres near the summit of the mount for the 'experimental culture of forest trees'. His

WILLIAM FERGUSON

intention was to plant considerable numbers of deodars, Himalayan spruce and silver firs, along with other European timber trees suitable for this high site.[69]

In 1875, he began to reafforest this site. He first cleared 'immense and heavy timber . . . laid in every direction', as well as hazel regrowth and rank ferns. When the site was ready, he had 4000 trees—*Cedrus deodara, Pinus insignis*, the Douglas fir, Himalayan spruce, silver firs, blue gums, an ash and the British oak[70]—brought in by pack horse from the nursery, a four-mile journey over the range.

With the ground so well prepared, the trees might have been expected to thrive, but this was not to be. First, wallabies and wild rabbits caused the plants 'considerable injury'. To control the pests, a fence was erected in the following year. Also in 1875, a bushfire destroyed 'five hundred pines, mainly *Pinus insignis*, planted in open spaces of forest on the summit and along the crest of the mountain'. Ferguson might have considered himself lucky, but the remaining pines were soon consumed by cattle grazing in the forest.

Yet nothing discouraged Ferguson from planting exotic trees to replace the native forest. By 1883, he had succeeded in planting 75 acres with more than 6500 firs, spruces and pines 'in great variety and rareness'. Large numbers of British and American oaks, ash and sycamores went in as well. He did not stop there. In 1886, the Macedon plantation was extended by 200 acres, giving Ferguson scope to create a forest landscape in accord with the picturesque precepts he had used at Flemington. He now chose his trees for aesthetic effect. Californian pines, he knew, would produce 'quite a skyline' when seen from the lower slopes, while groups of Indian cedars created 'beautiful outlines amongst the other conifers'. To the man of pines, these plantings gave 'great relief to the eye' by contrast with 'the dismal appearance' of the 'dead and dying indigenous timber'.[71]

If the new forests of Mount Macedon were envisaged as gardens in the landscape, other terrains were less malleable. In 1878 the Secretary of Agriculture, A. R. Wallis, approved a site

Catalpa syringifolia.

for a new State Nursery at Longeranong in the Wimmera, hundreds of miles from Melbourne.[72] Here, the climate was utterly different from that of Macedon: in summer, the sun was scorching and water was in short supply, even though the site was on Darlot's Swamp, which was fed by the Yarriambeack Creek in winter.[73] Despite this, Ferguson was optimistic that the trees he had acclimatised at Macedon could be grown successfully on the Wimmera plain. In 1878, he planted 3000 trees from Macedon, including English oaks, walnuts, planes, and English and Canadian elms; his only concession to the climate was to plant the Syrian carob bean tree (*Ceratonia siliqua*). Surprisingly, by 1884 Ferguson was claiming that the English ash and manna ash had succeeded in 'that dry climate', where they provided cattle fodder and 'grateful shade'.

Not all Ferguson's experiments succeeded. When a dam was thrown across the Yarriambeack to provide water in the summer, he seized the opportunity to plant hundreds of red, golden and basket willows.[74] They failed, and planting willows was never mentioned again. The 'hot and scorching winds' also lacerated the foliage of the Indian bean tree (*Catalpa speciosa*).

'By way of experiment', Ferguson also planted pines at Longeranong that once would only have been found in the gardens of Melbourne's well-to-do. Being well acquainted with the genus *Pinus*, he carefully selected the Aleppo pine of southern Europe (*Pinus halepensis*) and two Californian pines, *Pinus radiata* and the digger pine (*Pinus sabiniana*), as being most adaptable to the Wimmera.[75]

In 1882, the Department of Agriculture asked him to report if there were 'any portions of the state forests suitable for wattle plantations' to supply the tanning industry, and the next year he set aside sixty acres for wattles at Longeranong.[76] Thirty acres were sown with seed of the black wattle (*Acacia decurrens*), and the remaining thirty with the golden wattle (*Acacia pycnantha*). Within a year some of the trees were ten feet high. Encouraged, Ferguson sowed golden wattle seeds six miles on either side of the railway line between Jung Jung and

The Indian bean tree, *Catalpa speciosa*, which was lacerated by the hot winds of the Australian Wimmera

Catalpa syringifolia, from *Loddiges Botanical Cabinet*, vol. 13, plate 1282, State Library of Victoria

The You Yangs in 1861; twenty years after this photograph was taken, they had been completely denuded of timber

Richard Daintree, *You Yangs Looking East*, albumen print, 1861, La Trobe Picture Collection. State Library of Victoria

Doeen. It was the beginning of a project Ferguson envisaged stretching for 'many miles' in a colony where railway reserves were 'unoccupied and lying waste'.[77]

Ferguson soon began sowing wattle closer to Melbourne, along the length of the Geelong–Melbourne railway line. Borers 'caused the demise of some of the wattles' between the fifteenth and nineteenth miles, but the plantings from Werribee to the twenty-first mile were untouched.[78] Unfazed, Ferguson planted another two miles in autumn 1884, then three miles at Little River the following year. By that stage, the only stretch that 'awaited cultivation' was from Lara station to the forty-mile post.

These plantings were continued beyond Geelong. Ten miles of the Geelong–Queenscliff line were sown with golden wattle during 1883–84.[79] On the line running west from Geelong to Colac, a thousand acres of wattle plantations had been established by 1886 and another 200 acres were expected to be planted in the following year. These plantings became so overcrowded that they had to be thinned.[80] To the practised eye of George Smith of the Ballarat Royal Exotic Nursery, the 'acacias upon the Colac line were sowed by someone who had no idea what he was doing; they have sowed about ten times too much seed'.[81]

The aim of these plantations was to supply 'an immense quantity of bark for tanning purposes'. The demand for tannin was so great that there was lobbying to strip the wattles on the Colac railway prematurely. Ferguson held back these demands for a year, proposing to lease out some land sown with wattle at Colac. Yet demand soon outran the supply of bark from the plantations, compounding the pressure on the native forests. In the Grampians, 'valuable young [wattle] trees' on the Victoria Range were 'stripped of their bark before they had reached three inches in diameter'. In 1886, Ferguson visited the Rodney district and found 'a whole forest destroyed'—'wattles . . . as thick as your finger' stripped, and 'iron bark cut down in every direction'.[82] There were 200 to 300 timber-getters at work in the southern section of the forest alone.

The colony's remaining ironbark forests were also under threat from bark-hunters and timber-getters. To prevent 'the whole of this valuable timber from being destroyed', in 1883 an Order in Council was issued prohibiting 'the felling of trees for the purpose of obtaining only the bark'.[83] Yet this did not stop the ironbark forests from being cut for timber. On inspecting 'many hundred miles of timber country', Ferguson recorded that in the Rodney ironbark forest of Central Victoria the best timber had been taken out to make piles for Public Works projects.[84] In the timber reserves of the north-east, Ferguson also reported that the timber was 'fast disappearing' from Chiltern to Yackandandah, and recommended that what remained be conserved and protected.

These suggestions went unheeded, and Victoria's forests remained under threat. In Gippsland, Ferguson found that timber-splitters were laying waste to the mountain ash forest in the Upper Neerim reserve, which contained 'some of the finest timber in the colony'. Large trees that could have been gainfully used by sawmillers were being wantonly split for palings and firewood.

In Central Victoria there were some attempts to redress this destruction. Although most of the former Craigie State Forest had been thrown open to selectors, 400 acres remained, and these were sown with black and golden wattle in 1882–83. Meanwhile, Creswick forester John La Gerche was sowing blue gum seed in a small, abandoned garden in Jackass Gully in the Bullarook forest.[85] Since 1873, Ferguson had recommended that his foresters gather and sow 'seeds of our indigenous trees',[86] but La Gerche found that the land had to be ploughed for seed to germinate.[87] At nearby Daylesford, forester Chamberlain had no success growing blue gum from seed on un-cultivated land in the Wombat Forest. He too came to the conclusion that the seed would have a better chance to grow 'if a portion of the forest were cleared and the ground roughly ploughed'.[88] While 'the timber getters, like birds of passage', pursued the ever-diminishing supply of timber in the forest, Chamberlain was reduced to sowing blue gum seeds 'by way of experiment' in his own garden.[89] Like Ferguson, his foresters were returning to the garden as a model for understanding the country.

There were similar problems in the You Yangs, near Geelong. Here, the shire council had lobbied for forest trees to be planted to reduce the perceived climatic changes associated with the destruction of the forests.[90] Remembering the difficulties he had experienced with stock and wildlife in his early afforestation programme on Mount Macedon, Ferguson enclosed 1180 acres of the You Yangs with five miles of post-and-wire fence at a cost of £400. He then sowed pine, wattle, ironbark and red gum and planted 2000 pine trees in pits dug out of the rocky terrain. Although initially the seeds germinated, they succumbed to insufficient moisture and the ubiquitous rabbit, which by then had reached plague numbers.[91]

The selection of seeds planted in the You Yangs bears further examination. Ferguson's choice of ironbark and wattle suggests that he saw similarities between the You Yangs and the Craigie ironbark forest, where golden wattle had successfully been raised from seed sown *in situ*. By this time, wattle seeding was seen as a safe means of reafforesting the landscape and fulfilling the promise of economic gain. When La Gerche in Creswick asked Ferguson for stringybark seed, Ferguson replied that it would be 'useless to sow stringy bark seed during April', even if they cultivated the land with picks. After La Gerche pressed him further, Ferguson recommended that he sow golden wattle seed.[92] So the golden wattle spread across Victoria at the expense of the local vegetation.

South-west of the You Yangs, the selectors' demand for land had begun to threaten the pristine forests of the Otway Ranges. During 1879, while Ferguson was planting willows in the Wimmera, his political masters had excised 158 000 acres from this forest.[93] What remained became a magnet for middle-class adventurers seeking new lands to conquer close to home. In 1880, George Morrison, the precocious son of the Geelong College headmaster, traversed the forest on foot as part of a trek from Geelong to Adelaide—a kind of dress rehearsal for the imperial exploits that would later win him the nickname 'Morrison of Peking'. On his way, he encountered two 'celebrated men', university lecturers on a kind of sabbatical in the bush: William Kernot and John Burslem Gregory, lecturers in Civil Engineering and Common Law respectively at the University of Melbourne. (In the 1890s, Gregory would be instrumental in securing Wilson's Promontory as a national park.[94])

Morrison described Gregory as 'the very type of an explorer', replete with pith helmet; he was 'short, broad shouldered . . . with a long beard, slight stoop and handsome face'. By contrast, Kernot, 'although fairly tall, had a very round back, concave chest, narrow shoulders, knock-knees, red nose and spectacles'. Morrison was disappointed to observe that neither man 'much believed in roughing it'; they were carrying 'every conceivable luxury from a tent, to lime juice, sweet biscuits and figs'.[95] The whole kit was kept dry by a packhorse named Lorne, which Gregory had trained to cross creeks by walking on logs.[96] Yet large areas of the Otway forest remained unseen and unexplored.

About two years after Morrison's sortie, the Colac shire engineer, P. C. Moroney, discovered a beech forest fifteen miles from Mount Sabine, and in February 1883 Ferguson came to see it. The journey from Colac proved arduous. Ferguson traversed the 'poor scrubby timbered country' of Yahoo station (named after the uncouth land in Jonathan Swift's *Gulliver's Travels*), then ascended a steep range, where he came upon 'magnificent messmate of the very best description' between 250 and 300 feet high, interspersed with large white gums. The mountain ash (*Eucalyptus regnans*) and messmate (*E. obliqua*) filled him with awe.

Yet when Ferguson came upon the beech forest, he did not see it for what it was. Although he saw individual beech trees five feet in diameter, he described them merely as 'a few scattered trees interspersed throughout a great forest of mountain ash and messmate'. He did not understand that the

Well-heeled explorers: John Burslem
Gregory (left, in pith helmet),
Denis East (centre) and William
Kernot (right) with Lorne
the packhorse

*John Burslem Gregory, Denis East,
Professor Kernot with Lorne the
packhorse on returning home
(to Rosedale, St Kilda) from an
exploring excursion in the
mountains,* private collection

The Beech Forest railway in a
skeletal landscape

John Mont Arnest, *Beech Forest
Narrow Gauge Railway,* 1904,
La Trobe Picture Collection,
State Library of Victoria

beech trees were the remnants of an ancient forest succession. They had predominated until fire depleted their numbers, leaving only those in protected ravines.

In an attempt to make sense of what he saw, Ferguson fell back on European understandings of the landscape. His description of these remnant trees as 'occasional groups of not less than twenty trees of the same species' owed much to the language of landscape gardening. He also evoked the gothic, describing the locale as 'a ravine or deep dell where the sun never penetrates'.

And, in the midst of the forest, Ferguson dreamed of the clearing. He envisaged the forest's 'exceedingly rich vegetable matter' turned into productive farmland. In his dream, the state would assist the selectors by establishing an agricultural college and setting aside land for crop experimentation. There would be a railway through the precipitous country to allow timber to be taken to the mills. This vision began to be realised a year later, when the first selector entered the forest.[96]

The results were apparent by 1885, when the Melbourne journalist Julian Thomas explored the Otway Ranges. Thomas, who became famous as 'The Vagabond', was travelling with a local squatter and 'distinguished amateur photographer', William Robertson, along with P. C. Moroney, the intrepid Colac shire engineer who had escorted Ferguson. Thomas knew he was following in Ferguson's footsteps; he began his newspaper article by repeating Ferguson's opinion that the messmate and mountain ash forests 'appear to be as far as I have penetrated, inexhaustible'.

The party emerged from the tall timbers into a clearing where a selector had made a garden—a patch filled with flowers, vegetables, and remnant tree ferns. The 'Vagabond' was no stranger to the transformation of the wilderness, having accompanied the American photographer Edweard Muybridge to see the coffee plantations hewn out of the Guatemalan jungle in 1875.[98] In the Otways, the selector's clearing was on a smaller scale. Thomas was pleased to observe

that, even in this wild environment, the arrangement of plants suggested that 'the owner or owner's wife has some taste'.[99]

Yet this small clearing was a harbinger of greater destruction. By the turn of the century the beech forest was no longer. In its place was a skeletal landscape of ringbarked, fire-blackened messmate and mountain ash. Ironically, the only tree species still thriving was Ferguson's beloved wattle.[100] Knowing this, let us leave him standing in the forest, blinded by his vision, and ask ourselves: how do we inhabit the clearings created by a century of this kind of seeing?

Notes

Chapter I Sir William Macarthur

1   J. G. Veitch, 'Extracts from the Journal of Mr John Gould Veitch during a Trip to the Australian Colonies and the South Sea Islands' (henceforward 'Journal'), *Gardeners' Chronicle and Agricultural Gazette*, 27 January 1866, p. 76.

2   Plants sent from Veitch and Son of Exeter, October 1849, Macarthur papers, A2943, Mitchell Library.

3   S. Heriz-Smith, 'The Veitch Nurseries of Killerton and Exeter *c.* 1780 to 1863: Part 1', *Garden History*, vol. 16, no. 1, spring 1988, p. 47.

4   Macarthur papers, A2943, Mitchell Library.

5   J. G. Veitch, 'Extracts from Mr. J. G. Veitch's Letters on Japan' (henceforward 'Letters'), *Gardeners' Chronicle and Agricultural Gazette*, 15 December 1860, p. 1104.

6   James Veitch to Sir William Macarthur, 16 July 1860, and Harry Veitch to Sir William Macarthur, 18 May 1860, Macarthur papers, A2945, Mitchell Library.

7   Stephen Leslie and Sidney Lee (eds), 'James Bruce, eighth Earl of Elgin', *Dictionary of National Biography*, vol. 3, p. 105; F. L. Hawks, *Narrative of an Expedition of an American Squadron to the China Seas and Japan in the years 1852, 1853, 1854 under the command of Commodore M. C. Perry, United States Navy*, vol. 1.

8   Robert Fortune, 'Notes on the Botany of Japan', *Gardeners' Chronicle and Agricultural Gazette*, 16 February 1861, p. 145; Veitch, 'Letters', 11 January 1862, p. 23.

9   Veitch, 'Letters', 15 December 1860, p. 1104.

10 Veitch, 'Letters', 15 December 1860, p. 1104; 22 December 1860, p. 1126.

11 Veitch, 'Letters', 15 December 1860.

12 R. Alcock, *The Capital of the Tycoon. A Narrative of a Three Years' Residence in Japan*, vol. 1, pp. 397–8.

13 Alcock, *The Capital of the Tycoon*, vol. 1, p. 400.

14 Alcock, *The Capital of the Tycoon*, vol. 1, pp. 397–8.

15 J. G. Veitch, 'Diary kept by J. G. Veitch, during his Trip to Mount Fusi Yama, September 1860' (henceforward 'Diary'), *Gardeners' Chronicle and Agricultural Gazette*, 19 January 1861, p. 50.

16 Alcock, *The Capital of the Tycoon*, vol. 1, pp. 411–12.

17 Veitch, 'Diary', 19 January 1861, pp. 49–50.

18 Alcock, *The Capital of the Tycoon*, vol. 2, p. 482.

19 J. G. Veitch, 'Notes on the Vegetation of Japan', *Gardeners' Chronicle and Agricultural Gazette*, 22 December 1860, p. 1126.

20 Alcock, *The Capital of the Tycoon*, vol. 1, p. 412.

21 Veitch, 'Notes', 22 December 1860, pp. 1126–7; Veitch, 'Diary', 19 January 1861, p. 49.

22 Veitch, 'Letters', 12 January 1861, p. 24.

23 Veitch, 'Letters', 2 February 1861, p. 97.

24 John Gould Veitch to Joseph Hooker, 19 June 1861, Supplementary Foreign Letters, vol. 218, Royal Botanic Gardens, Kew.

25 Veitch, 'Letters', 1 February 1862, p. 93; D. A. Griffiths, 'A Garden on the Edge of China: Hong Kong, 1848', *Garden History*, vol. 16, no. 2, autumn 1988, p. 190.

26 Sue Shephard, *Seeds of Fortune: A Gardening Dynasty*, p. 146.

27 James Veitch to Sir William Macarthur, 26 January 1864, Macarthur papers, A2945, Mitchell Library.

28 Veitch, 'Journal', 6 January 1866, p. 7.

29 Veitch, 'Journal', 27 January 1866, p. 76.

30 Veitch, 'Journal', 27 January 1866, p. 76.

31 Veitch, 'Journal', 3 February 1866, p. 101.

32 *Curtis's Botanical Magazine*, 1 October 1865, tab. 553; 1 January 1867, tab. 5620.

33 Veitch, 'Journal', 24 February 1866, p. 172; L. Gilbert, *The Royal Botanic Gardens, Sydney. A History 1816–1985*, p. 84.

34 J. Kerr (ed.), *The Dictionary of Australian Artists*, 'Henry Kerr', p. 424.

35 Veitch, 'Journal', 24 February 1866, p. 172.

36 Veitch, 'Journal', 17 February 1866, pp. 147–8, 24 March 1866, p. 267; J. Brenchley, *The Voyage of the 'Curaçao'*, pp. 217–19.

37 Veitch, 'Journal', 24 March 1866, p. 267.

38 Veitch, 'Journal', 3 March 1866, p. 195.

39 Veitch, 'Journal', 10 March 1866, p. 220.

40 Veitch, 'Journal', 10 March 1866, p. 220.

41 Veitch, 'Journal', 24 March 1866, p. 267.

42 C. G. S. Foljambe, *Three Years on the Australian Station*, p. 237.

43 John Veitch to Sir William Macarthur, 1
    November 1866, Macarthur papers, A2945,
    Mitchell Library.

44 *Curtis's Botanical Magazine*, 1 October 1865,
    tab 5540.

45 Harry Veitch to Sir William Macarthur, 29
    October 1867, Macarthur papers, A2945, Mitchell
    Library.

46 John Veitch to Sir William Macarthur,
    12 December 1868, Macarthur papers, A2945,
    Mitchell Library.

47 John Veitch to Sir William Macarthur, 21 February
    1870, Macarthur papers, A2945, Mitchell Library.

48 John Veitch to Sir William Macarthur, 26 February
    1870, Macarthur papers, A2945, Mitchell Library.

49 Harry Veitch to Sir William Macarthur, 20 August
    1873, Macarthur papers, A2945, Mitchell Library.

50 Harry Veitch to Sir William Macarthur, 23 January
    1872, Macarthur papers, A2945, Mitchell Library.

51 Harry Veitch to Sir William Macarthur, 14 April
    1874, Macarthur papers, A2945, Mitchell Library.

52 Harry Veitch to Sir William Macarthur, 20 August
    1873, Macarthur papers, A2945, Mitchell Library.

53 Harry Veitch to Sir William Macarthur, 15 April
    1875, Macarthur papers, A2945, Mitchell Library.

54 Harry Veitch to Sir William Macarthur,
    25 November 1874, Macarthur papers, A2945,
    Mitchell Library.

55 S. Heriz-Smith, 'The Veitch Nurseries of Killerton
    and Exeter *c.* 1780 to 1863: Part 2', *Garden History*,
    vol. 16, no. 2, Autumn 1988, p. 180.

56 Ferdinand von Mueller to William Macarthur,
    17 March 1875, Macarthur papers, A2944,
    Mitchell Library.

57 Harry Veitch to Sir William Macarthur, 1 June
    1875, Macarthur papers, A2945, Mitchell Library.

58 Ferdinand von Mueller to William Macarthur,
    17 March 1875, Macarthur papers, A2944,
    Mitchell Library.

59 David Macmillan, *A Squatter Went to Sea*, p. 144.

60 C. G. G. J. van Steenis (ed.), *Flora Malesiana*, vol. 1,
    p. 429.

61 Macmillan, *A Squatter Went to Sea*, pp. 137, 154.

62 van Steenis (ed.), *Flora Malesiana*, vol. 1, p. 429;
    The Garden, 1 April 1876, p. 311.

63 Ferdinand von Mueller, *Descriptive Notes on
    Papuan Plants*, 1875, pp. 3–4.

65 van Steenis (ed.), *Flora Malesiana*, vol. 1, pp. 43–5;
    The Garden, 1 April 1876, p. 311.

65 Ray Desmond, *Dictionary of British and Irish
    Botanists and Horticulturalists: Including Plant
    Collectors, Flower Painters and Garden Designers*,
    p. 248.

66 Andrew Goldie to William Macarthur, 13 October
    1875, Macarthur papers, A2944, Mitchell Library.

67 For details of Goldie's subsequent career in New
    Guinea, see Paul Fox, 'In Search of Birds and
    Beetles: Scientific Imagination and New Guinea',
    Meanjin, vol. 49, no. 4, summer 1990, pp. 678–81.

68 Harry Veitch to Sir William Macarthur,
    25 November 1874, Macarthur papers, A2945,
    Mitchell Library.

69 Harry Veitch to Sir William Macarthur, 1 June
    1875, Macarthur papers, A2945, Mitchell Library.

70 J. H. Veitch, *Hortus Veitchii*, pp. 67–78.

71 Peter Veitch to Sir William Macarthur,
    13 September 1875, Macarthur papers, A2945,
    Mitchell Library.

72 Harry Veitch to Sir William Macarthur,
    24 December 1875, Macarthur papers, A2945,
    Mitchell Library.

73 Ferdinand von Mueller to Sir William Macarthur,
    n.d. [1876], Macarthur papers, A2944,
    Mitchell Library.

74 Ferdinand von Mueller to Sir William Macarthur,
    23 May 1876, Macarthur papers, A2944,
    Mitchell Library.

75 Charles Moore to William Macarthur, 28 May
    1876, Macarthur papers, A2944, Mitchell Library.

76 Orchids requested from Messrs Veitch in return
    for *Chevert* plants valued at £800, 2 October
    1876, Macarthur papers, A2948, Mitchell Library.

77 Peter Veitch to Sir William Macarthur,
    15 November 1876, Macarthur papers, A2945,
    Mitchell Library.

78 Peter Veitch to Sir William Macarthur, 3 October
    1876, Macarthur papers, A2945, Mitchell Library.

79 Peter Veitch to Sir William Macarthur, 3 October
    and 6 November 1876, Macarthur papers, A2945,
    Mitchell Library.

80 Peter Veitch to Sir William Macarthur, 22 January 1877, Macarthur papers, A2945, Mitchell Library.

81 Harry Veitch to Sir William Macarthur, 22 December 1876, Macarthur papers, A2945, Mitchell Library.

82 Peter Veitch to Sir William Macarthur, 13 April 1877, Macarthur papers, A2945, Mitchell Library.

83 Auction list of *Dendrobium superbiens*, n.d., Macarthur papers, A2496, Mitchell Library; Harry Veitch to Sir William Macarthur, 15 November 1877, A2945, Macarthur papers, Mitchell Library.

84 Harry Veitch to Sir William Macarthur, 15 November 1877, Macarthur papers, A2945, Mitchell Library.

85 Harry Veitch to Sir William Macarthur, 15 November 1877, Macarthur papers, A2945, Mitchell Library.

86 Peter Veitch to Sir William Macarthur, 13 April 1877, Macarthur papers, A2945, Mitchell Library.

87 Harry Veitch to Sir William Macarthur, 15 November 1877, Macarthur papers, A2945, Mitchell Library.

88 Peter Veitch to Sir William Macarthur, 30 July 1879, Macarthur papers, A2945, Mitchell Library.

Chapter II Thomas Lang

1 Thomas Lang and Company, *Catalogue of Plants Cultivated for Sale by Thomas Lang and Company*, 1870, p. 5.

2 George Smith, Evidence, 18 June 1886, *Royal Commission on Vegetable Products, Second Progress Report*, 1886, p. 110.

3 W. J. Bean, *Trees and Shrubs Hardy in the British Isles*, vol. 4, p. 266; List of Plants received into Lang's Nursery 1860–67, Cont Q/10, 5 January 1863 per Great Britain, arrived April 1863, Ballarat Historical Parks Association.

4 *Ballarat Star*, 9 April 1862, supplement, p. 1. Lang presented one redwood (*Wellingtonia gigantea*) to the Melbourne Botanic Gardens and another to Mr Thomas Bath, whose farm Ceres at Learmonth was named after the Roman goddess of agriculture; a third Lang planted at his own Warrenheip Nursery. This is a different number from the six he imported from Hugh Low and Company in May 1860, and the twenty he ordered from the same nursery in July 1860. This suggests that the three mentioned by Lang in his lecture were received before 1860. Alternatively, Lang may have imported seed into the colony before 1860 and raised the first *Wellingtonia* from seed; this appears to be borne out by the fact that Lang offered 'small plants' to the public in May 1860 for 42 shillings each. (Hugh Low & Co. May 1860 & 13 July 1860, List of Plants received into Lang's Nursery 1860–67, Ballarat Historical Parks Association. (I am indebted to Margaret and Clive Windmill for drawing my attention to this List of Plants), and *Victorian Agricultural and Horticultural Gazette*, 21 May 1860, pp. 32, 43.) As an indication of how this Californian redwood fired the imagination, one Ballarat mining company named its mine Wellingtonia gigantea, presumably to describe the stupendous amount of gold the company expected to find (*Ballarat Star*, 6 October 1860, p. 1).

5 Thomas Lang, 'On Wardian or Plant Cases', *Ballarat Star*, 9 April 1862, supplement, p. 1.

6 Ray Desmond, *Dictionary of British and Irish Botanists and Horticulturalists: Including Plant Collectors, Flower Painters and Garden Designers*, p. 459.

7 Miles Hadfield, *A History of British Gardening*, p. 326.

8 I am indebted to Barney Hutton for this information.

9 Lang, 'On Wardian or Plant Cases', *Ballarat Star*, 9 April 1862, supplement, p. 1.

10 Hutton, 'Thomas Lang, Nurseryman', p. 96; Thomas Lang, Record of Plants Received into Lang's Nursery, 1856–59, 1 July 1856, Ballarat Historical Parks Association.

11 *Report of the Trustees, Public Library, Museums and National Gallery of Victoria for 1883*, p. 15. (Lang's copies of the *Gardeners' Chronicle and Agricultural Gazette* are now held in two locations: 1848–1857 in the library of the Herbarium, Royal Botanic Gardens, Melbourne; the remainder in the State Library of Victoria.) Evidence of his reading the *Florist* is provided by *Catalogue of Flowering Bulbs, Tubers Cultivated by Thomas Lang and Company*, 1872, p. 12.

12 *Florist*, November 1861, p. 321; *Catalogue of Plants Cultivated for Sale by Thomas Lang and Company*, 1868, p. 51.

13 *Florist and Pomologist*, April 1862, p. 49. This petunia was known as 'Eliza Mathieu'. The *Catalogue of Plants Cultivated for Sale by Thomas Lang and Company*, 1870 (p. 5) mentions that 'Elsie Mathieu' was among Lang's introductions. I have assumed that this is the same variety, as Lang's 1867 catalogue describes 'Elise Matthieu' as purple spotted with white, which accords with the *Florist and Pomologist*'s description.

14 *Ballarat Times*, 24 March 1860. p. 3.

15 Lang's araucarias included *Araucaria imbricata*, *bidwillii*, *excelsa* and *cunninghamii* (*Ballarat Times*, 24 March 1860; reprint of article in *Victorian Agricultural and Horticultural Gazette*, 21 March 1860, pp. 10–11).

16 *Victorian Agricultural and Horticultural Gazette*, 12 November 1860, p. 116. Before becoming Lang's partner, Elliott had been proprietor of the Creswick Road Nursery, Ballarat.

17 *Ballarat Star*, 13 May 1865, supplement, p. 1.

18 Thomas Lang, List of Plants received into Lang's Nursery 1860–67, Cont. Y/9 per Great Britain arrived May 1861, Ballarat Historical Parks Association.

19 Lang, List of Plants, loc. cit; W. J. Bean, *Trees and Shrubs Hardy in the British Isles*, vol. 2, pp. 658, 672. Bean identifies *Magnolia glauca* as *Magnolia virginiana*.

20 *Ballarat Star*, 13 May 1865, supplement, p. 1.

21 *Ballarat Star*, 11 January 1862, p. 2.

22 Hutton, 'Thomas Lang, Nurseryman', p. 95.

23 Sebastian Rennie, Evidence, 18 June 1886, Royal Commission on Vegetable Products, *Second Progress Report*, 1886, p. 111.

24 J. G. Veitch, 'Extracts from the Journal of John Gould Veitch during a Trip to the Australian Colonies and the South Sea Islands' (henceforward 'Journal'), *Gardeners' Chronicle and Agricultural Gazette*, 14 April 1866, p. 339.

25 Rennie, Evidence, 18 June 1886, Royal Commission on Vegetable Products, *Second Progress Report*, 1886, p. 111.

26 Veitch, 'Journal', 14 April 1866, p. 339.

27 Thomas Lang to Sir William Macarthur, 11 January 1866, Macarthur papers, A2943, Mitchell Library.

28 Thomas Lang, 'Melons', *Victorian Agricultural and Horticultural Gazette*, 21 August 1858, pp. 58–9.

29 *Ballarat Times*, 24 March 1860, p. 3. Reprint of article from the *Victorian Agricultural and Horticultural Gazette*, 21 March 1860, pp. 10–11. For details of van Houtte see 'M. Louis van Houtte', *The Garden*, 15 July 1876, supplement, pp. xi-xii.

30 On the Chinese labels, see *Ballarat Star*, 11 November 1861, p. 2; on melons, Thomas Lang, 'Melons', *Victorian Agricultural and Horticultural Gazette*, 21 August 1858, pp. 58–9.

31 *Town and Country* (Melbourne), 19 July 1873.

32 Hazel Conway, *People's Parks. The Design and Development of Victorian Parks in Britain*, pp. 20, 21, 33.

33 *Ballarat Star*, 6 July 1860. I am indebted to Barney Hutton for this reference.

34 Thomas Lang, 'Eastern Municipal Trees', *Ballarat Star*, 7 November 1860, p. 3.

35 Honour Board of Past Presidents of Ballarat Mechanics Institute, sighted Ballarat, October 2000.

36 I am indebted to Barney Hutton for information about the school; on Matilda's washing machine, see Thomas Lang and Company, *Catalogue of Flowering Bulbs, Tubers Cultivated by Thomas Lang and Company*, 1872, pp. 21–3.

37 Thomas Lang to Sir William Macarthur, 11 January 1866, Macarthur papers, A2943, Mitchell Library.

38 Cont Q/10, 6 January 1863, Thomas Lang, List of Plants received into Lang's Nursery 1860–67, Ballarat Historical Parks Association; Thomas Lang, 'Introduction' in W. H. Treen, *The Majetin v Apple Blight*, A. L. Henriques, Melbourne, 1871, pp. 3, 9.

39 *Australasian*, 6 November 1886, p. 876. The *Australasian*'s account differs in detail from Lang's foreword to Treen's *The Majetin v Apple Blight*. The latter has been given weight over the *Australasian* report.

40 Horticultural Pamphlets, Macarthur papers, A2947, Mitchell Library.

41 Thomas Lang, 'Introduction' in W. H. Treen, *The Majetin v Apple Blight*, p. 4.

42 Thomas Lang and Company, *Apples on Majetin Stocks offered for sale by Thomas Lang and Company, Nurserymen Ballarat and Melbourne*, 1 February 1871; *Australasian*, 6 November 1886, p. 876.

43 Lang's grandfather, Gilbert Lang, was born at Greenoak in 1725, studied at Glasgow University and was minister of the parish of Largs from August 1756 until his death in December 1791 (Hew Scott (ed.), *Fasti Ecclesiae Scoticanae*, vol. 3, pp. 215–16. I am indebted to Barney Hutton for this information). On Lang's background, see Barney Hutton, 'Thomas Lang, Nurseryman', *Australian Garden Journal*, April 1985, p. 95.

44 Thomas Lang to Sir William Macarthur, 9 August 1870, Macarthur papers, A2943, Mitchell Library.

45 *Geelong Advertiser*, 11 August 1870, p. 2.

46 Thomas Lang, *Phonetic Printing or the Reformation of Printing*, p. 5; *Phonetic Journal*, 8 May 1858, p. 163; Leslie Stephen and Sidney Lee (eds), *Dictionary of National Biography*, vol. 8, p. 548; vol. 19, p. 1137.

47 *Phonetic Journal*, 10 September 1853, p. 290; 23 October 1852, pp. 339–40; 21 February 1852, p. 58. Lang presented his collection of the *Phonetic Journal* 1842–1877 (non-consecutive) to the Melbourne Public Library in February 1887.

48 *Kilmarnock Directory*, 1851. Letter to H.B. from Chief Librarian, Kilmarnock and Loudon District Council, 31 May 1983. I am indebted to Barney Hutton for this reference.

49 Lang, *Phonetic Printing*, pp. 9–10.

50 On Lang's dealings with the great houses, see Ellison Harvie to H. B. Hutton, 4 September 1982. His views on British gardeners are outlined in Thomas Lang, 'Plea for Gardeners' *Horticultural Calendar*, May 1874. I am indebted to Barney Hutton for these references.

51 Hazel Le Rougetel, 'The First Rose Grower in England', *Country Life*, 25 June 1981, p. 183; 'Trade Lists Reviewed: T. Rivers (Sawbridgeworth), 'A Descriptive Catalogue of Fruits for the Seasons 1858–59', *Gardeners' Chronicle and Agricultural Gazette*, 6 November 1858, p. 816.

52 Thomas Rivers, 1 January 1858, List of Plants received into Lang's Nursery 1860–67, Ballarat Historical Parks Association. Among the plums were 'Ickworth Imperatrice', 'Washington', 'Coe's Golden Drop', 'Kirke's', 'Jefferson', 'Prince Englebert,' 'Lawrence's Gage' and 'Guthrie's Late Green'.

53 Veitch, 'Journal', 14 April 1866, p. 339.

54 Desmond, *Dictionary of British and Irish Botanists and Horticulturalists*, p. 439.

55 Lang, List of Plants received into Lang's Nursery 1860–67, May 1860, Ballarat Historical Parks Association.

56 *Ballarat Star*, 11 January 1862, p. 2; Lang, List of Plants received into Lang's Nursery 1860–67, March 1866, Ballarat Historical Parks Association.

57 The Douglas fir (*Abies douglasii*, now *Pseudotsuga menziesii*) and Western red cedar (*Thuja gigantea*, now *Thuja plicata*) are included in Lang, List of Plants received into Lang's Nursery 1860–67, August 1862, Ballarat Historical Parks Association. For Low's advertisement, see *Gardeners' Chronicle and Agricultural Gazette*, 6 July 1861, p. 621.

58 *Ballarat Star*, 11 January 1862, p. 2.

59 *Florist*, November 1859, p. 321; Lang, List of Plants received into Lang's Nursery 1860–67, 23 January 1864, Ballarat Historical Parks Association.

60 'Greenhouse plants at Ballarat', *Weekly Times*, 18 November 1871, p. 6.

61 William Guilfoyle to Clement Hodgkinson, 23 August 1873, VPRS. 44/P, Unit 000750, File 73/M18742, Public Record Office Victoria (henceforward PROV).

62 The 1863 consignment from Low included *Rhododendron* 'Album', the rosy crimson-and-white blotched 'Fleur de Marie', 'Leopardi' with lilac flowers and chocolate spots, the cherry rose flowering 'Georgina', the dark plum 'Victoria (Waterer's)' and the bright rose-scarlet flowering 'Titan'. Lang, List of Plants received into Lang's Nursery 1860–67, Hugh Low, 9 October 1863. For the 1866 consignment, see Lang, List of Plants received into Lang's Nursery 1860–67, James Veitch, 19 May 1866, Ballarat Historical Parks Association.

63 Joseph Dalton Hooker, *The Rhododendrons of Sikkim-Himalaya: Being an Account, Botanical and Geographic, of Rhododendrons Recently Discovered in the Mountains of the Eastern Himalaya from Drawings and Descriptions made on the spot during a Government Mission to that Country*, pp. 12, 14.

64 Lang, List of Plants received into Lang's Nursery 1860–67, Hugh Low, 5 November 1866, Ballarat Historical Parks Association. On Waterer, see Desmond, *Dictionary of British and Irish Botanists and Horticulturalists*, p. 720. On the rhododendron varieties, see Bean, *Trees and Shrubs Hardy in the British Isles*, vol. 3, p. 864. Anthony Waterer's varieties included *Rhododendron* 'Barclayana', 'Stella', 'Mirandum' and 'Alarm'. See 'Messrs. T. Lang & Co.'s Exhibition of Rhododendrons', *Weekly Times*, 5 December 1874, p. 7; J. G. Millias, *Rhododendrons in which is Set Forth an Account of All Species of the Genus Rhododendron including Azalea and the Various Hybrids*, pp. 34–44.

65 Thomas Lang and Company, *Catalogue of Plants, 1868*, p. 44.

66 William Watson, *Rhododendrons and Azaleas*, pp. 30–1.

67 'Greenhouse Plants at Ballarat', *Weekly Times*, 18 November 1871, p. 6; Lang and Company, *Catalogue of Plants, 1868*, p. 44.

68 Desmond, *Dictionary of British and Irish Botanists and Horticulturalists*, p. 540; *Florist*, November 1860, p. 323.

69 See annotations to Thomas, List of Plants received into Lang's Nursery 1860–67, 5 December 1862, Ballarat Historical Parks Association. For comment on the strategy of importing roses in autumn, see Thomas Rivers to Sir William Macarthur, 28 January 1869, Macarthur papers, A2943, Mitchell Library.

70 Paul, 'Roses: No. III', *Gardeners' Chronicle and Agricultural Gazette*, 21 March 1863 p. 270; 'Roses No. IV', *Gardeners' Chronicle and Agricultural Gazette*, 2 May 1863, p. 389.

71 *Florist*, January 1861, pp. 22–3.

72 Desmond, *Dictionary of British and Irish Botanists and Horticulturalists*, p. 261. Lang, List of Plants received into Lang's Nursery 1860–67, December 1861, Ballarat Historical Parks Association.

73 Lang, Record of Plants received into Lang's Nursery 1856–59, John J. Rule, 31 August 1859, Ballarat Historical Parks Association; *Florist*, June 1857, p. 161.

74 Desmond, *Dictionary of British and Irish Botanists and Horticulturalists*, p. 476; *Gardeners' Chronicle*, 6 December 1884, pp. 729–30.

75 *Florist and Pomologist*, September 1862, p. 129.

76 Lang, List of Plants received into Lang's Nursery 1860–67, James Veitch, 16 December 1863, Ballarat Historical Parks Association.

77 Lang and Company, *List of Flowering Bulbs Cultivated by Thomas Lang and Company, 1868*, p. 4. I am indebted to Richard Aitken for this reference.

78 Lang, List of Plants received into Lang's Nursery 1860–67, James Veitch, 18 October 1865, Ballarat Historical Parks Association.

79 Thomas Lang, *List of Flowering Bulbs and Tubers Cultivated by Thomas Lang and Company*, 1867, p. 17; Lang to Sir William Macarthur, 22 January 1868, Macarthur papers, A2943, Mitchell Library.

80 *Argus*, 14 February 1868, p. 5.

81 'Greenhouse Plants at Ballarat', *Weekly Times*, 18 November 1871, p. 6.

82 *Gardeners' Chronicle and Agricultural Gazette*, 23 March 1861. Among the introductions were *Retinispora pisifera* and *obtusa*; ibid., 18 July 1863, p. 679. They also included the parasol fir and the green-leafed Aucuba.

83 Veitch, 'Journal', 14 April 1866, p. 339.

84 Lang, List of Plants received into Lang's Nursery 1860–67, James Veitch, 19 May 1866, Ballarat Historical Parks Association; Thomas Lang & Co., *List of Coniferous Trees, Japanese Plants, Hardy Trees and Shrubs, Climbers, Greenhouse Plants, Herbaceous Plants, Roses, Fruit Trees and Hedge Plants*, no. 17, 1867, p. 4, includes *Retinispora pisifera* and *R. obtusa*, *Aucuba japonica*, *Cryptomeria elegans*, *Juniperus rigida*, and *Thuja dolabrata*, *T. variegata* and *T. loetevirens*.

85 Lang, List of Plants 1860–67, James Veitch, 19 May 1866, Ballarat Historical Parks Association; *Gardeners' Chronicle and Agricultural Gazette*, 23 March 1861, p. 265.

86 Lang, List of Plants 1860–67, Sir William Macarthur, 5/12 July 1866 includes *Retinispora obtusa* and *R. pisifera*, *R. lycopodioides. Osmanthus ilicifolius*, *Abies alcoquiana* and *A. polita*, and *Clematis patens* 'Standishii'; many of these are listed for sale in Lang, *List of Coniferous Trees*, p. 4.

87 'Mount Warrenheip Nurseries, Ballarat, Ballarat. No. 1', *Weekly Times*, 23 December 1871, p. 6.

88 Thomas Lang to Sir William Macarthur, 14 March 1871, Macarthur Papers, A2943, Mitchell Library For examples of gladioli supplied by Lang to Sir William Macarthur, see invoice, 28 June 1871, Macarthur papers, A2943, Mitchell Library. Among the eighteen varieties forwarded by Lang were 'Crystal Palace', 'James Veitch', 'Galileo', 'Prince of Wales' and 'Princess of Wales'.

89 Thomas Lang to Sir William Macarthur, 14 May 1879, Macarthur papers, A2944, Mitchell Library.

90 Thomas Lang to Sir William Macarthur, 11 January 1866, Macarthur papers, A2944, Mitchell Library.

91 *Portland Guardian*, 29 June 1865, p. 2; Paul Fox, 'For Our Treed Vistas, Thank Early Settlers with Vision' *Age*, 5 August 1986; Paul Fox, 'Over the Garden Fence', *Historic Environment*, vol. 4, no. 3, 1985, p. 34.

92 Thomas Lang & Co. to Niel Black, 8 April 1875, Niel Black papers, MS8996, SLV.

93 *Kyneton Guardian*, 1 June 1893, p. 4. I am indebted to Barney Hutton for this reference.

94 *Kyneton Guardian*, 5 January 1893, p. 4.

95 Thomas Lang, *Phonetic Spelling*, p. 22.

Chapter III Daniel Bunce

1   *Geelong Advertiser*, 3 July 1872, p. 5.

2   George Jones, 'Daniel Bunce', in R. Aitken and M. Looker (eds), *The Oxford Companion to Australian Gardens*, p. 113.

3   Daniel Bunce, *Manual of Practical Gardening Adapted to the Climate of Van Diemen's Land*, p. i.

4   Bunce, *Manual of Practical Gardening*, p. 41; Daniel Bunce, *Catalogue of Seeds and Plants Indigenous and Exotic, Cultivated and on Sale at Denmark Hill Nursery*.

5   E. M. Webster, *Whirlwinds in the Plain*, p. 73.

6   Daniel Bunce, *Travels with Dr Leichhardt*, p. 59.

7   'Report on the Progress of the Horticultural Society from May 1, 1830 to April 30, 1840', *Transactions of the Horticultural Society of London*, second series, vol. 2, 1835–1841, pp. 418–19; Bunce, *Travels*, p. 10.

8   Webster, *Whirlwinds in the Plain*, p. 74.

9   Bunce, *Travels*, p. 58.

10 T. E. Burns and J. R. Skemp, *Van Diemen's Land Correspondents: Letters from R. C. Gunn, R. W. Laurence, Jorgen Jorgenson, Sir John Franklin and Others to Sir William Hooker, 1827–1849*, p. xiv; *Annales des Sciences Naturelles*, second series, vols. 9, 10, 1838. Contains Ronald C. Gunn plate and sticker 'Bound by G. Rolwegan Hobart Town' (in author's possession).

11 E. E. Pescott, 'The Writings of Daniel Bunce, 1813–1872', *Victorian Historical Magazine*, vol. 23, September 1950, p. 118.

12 Bunce, *Travels*, pp. 32, 33, 42.

13 Bunce, *Travels*, pp. 34.

14 Bunce, *Travels*, pp. 56–7.

15 Bunce, *Travels*, p. 62.

16 Bunce, *Travels*, pp. 64–7.

17 Bunce, *Travels*, pp. 69–71.

18 Bunce, *Travels*, pp. 74–5.

19 *Port Phillip Patriot*, 14 March 1842, p. 2; Webster, *Whirlwinds in the Plain*, pp. 75–6; *Port Phillip Gazette*, 15 November 1845, p. 2.

20 Webster, *Whirlwinds in the Plain*, p. 79.

21 Bunce, *Travels*, p. 109.

22 Bunce, *Travels*, p. 126.

23 Bunce, *Travels*, p. 117.

24 Bunce, *Travels*, pp. 137–8.

25 Bunce, *Travels*, p. 156.

26 Webster, *Whirlwinds in the Plain*, p. 192.

27 Leichhardt to Sir William Macarthur, 15 February 1848, in M. Aurousseau (ed.), *The Letters of F. W. Ludwig Leichhardt*, vol. 3, p. 1001.

28 Leichhardt to Sir William Macarthur, 10 October 1847, in Aurousseau (ed.), *The Letters of F. W. Ludwig Leichhardt*, vol. 3, p. 941.

29 Daniel Bunce, *Language of the Aborigines of the Colony of Victoria and Other Districts*, p. 57; Leichhardt to Bunce, end of November 1848, in Aurousseau (ed.), *The Letters of F. W. Ludwig Leichhardt*, vol. 3, p. 976.

30 Leichhardt to Bunce, end of November 1848, in Aurousseau (ed.), *The Letters of F. W. Ludwig Leichhardt*, vol. 3, p. 975.

31 Leichhardt to G. Durando, 6 January 1844, in Aurousseau (ed.), *The Letters of F. W. Ludwig Leichhardt*, vol. 2, p. 704.

32 Bunce, *Language of the Aborigines*, p. 59; *Travels*, pp. 112–13.

33 Leichhardt to G. Durando, 6 January 1844, in Aurousseau (ed.), *The Letters of F. W. Ludwig Leichhardt*, vol. 2, p. 705.

34 Leichhardt to Sir William Macarthur, 15 February 1848, in Aurousseau (ed.), *The Letters of F. W. Ludwig Leichhardt*, vol. 3, p. 1001.

35 *Argus*, 16 March 1850, p. 2.

36 *Argus*, 25 December 1849, p. 2.

37 *Argus*, 7 March 1850, p. 2; Bunce, *Travels*, p. 64.

38 *Argus*, 22 March 1850, p. 2.

39 W. H. Bacchus, 'A Description of some Victorian and other Australian Grasses' in Victorian Department of Lands and Agriculture, *Second Annual Report of the Secretary of Agriculture*, 1874, p. 128.

40 *Argus*, 11 March 1850, p. 2; 14 March 1850, p. 2.

41 *Argus*, 22 March 1850, p. 2; R. V. Billis and A. S. Kenyon, *Pastoral Pioneers of Port Phillip*, p. 27.

42 *Argus*, 28 March 1850, p. 2; 30 March 1850, p. 2.

43 Billis and Kenyon, *Pastoral Pioneers of Port Phillip*, p. 20.

44 *Argus*, 4 April 1850, p. 2; 19 April 1850, p. 2.

45 *Argus*, 4 May 1850, p. 2.

46 *Argus*, 20 May 1850, p. 2.

47 Robertson in T. F. Bride (ed.), *Letters from Victorian Pioneers*, pp. 167–9.

48 W. E. Stanbridge, 'General Characteristics, Astronomy and Mythology of the Tribes in the Central Part of Victoria', *Ethnographical Society Transactions*, vol. 1, 1861, p. 300. For a subsequent telling of this story, see A. Massola, 'Two Aboriginal Legends of the Ballarat District', *Victorian Naturalist*, vol. 79, no. 4, August 1962, pp. 110–11.

49 *Argus*, 20 May 1850, p. 2.

50 *Argus*, 18 April 1850, p. 2.

51 *Argus*, 21 February 1850, p. 2.

52 Ronald Gunn to unknown recipient, n.d., cited in E. E. Pescott, 'The Writings of Daniel Bunce', p. 119.

53 *Argus*, 18 April 1850, p. 1.

54 *Argus*, 13 May 1850, p. 1.

55 Bunce, *Language of the Aborigines*, p. i.

56 *Geelong Advertiser*, 3 July 1872, p. 5.

57 *Argus*, 20 December 1851, p. 2.

58 Pescott, 'The Writings of Daniel Bunce', p. 125.

59 Webster, *Whirlwinds in the Plain*, p. 304; Daniel Bunce, 'Tree Planting in Victoria Parade', *The Rural Magazine*, 1 May 1855, pp. 25–6. Unsigned but authorship assigned in *The Rural Magazine*, 1 August 1885, p. 88.

60 Daniel Bunce, 'Indigenous Plants', *The Rural Magazine*, 1 August 1855, p. 85.

61 *Ballarat Star*, 12 April 1865, p. 3.

62 *Geelong Advertiser*, 26 May 1863, p. 2.

63 *Ballarat Star*, 12 April 1865, p. 3; 'A Visit to the Geelong Botanic Gardens', *Yeoman and Acclimatiser*, 18 July 1863, p. 656.

64 Stephen Daniels, *Humphry Repton: Landscape and the Geography of Georgian England*, pp. 149–205.

65 *Victorian Agricultural and Horticultural Gazette*, 21 September 1858, p. 87.

66 *Yeoman and Acclimatiser*, 21 December 1859; 18 July 1863, p. 656.

67 Daniel Bunce, *Catalogue of Plants under Cultivation in the Botanical Gardens*, pp. 1, 2, 14–15.

68 Bunce, *Catalogue of Plants under Cultivation*, pp. 9, 14, 15, 24.

69 See for example *Victorian Agricultural and Horticultural Gazette*, 21 February 1859, p. 151; *Geelong Advertiser*, 24 March 1868, p. 2.

70 George Jones, *Growing Together: A Gardening History of Geelong—Extending to Colac and Camperdown*, p. 60.

71 Bunce to President, Board of Land and Works, 4 November 1868, VPRS 44/P, Unit 675, File 68/Q17749, PROV; W. R. Brownhill, *History of Geelong and Corio Bay*, p. 112; *Geelong Advertiser*, 18 April 1868, p. 2.

72 *Geelong Advertiser*, 5 June 1866, p. 3.

73 Henry J. Wilkinson to Bunce, 29 March 1871, M5088, State Library of Victoria (henceforward SLV).

74 Jones, *Growing Together*, p. 208; *Geelong Advertiser*, 7 June 1866, p. 2.

75 Henry Nicoll, 15 February 1864 and 26 October 1868, Nicoll papers, MS6329, SLV.

76 J. Campbell Carey to Bunce, 20 September 1867, Australian Autograph Collection, M5088, SLV.

77 *Geelong Advertiser*, 15 May 1868, p. 2.

78 Not all commentators were as complimentary. Schomburgk, the director of the Adelaide Botanic Gardens, described Driffield merely as 'a thoroughly practical amateur gardener' who as a florist had 'maintained a leading position' in Adelaide. A more flattering assessment was given by the Adelaide magnate Robert Barr Smith, who opined that, unlike other newcomers with good English reputations, Driffield had 'nothing to unlearn as to the treatment of plants in this climate'. R. Barr Smith to F. C. Driffield, 30 September 1872, VPRS 44/P, Unit 352, File 72/G24264, PROV; Driffield to J. J. Casey, 29 October 1872, VPRS 44/P, Unit 352, File 72/G24264, PROV.

79 J. Campbell Carey to Bunce, 29 October 1867, Australian Autograph Collection, M5088, SLV.

80 J. Tomkinson to Bunce, 3 August 1865 and 8 November 1870, Australian Autograph Collection, M5088, SLV.

81 *Ballarat Star*, 12 April 1865, p. 3. The site had been selected by September 1864 (*Geelong Chronicle*, 10 September 1864, p. 2). For the prohibition on dogs, see *Geelong Advertiser*, 20 April 1868, p. 2.

82 *Geelong Advertiser*, 5 June 1866, p. 2.

83 *Argus*, 27 February 1867, p. 5; 9 December 1867, p. 5; Brownhill, *History of Geelong and Corio Bay*, p. 215; *Argus*, 9 December 1867, p. 5; 4 September 1868, p. 5.

84 Ray Desmond, *Dictionary of British and Irish Botanists and Horticulturalists: Including Plant Collectors, Flower Painters and Garden Designers*, p. 699; *Gardeners' Chronicle*, vol. 2, 1889, p. 639; *Geelong Advertiser*, 18 April 1868, p. 2; *Argus*, 9 July 1868, p. 5.

85 Jones, *Growing Together*, p. 64; *Geelong Register*, 9 November 1867, p. 2.

86 *Yeoman and Acclimatiser*, 5 March 1864, p. 357; 'The Geelong Botanic Gardens', *Geelong Chronicle*, 10 September 1864, p. 2; *Ballarat Star*, 12 April 1865, p. 3; *Argus*, 9 July 1868, p. 5.

87 Bunce, *Manual of Practical Gardening*, p. iii.

88 Thomas Gordon to Bunce, 28 November 1867, Australian Autograph Collection, M5088, SLV; Jones, *Growing Together*, pp. 41, 57.

89 N. C. Henley to Bunce, 21 October 1863, Australian Autograph Collection, M5088, SLV.

90 Dunn, Wilson & Botterill (late Batchelder & O'Neill) to Bunce, 27 July 1865, Australian Autograph Collection, M5088, SLV.

91 On Thomas Chuck, see Paul Fox and Joan Kerr, 'Thomas Foster Chuck' in Joan Kerr (ed.), *The Dictionary of Australian Artists: Painters, Sketchers, Photographers and Engravers to 1870*, p. 151; for his letter, see T. Chuck to Bunce, 9 August 1870, Australian Autograph Collection, M5088, SLV.

92 *Yeoman and Acclimatiser*, 18 June 1864, p. 602.

93 *Geelong Advertiser*, 27 April 1872, p. 2.

94 Jones, *Growing Together*, p. 46; *Geelong Advertiser*, 16 July 1860, p. 3. Governor was acquitted and Billy sentenced for four months (in addition to the eight months he had already been in jail).

95 Jones, *Growing Together*, p. 64; *Geelong Advertiser*, 5 July 1872, p. 3. To mark the royal visit, Bunce also erected an arch at the entrance of the gardens (*Geelong Register*, 9 November 1867, p. 2).

96 George Rolfe to Bunce, 7 July 1860, Australian Autograph Collection, M5088, SLV.

97 I have based this view on an examination of the material by Davis in the SLV. None showed a connection with Bunce. The only connection with Victoria may be found in J. B. Davis, *Contributions Towards Deferring the Weight of the Brain in Different Races of Men*, p. 524, which acknowledges Ludwig Becker. However, other works by Davis not found in the Library's collection may lead to a reconsideration of this conclusion.

98 *Geelong Advertiser*, 5 July 1872, p. 3. Identified by Brownhill as Billy Gore, who died on 11 November 1885 (Brownhill, *History of Geelong and Corio Bay*, p. 36).

99 *Geelong Advertiser*, 5 July 1872, p. 3.

Chapter IV William Guilfoyle

1 *Australasian Town and Country Journal*, 18 July 1874. p. 96; on Joseph Knight (*c.* 1777–1855), see Miles Hadfield, Robert Harling and Leonie Highton (eds), *British Gardeners: A Biographical Dictionary*, p. 294.

2 R. Clough, 'Michael Guilfoyle', in Aitken and Looker (eds), *The Oxford Companion to Australian Gardens*. I am also indebted to Eve Almond for this information.

3 *Australasian Town and Country Journal*, 18 July 1874, p. 96; J. G. Veitch, 'Extracts from the Journal of John Gould Veitch during a Trip to the Australian Colonies and the South Sea Islands' (henceforward 'Journal'), *Gardeners' Chronicle and Agricultural Gazette*, 20 January 1866, p. 53.

4 Select Committee on the Botanic Gardens, Minutes of Evidence , 10 August 1855, *Votes and Proceedings of the NSW Legislative Council*, 1855, vol. 1, p. 1170.

5 Veitch, 'Journal', 20 January 1866, p. 53.

6 Lionel Gilbert, *The Royal Botanic Gardens, Sydney: A History 1816–1985*, pp. 74–7.

7 'Petition of T. W. Shepherd and M. Guilfoyle', *Votes and Proceedings of the NSW Legislative Council*, 1854, vol. 2, pp. 1295–97.

8 'Petition of T. W. Shepherd and M. Guilfoyle', *Votes and Proceedings of the NSW Legislative Council*, 1854, vol. 2, pp. 1295–97.

9 *Argus*, 26 June 1912, p. 13; K. J. Cable, 'William Woolls', in B. Nairn (ed.), *Australian Dictionary of Biography*, vol. 6, pp. 437–8.

10 Desmond, *Dictionary of British and Irish Botanists and Horticulturalists*, p. 45.

11 J. MacGillivray, *Narrative of HMS Rattlesnake*, vol. 1, pp. 207–8.

12 Veitch, 'Journal', 24 March 1866, p. 267.

13 I am indebted to Richard Aitken for this information.

14 *Argus*, 26 June 1912, p. 13.

15 Veitch, 'Journal', 13 January 1866, p. 31; Jennifer Stackhouse, *Mr Macleay's Garden*, p. 5.

16 Mueller to William Guilfoyle, 18 March 1867, Pescott papers, MS439C, Archives of the Royal Botanic Gardens, Melbourne (henceforward ARBGM).

17 W. R. Guilfoyle, 'A Botanical Tour Among the South Sea Islands', *Journal of Botany*, vol. 7, pp. 131–2.

18 Guilfoyle, 'A Botanical Tour', p. 125.

19 Guilfoyle and Sons, *Catalogue*, 1866, pp. 3, 33.

20 Guilfoyle, 'A Botanical Tour', pp. 120, 125.

21 Guilfoyle, 'A Botanical Tour', p. 126.

22 Guilfoyle, 'A Botanical Tour', p. 120.

23 Guilfoyle, 'A Botanical Tour', pp. 130–1.

24 Guilfoyle, 'A Botanical Tour', pp. 129–30.

25 Guilfoyle, 'A Botanical Tour', p. 124.

26 Guilfoyle, 'A Botanical Tour', pp. 122–3.

27 Fox, 'Portraits of Oceania', *Portraits of Oceania*, p. 24.

28 Guilfoyle, 'A Botanical Tour', pp. 131–2.

29 Guilfoyle, 'A Botanical Tour', pp. 132–3.

30 Guilfoyle, 'A Botanical Tour', pp. 126, 131.

31 Guilfoyle, 'A Botanical Tour', pp. 134–5.

32 Guilfoyle, 'A Botanical Tour', p. 136.

33 Von Mueller to Michael Guilfoyle, 11 February 1869, Pescott, papers, MS439C, ARBGM.

34 Von Mueller to William Guilfoyle, 21 April 1869, Pescott papers, MS439C, ARBGM. Mueller was known as von Mueller from 20 December 1867 (Rod Home, personal communication).

35 Von Mueller to William Guilfoyle, 27 January 1869, Pescott papers, MS439C, ARBGM.

36 Von Mueller to William Guilfoyle, 20 March 1869, Pescott papers, MS439C, ARBGM.

37 R. M. Baker and W. R. Baker, 'Botanical Contributions Overlooked: The Role and Recognition of Collectors, Horticulturalists, Explorers and Others in the Early Documentation of the Australian Flora', in P. S. Short (ed.), *History of Systematic Botany in Australasia*, pp. 66–7.

38 Von Mueller to William Guilfoyle, 20 March 1869, Pescott papers, MS439C, ARBGM.

39 Von Mueller to William Guilfoyle, 15 May 1869, Pescott papers, MS439C, ARBGM.

40 Fox, 'What's in a Historic Garden?', p. 14.

41 W. R. Guilfoyle, 'Sydney Botanic Gardens,' *Leader*, 28 May 1870, pp. 7–8.

42 'The Tweed River', *Australasian Town and Country Journal*, 14 December 1872, p. 784.

43 William Robinson, *The Wild Garden: The Naturalisation and Natural Groupings of Hardy*

Exotic Plants; William Robinson, *The Subtropical Garden: or Beauty of Form in the Flower Garden*.

44 W. R. Guilfoyle, 'Vegetation and Scenery of the Tweed River', *Sydney Mail*, 14 September 1872, p. 329.

45 W. R. Guilfoyle, 'The Tweed River and District from the top of Mount Warning', *Australasian Town and Country Journal*, 17 May 1873, p. 625.

46 Von Mueller to William Guilfoyle, 25 May 1873, Pescott papers, MS439C, ARBGM.

47 R. T. M. Pescott, *W. R. Guilfoyle 1840–1912*, p. 46. See also von Mueller to William Guilfoyle, 23 August 1870, Pescott papers, MS439C, where von Mueller regretted that he 'never had the pleasure to read your father's account of Tweed vegetation in the Herald'.

48 Guilfoyle and Sons, *Catalogue*, 1866, p. 6.

49 Von Mueller to William Guilfoyle, 23 March 1870, Pescott papers, MS439C, ARBGM.

50 F. Von Mueller to [Michael or William] Guilfoyle, 28 July 1870, Pescott papers, MS439C.

51 Von Mueller to William Guilfoyle, 23 August 1870, Pescott papers, MS439C.

52 F. Von Mueller to [Michael or William] Guilfoyle, 26 March 1873 and 15 May 1871, Pescott papers, MS439C, ARBGM.

53 Von Mueller to William Guilfoyle, 3 September 1871 (cow-itch bean), 1 March 1872 and 15 April 1873 (belum wood), Pescott papers, MS439C, ARBGM.

54 Von Mueller to William Guilfoyle, n.d. (but post 1870), Pescott papers, MS439C, ARBGM.

55 Von Mueller to Michael Guilfoyle, 23 August 1870, 3 September 1871, Pescott papers, MS439C, ARBGM.

56 Von Mueller to William Guilfoyle, 15 September 1870, Pescott papers, MS439C, ARBGM.

57 W. R. Guilfoyle, 'Vegetation and Scenery of the Tweed River', *Sydney Mail*, 14 Sepetember 1872, p. 329.

58 Von Mueller to William Guilfoyle, 15 September 1870, 14 August 1871, Pescott papers, MS439C, ARBGM.

59 Von Mueller to [William or Michael] Guilfoyle, 20 March 1873, Pescott papers, MS439C, ARBGM.

60 Von Mueller to William Guilfoyle, 12 October 1871, Pescott papers, MS439C, ARBGM.

61 Pescott, *W. R. Guilfoyle 1840–1912*, p. 63.

62 Von Mueller to William Guilfoyle, n.d. (but 1873), Pescott papers, MS439C, ARBGM.

63 Helen Cohn and Sara Maroske, 'Relief from Duties of Minor Importance—The Removal of Baron von Mueller from the Directorship of the Royal Botanic Gardens', *Victorian Historical Journal*, vol. 67, no. 1, April 1996, pp. 113–15; Margaret Willis, *By Their Fruits: A Life of Ferdinand von Mueller, Botanist and Explorer*, p. 92.

63 Pescott, *W. R. Guilfoyle 1840–1912*, p. 57.

65 William Greig, Josiah Mitchell and William Sangster, 'Report on the Changes that Might be Necessary to Bring into Operation an Organisation which will Secure the Gardens being Kept in the Best Possible Condition without Interfering with Valuable Services Rendered to the Colony by Dr Von Mueller', *Leader*, 30 December 1871, p. 19.

66 *Weekly Times*, 6 February 1875, p. 7.

67 Guilfoyle to Hodgkinson, 9 July 1873, VPRS 44/P, Unit 750, File 73/13988, PROV. I have attributed the 'Notes on the Botanic Gardens' to Guilfoyle because their contents closely match the accounts found in his earlier writings. The fact that the same column appeared in the *Weekly Times* also suggests the column was not written by a journalist attached to a particular paper; see *Weekly Times*, 27 November 1880, p. 11. Moreover, Guilfoyle used the same title in an article published in 1902 (W. R. Guilfoyle, 'Notes from the Botanic Gardens', *Garden Gazette*, December 1902, p. 118).

68 Guilfoyle to Hodgkinson, 9 July 1873, VPRS 44/P, Unit 750, File 73/13988, PROV.

69 *Age*, 12 July 1873, p. 8.

70 Guilfoyle to Hodgkinson, 9 July 1873, VPRS 44/P, Unit 750, File 73/K13988, PROV.

71 Guilfoyle to Hodgkinson, 5 September 1873, VPRS 44/P, Unit 750, File 73/M19713 PROV.

72 Whitehead, *Civilising the City*, pp. 9–12.

73 File note attached to Guilfoyle to Hodgkinson, 30 September 1873, VPRS 44/P, Unit 750, File 73/L21660, PROV.

74 Guilfoyle to Hodgkinson, 11 November 1873, VPRS 44/P, Unit 750, File 73/J26053, PROV.

75 Edmund Burke, *Choice Pieces: Including On the Sublime and the Beautiful*, Inscribed: 'W. R. Guilfoyle Melbourne 12/9/73'. In author's possession.

76 Hortus, 'The Formation of Parks and Gardens', *Weekly Times*, 2 May 1874, pp. 6–7; 9 May 1874, p. 6; 16 May 1874, p. 6; 23 May 1874, p. 6; 30 May 1874, p. 6. For discussion of these see Fox, Images of the Mind: Worlds within Gardens, Master of Landscape Architecture, University of Melbourne, 1980. The lake in Bendigo is now known as Lake Weeroona, and was laid out by Guilfoyle in 1878; the local council opted to wait until he was available. See William Guilfoyle to Sandhurst Town Clerk, 22 April 1874, Bendigo Council Archives; *Bendigo Advertiser*, 2 July 1878, p. 2.

77 Guilfoyle to Hodgkinson, 9 July 1873, VPRS 44/P, Unit 750, File 73/13988, PROV.

78 Guilfoyle to Hodgkinson, 17 July 1873, VPRS 44/P, Unit 750, File 73/14783, PROV.

79 Guilfoyle to Hodgkinson, 9 July 1873, VPRS 44/P, Unit 750, File 73/13988, PROV.; Hodgkinson conveyed Guilfoyle's views to the minister, J. J. Casey; see *Argus*, 12 July 1873, p. 6.

80 Guilfoyle to Hodgkinson, 17 July 1873, VPRS 44/P, Unit 750, File 73/14783, PROV.

81 W. R. Guilfoyle, 'Monthly Report of the Curator of the Botanical and Domain Gardens 1873', *Report of the Inspector-General of Gardens, Parks and Reserves*, p. 23.

82 W. R. Guilfoyle, 'Vegetation and Scenery of the Tweed River', *Sydney Mail*, 14 September 1872, p. 329; W. R. Guilfoyle, *Australian Botany for the Use of Schools*, frontispiece.

83 A. R. Wallis, 'Memorandum by the Secretary for Agriculture Relative to Works in the Government House Domain prior to 1st July 1873', *Report of the Inspector-General of Gardens, Parks and Reserves*, pp. 12–13.

84 Guilfoyle to Hodgkinson, 17 July 1873, VPRS 44/P, Unit 750, File 73/14783, PROV.

85 Guilfoyle to Hodgkinson, Curator's Monthly Report, 5 October 1873, VPRS44/P, Unit 750, File 73/22541, PROV.

86 H. Pitt to W. Archer, 2 March 1876, William Archer papers, MS64/10, University of Melbourne Archives.

87 W. R. Guilfoyle, Draft Plan, Government House Grounds. Showing Important Works Necessary to be Carried Out at Once, 19 July 1876, VPRS 44/P, Unit 433, File 9835, PROV.

88 W. R. Guilfoyle, *Annual Report on the Melbourne Botanic Gardens with a Plan of the Garden*, 1875, p. 7.

89 On the Macedon ferns, see Guilfoyle to Hodgkinson, 13 September 1873, VPRS 44/P, Unit 750, File 173/20339, PROV; on Sayce's design, see Guilfoyle to Hodgkinson, 9 July 1873, VPRS 44/P, Unit 750, File 73/13988, PROV; *Age*, 12 July 1873, p. 8.

90 Sketch of Tree Ferns & Giant Gum Tree (*Eucalyptus amygdalina*) Black Spur Gippsland, signed 'W R G' and dated '1873' in W. R. Guilfoyle, Australian Vegetation. Articles, Lectures etc., W. R. Guilfoyle papers, MS75/104, University of Melbourne Archives; W. R. Guilfoyle, *Annual Report on the Melbourne Botanic Gardens*, 1875, p. 3.

91 W. R. Guilfoyle (attrib.), 'Notes from the Botanic Gardens', *Australasian*, 3 July 1880, p. 28.

92 W. R. Guilfoyle (attrib.), 'Notes from the Botanic Gardens', *Australasian*, 3 April 1880, p. 441; J. H. Veitch, *Gardeners' Chronicle*, 15 September 1894, p. 308.

93 W. R. Guilfoyle, *Annual Report on the Melbourne Botanic Gardens*, 1875, p. 4.

94 W. R. Guilfoyle, 'Vegetation and Scenery of the Tweed River', *Sydney Mail*, 14 September 1872, p. 329.

95 W. R. Guilfoyle (attrib.), 'Notes from the Botanic Gardens', *Australasian*, 3 April 1880, p. 441.

96 W. R. Guilfoyle (attrib.), 'Notes from the Botanic Gardens', *Australasian*, 24 January 1880, p. 122.

97 J. H. Veitch, 'A Traveller's Notes', *Gardeners' Chronicle*, 15 September 1894, pp. 308–9.

98 W. R. Guilfoyle, *Annual Report on the Melbourne Botanic Gardens*, 1875, pp. 4, 8.

99 W. R. Guilfoyle (attrib.), 'Notes from the Botanic Gardens', *Australasian*, 10 January 1880, p. 58.

NOTES

100 *Australasian*, 28 February 1880, p. 281. See also
Sharon Sullivan, 'Aboriginal Diet and Food
Gathering Methods in the Richmond and Tweed
River Valleys, As Seen in Early Settler Records' in
Isabel McBryde (ed.), *Records of Times Past:
Ethnohistorical Essays on the Culture and Ecology
of the New England Tribes*, pp. 101–15.

101 W. R. Guilfoyle (attrib.), 'Notes from the
Botanic Gardens', *Australasian*, 28 February 1880,
p. 281.

102 W. R. Guilfoyle (attrib.), 'Notes from the Botanic
Gardens', *Australasian*, 10 January 1880, p. 58.

103 W. R. Guilfoyle (attrib.), 'Notes from the Botanic
Gardens', *Weekly Times*, 27 November 1880, p. 11.

104 W. R. Guilfoyle (attrib.), 'Notes from the Botanic
Gardens', *Australasian*, 7 February 1880, p. 185.

105 W. R. Guilfoyle (attrib.), 'Notes from the Botanic
Gardens', *Australasian*, 24 January 1880, p. 122.

106 W. R. Guilfoyle, 'Notes on the Dracaena and
Cordyline', *Weekly Times*, 30 January 1875, p. 6.

107 *Garden Gazette*, July 1903, p. 260.

108 Pescott, *W. R. Guilfoyle 1840–1912*, p. 98; Fox,
'Discovering Port Phillip' in J. Phipps (ed.), *La
Trobe and his Circle: An Exhibition to Mark the
150th Anniversary of the Arrival of Victoria's First
Lieutenant Governor*, p. 49.

109 *Garden Gazette*, January 1903, p. 133.

110 'Recent Improvements at the Botanical Gardens',
Weekly Times, 6 February 1875, p. 7.

111 W. R. Guilfoyle (attrib.), 'Notes from the Botanic
Gardens', *Australasian*, 31 January 1880, p. 154.

112 W. R. Guilfoyle, 'Vegetation and Scenery of the
Tweed River', *Sydney Mail*, 14 September 1872, p. 329.

113 A. R. Wallis, 'Report of the Present State of the
Botanical Gardens and to Make Suggestions for
Rendering it in Future More Subservient for the
Purpose of Affording Practical and Scientific
Information in Plants Useful to the Country and
Novel Industries', 20 March 1873, VPRS 44/P Unit
750, File 73/K5085, PROV.

114 J. H. Veitch, 'A Traveller's Notes', *Gardeners'
Chronicle*, 15 September 1894, p. 310;
W. R. Guilfoyle, *Fibres from Plants Indigenous and
Introduced Eligible for Industrial Culture and
Experiment in Victoria*, pp. 32–4.

115 'The Medicinal Garden', *Garden Gazette*,
February 1903, pp. 152–5.

116 *Garden Gazette*, October 1902, p. 56.

117 *Australasian*, 21 October 1882, p. 9; W. R. Guilfoyle,
Evidence, 5 April 1886, Royal Commission on
Vegetable Products, *Second Progress Report*,
1886, p. 54.

118 *Leader*, 31 October 1885, p. 13.

119 W. R. Guilfoyle (attrib.), 'Notes from the
Botanic Gardens', *Australasian*, 28 February 1880,
p. 231.

120 J. H. Veitch, *A Traveller's Notes: or Notes of a Tour
through India, Malaysia, Japan, Corea, The
Australian Colonies and New Zealand during
1891–1893*, pp. 186–7.

121 Pescott, *W. R. Guilfoyle 1840–1912*, p. 100.

122 See also W. R. Guilfoyle, 'Notes from the
Botanic Gardens', *Garden Gazette*, December
1902, p. 118.

123 W. R. Guilfoyle 'Some Glimpses of Some
Botanical Gardens and their Conservatories',
11 August 1893, in Australian Vegetation. Articles,
Lectures etc., W. R. Guilfoyle papers, MS75/104,
University of Melbourne Archives.

124 W. R. Guilfoyle, 'New Zealand's Wonderland',
Argus, 25 April 1908, p. 6.

125 W. R. Guilfoyle (attrib.), *Australasian*, 24 January
1880, p. 122.

126 Veitch, 'A Traveller's Notes', *Gardeners' Chronicle*,
15 September 1894, p. 309.

127 Gertrude Jekyll, *Colour in the Flower Garden*.

128 W. R. Guilfoyle to Sir Joseph Hooker, 12 March
1900, Letters to J. D. Hooker, vol. 10, ff. 70, Royal
Botanic Gardens, Kew.

129 Paul Fox, Images of the Mind, pp. 35, 37.

130 W. R. Guilfoyle, Report on the Remodelling and
Development of the Colac Botanic Gardens
Prepared for the Colac Shire Council, 14 April 1910.

131 *Argus*, 26 June 1912, p. 13.

132 On Rudinoff, see E. Benezit, *Dictionnaire des
Peintres, Sculptures, Desinateurs et Graveurs*,
vol. 12, p. 82; on his opinion of the gardens, 'M.
Rudinoff, His Opinions on Art in General and
on our Botanic Gardens in Particular', *Garden
Gazette*, May–June 1903, p. 239.

Chapter V Josiah Mitchell

1   *Leader*, 23 April 1881, supplement, p. 1.

2   *Gardeners' Chronicle and Agricultural Gazette*, 6 January 1864, p. 50.

3   Miles Hadfield, Robert Harling and Leonie Highton, *British Gardeners: A Biographical Dictionary*, p. 199.

4   Charles McIntosh, *Flora and Pomona or the British Fruit Garden*, introductory remarks, n.p.

5   *Gardeners' Magazine*, 15 January 1839, p. 27.

6   *Leader*, 23 April 1881, supplement, p. 1; on early Victorian English attitudes toward Australian flora in England, see E. Charles Nelson, 'And Flowers for our Amusement: The Early Collecting and Cultivation of Australian Plants in Europe and the Problems Encountered by Today's Taxonomists', in P. S. Short (ed.), *History of Systematic Botany in Australasia*, pp. 285–96.

7   *Leader*, 23 April 1881, supplement, p. 1; Sarah Maroske, 'Planting the Melbourne General Cemetery: The Contribution of Ferdinand von Mueller', *Journal of the Australian Garden History Society*, vol. 2, no. 5, March–April 1991, pp. 3–4.

8   James Sinclair, *The Victorian Landscape Gardeners' Guide*, p. 11.

9   Carlotta Kellaway, 'Useful Documentary Sources for Researching Gardens', *Papers Presented at the Historic Gardens Conference 1986*, n.p. (inserted after p. 72); T. R. Garnett, *Man of Roses: Alister Clark of Glenara and his Family*, p. 18; John Patrick Pty. Ltd. in association with Allom Lovell and Associates Pty. Ltd., *Glenara, Bulla: Conservation Study and Management Plan*, Appendix H. I am indebted to Richard Aitken and John Hawker for this reference.

10 Victorian Horticultural Improvement Society, Minutes, 9 June 1860, p. 28, MS12521, SLV. The minutes record that Mitchell began planting at the Saltwater River 'about eight years ago'.

11 Josiah Mitchell, 'The Application of Known Principles in this Colony', Victorian Gardeners' Mutual Improvement Society, Essay Book, 1860, pp. 1–4, MS12521, SLV.

12 Victorian Horticultural Improvement Society, Minute Book 19 November 1859–10 March 1873, Minutes of Monthly Meetings held 9 June 1860, p. 28, and 16 December 1861, pp. 124–5, MS12521, SLV.

13 *Yeoman and Acclimatiser*, 17 January 1863, pp. 124–5.

14 *Weekly Times*, 22 January 1881, p. 11.

15 *Leader*, 23 April 1881, supplement, p. 1.

16 'Report of the Farm Committee to the Council of the Board of Agriculture', *Eleventh Annual Report of the Secretary of Agriculture*, 1870, p. 38.

17 *Argus*, 3 October 1863, p. 6.

18 *Leader*, 24 September 1870, p. 7.

19 Josiah Mitchell, 'Report of the Tenant of the Experimental Farm', *Fifth Annual Report of the Secretary of Agriculture*, 1864, pp. 22–3.

20 Josiah Mitchell, 'Report of the Lessee of the Experimental Farm', *Tenth Annual Report of the Secretary of Agriculture*, 1869, p. 45.

21 Josiah Mitchell, 'Report of the Lessee of the Experimental Farm', *Eleventh Annual Report of the Secretary of Agriculture*, 1870, p. 41.

22 Josiah Mitchell, 'Lecture on the Rotation of Crops at the New Presbyterian Church Brunswick', *Seventh Annual Report of the Secretary of Agriculture*, 1866, p. 35.

23 James Johnson, *The Chemistry of Common Life*.

24 Mitchell, 'Lecture on the Rotation of Crops', *Seventh Annual Report of the Secretary of Agriculture*, 1866, pp. 36–7. The lecture was also reported in the daily press: Josiah Mitchell, 'The Rotation of Crops', *Australasian*, 28 April 1866, p. 122.

25 Mitchell, 'Lecture on the Rotation of Crops', p. 35.

26 Mitchell, 'Lecture on the Rotation of Crops', pp. 37–8, 41.

27 Mitchell, 'Lecture on the Rotation of Crops', pp. 34–5.

28 Mitchell, 'Lecture on the Rotation of Crops', p. 38; John Macadam, 'Second and Supplementary Report. Government Analytical Laboratory, 9 February 1865', *Sixth Annual Report of the Secretary of Agriculture*, pp. 42–63.

29 Mitchell, 'Report of the Lessee of the Experimental Farm', *Tenth Annual Report of the Secretary of Agriculture*, p. 13.

30 Paul Fox, 'Victorian Historic Gardens: Cultural Background and Issues of Interpretation', in 'Open to View: Historic Gardens and the Public', *Proceedings of the Ninth Annual Conference of the Australian Garden History Society*, 1990, p. 8.

31 Josiah Mitchell, 'What is Rational Agriculture?', *Leader*, 14 May 1870, p. 6.

32 Josiah Mitchell, 'The Sydney Exhibition', *Leader*, 22 October 1870, p. 7.

33 Mitchell, 'What is Rational Agriculture?', *Leader*, 14 May 1870, p. 6.

34 *Leader*, 24 December 1870, p. 7.

35 F. H. Noble and R. Morgan, *Speed the Plough*, pp. 19–20; *Leader*, 14 January 1871, p. 7; Michael Clarke, *Clarke of Rupertswood 1831–1897*, pp. 111–14, 129–30.

36 *Leader*, 22 January 1870, p. 8.

37 Josiah Mitchell, 'The Sydney Intercolonial Exhibition', *Leader*, 24 September 1870, pp. 7–8.

38 Josiah Mitchell, 'The Sydney Exhibition', *Leader*, 22 October 1870, p. 7.

39 Mitchell, 'The Sydney Intercolonial Exhibition', *Leader*, 24 September 1870, p. 8.

40 Von Mueller to [Michael] Guilfoyle, 29 September 1870, Pescott papers, MS439C. While the recipient of this letter is not clearly identified, von Mueller would presumably have been more inclined to seek political support from the elder Guilfoyle rather than from his less experienced son.

41 Charles Moore, 'The Sydney Exhibition', *Leader*, 15 October 1870, p. 7.

42 Mitchell, 'The Sydney Exhibition', *Leader*, 22 October 1870, p. 7.

43 *Australasian*, 6 January 1872, p. 26.

44 *Argus*, 10 November 1869, p. 7.

45 *Daily Telegraph* (Melbourne), 12 June 1872, p. 3.

46 *Daily Telegraph* (Melbourne), 12 June 1872, p. 3.

47 *Australasian*, 6 January 1872, p. 26.

48 *Geelong Advertiser*, 28 October 1872, p. 2.

49 Mitchell appears to have continued to reside at the Model Farm after this time. See A. R. Wallis,

Memo, 17 July 1873, VPRS 44/P, Unit 750, File 73/J15097, PROV.

50 *Leader*, 23 April 1881, supplement, p. 1.

51 *Leader*, 10 May 1873, p. 6.

52 Henry Byron Moore, *A Brief Report on the Land System of Victoria, 24 April 1868*, pp. 7, 13; Weston Bate, *Lucky City*, p. 121.

53 Ray Wright, 'Dispensed With: A. R. Wallis, First Secretary for Agriculture in Victoria 1827–1882', p. 3. For a listing of Wallis's *Australasian* articles see Wright, ibid., Appendix A.

54 Wright, 'Dispensed With', pp. 2–3.

55 *Age*, 12 June 1872, p. 8.

56 A. R. Wallis, 'A Department of Agriculture: Its Benefits to the Community, Functions and Management', *Australasian*, 16 November 1872, pp. 633–4.

57 *Leader*, 24 May 1873, p. 6. I have attributed this article to Mitchell on internal evidence, especially its mention of rational agriculture and the fact that it appeared in the agricultural columns of the *Leader* while Mitchell was editor of the paper.

58 Wallis, 'A Department of Agriculture'.

59 *Leader*, 4 January 1873, p. 6; 24 May 1873, p. 6.

60 *Australasian Town and Country Journal*, 27 May 1876, p. 856.

61 Clarke, *Clarke of Rupertswood 1831–1897*, pp. 111, 130.

62 'Judges' Report on Prize Farms in the Smeaton Agricultural District', *Third Annual Report of the Secretary of Agriculture*, 1875, p. 211.

63 William Evans (ed.), *Diary of a Welsh Swagman*, p. 23.

64 Judges' Report, *Third Annual Report of the Secretary of Agriculture*, 1875, pp. 214, 215–16, 222.

65 Josiah Mitchell, 'Orange Culture' in Department of Lands and Agriculture Victoria, *Second Annual Report of the Secretary of Agriculture*, 1874, pp. 172–7.

66 Josiah Mitchell, 'The Orange Groves of Parramatta', *Leader*, 29 October 1870, pp. 7–8.

67 *Lancefield Examiner*, 9 July 1874, p. 3; Josiah Mitchell, 'Discussion following J. Riddell, 'Shorthorns. A Paper Read to the Romsey Farmers' Club on 6 June 1874', *Third Annual Report of the Secretary of Agriculture*, 1875, p. 190.

68   *Leader*, 30 January 1875, p. 6; 27 February 1875,
       p. 8; *Geelong Advertiser*, 16 February 1875, p. 2.

69   *Leader*, 23 April 1881, supplement, p. 1.

70   Morton acquired Skelsmergh Hall in 1872 from
       William Degraves, who had named the property
       Montpellier. J. O. Randall, *Pastoral Settlement in
       Northern Victoria: The Coliban District*, p. 323.

71   *Leader*, 9 January 1875, p. 6.

72   *Lancefield Examiner*, 1 April 1875, p. 3.

73   John Reid (ed.), *When Memory Turns the Key: The
       History of the Shire of Romsey*, p. 230.

74   *Lancefield Examiner*, 8 April 1875, p. 3.

75   Josiah Mitchell, 'Pasturelands', *Kyneton Guardian*,
       6 September 1876, pp. 2–3. Also published in
       Lancefield Examiner, 14 September 1876, p. 3.

76   *Lancefield Examiner*, 25 May 1876, p. 3.

77   *Australasian*, 27 May 1876, p. 697.

78   *Australasian*, 21 June 1879, p. 701.

79   *Argus*, 10 July 1880, p. 6.

80   *Argus*, 9 October 1879, p. 6.

81   *Kyneton Guardian*, 23 August 1879, p. 2;
       6 September 1879, p. 3.

82   *Gippsland Times*, 4 August 1880, p. 3.

83   *Lancefield Mercury and West Bourke Agricultural
       Record*, 7 September 1876, p. 3.

84   *Australasian*, 10 April 1880, p. 472; *Town and
       Country* (Melbourne), 10 April 1875, p. 15.

85   *Australasian*, 23 October 1880, pp. 536–7.

86   *Argus*, 7 July 1880, p. 7.

87   *Australasian*, 10 April 1880, p. 472.

88   *Australasian*, 10 July 1880, p. 50.

89   *Kyneton Guardian*, 6 September 1879, p. 3.

90   *Australasian*, 10 July 1880, p. 50.

91   *Argus*, 7 July 1880, p. 7.

92   *Warragul Guardian*, 8 July 1880, p. 3.

93   *Argus*, 15 July 1880, p. 6.

94   *Australasian*, 3 September 1881, p. 311. I am
       indebted to Richard Aitken for this reference.

95   *Leader*, 23 April 1881, supplement, p. 1;
       Australasian, 9 October 1880, p. 472.

96   *Australasian*, 9 October 1880, p. 472; 23 October
       1880, pp. 536–7.

97   John Foster, *Victorian Picturesque. The Colonial
       Gardens of William Sangster*, p. 1.

98   *Kyneton Guardian*, 23 August 1879, p. 2.

Chapter VI   William Ferguson

1   *Leader*, 31 October 1885, p. 9; J. G. Veitch, 'Extracts
      from the Journal of Mr John Gould Veitch during
      a Trip to the Australian Colonies and South Sea
      Islands' (henceforward 'Journal'), *Gardeners'
      Chronicle and Agricultural Gazette*, 14 April 1866,
      p. 339.

2   W. J. Bean, *Trees and Shrubs Hardy in the British
      Isles*, vol. 4, pp. 360, 584.

3   J. C. Loudon, *An Encyclopaedia of Gardening*,
      p. 1171.

4   One of these immigrants was Charles Smith,
      an Edinburgh landscape gardener and garden
      architect to bishops, earls and knights of the
      realm. In 1852, Smith promoted the virtues of
      the pinetum in a book entitled *Parks and
      Pleasure Grounds*. In 1860, after migrating to
      Victoria, he presented a copy of his book to the
      Melbourne Public Library. By the 1860s, this
      'practical man' of 'much good sense' was
      advising the governor and his vicereine on the
      siting of a new Government House. (See *Parks
      and Pleasure Grounds. Opinions of the Press*,
      VPRS 44/P, Unit 351, File 72/15619, PROV; C. H. J.
      Smith to J. J. Casey, 4 July 1872, *idem*, PROV;
      bookplate in Charles H. J. Smith, *Parks and
      Pleasure Grounds*, reading: 'Presented to the
      Melbourne Public Library, 1860, By Charles H. J.
      Smith Esq.' SLV.)

5   Veitch, 'Journal', 14 April 1866, p. 339.

6   Daniel Bunce, 'Planting of Trees in Towns',
      Victorian Agricultural and Horticultural Gazette,
      23 June 1861, p. 79.

7   William Ferguson, 'Notes on Ornamental
      Planting', *Victorian Agricultural and
      Horticultural Gazette*, 23 June 1861, pp. 102–3.
      Whether all eighty-one species were correctly
      named is open to doubt.

8   Bean, *Trees and Shrubs Hardy in the British Isles*,
      vol. 3, p. 281.

9   Ferguson, 'Notes on Ornamental Planting', 1861,
      pp. 102–3. The junipers were *Juniperus excelsa*
      (Balkans), *Juniperus oxycedrus* (Central and
      Southern Europe), *Juniperus recurva* (the
      Himalayas) and *Juniperus japonica* (Japan).

10 In 1862 it was estimated that Glass was worth some £800 000; see J. E. Senyard, 'Hugh Glass' in D. Pike (ed.), *Australian Dictionary of Biography*, vol. 4, p. 254.

11 James Sinclair, 'The Victorian Landscape Gardening Guide', *Gardener's Magazine and Journal of Rural Economy*, 1855–56, p. 12.

12 Anne Neale, 'Edward La Trobe Bateman', *Australian Garden History*, vol. 9, no. 4, January–February 1998, p. 24; Anne Neale, 'Ornamental Gardening and Architecture. The Private Gardens of E. L. Bateman', in Sean Pickersgill (ed.), *On What Ground(s)?*, pp. 178, 181.

13 Veitch, 'Journal', 14 April 1866, p. 339.

14 William Ferguson, 'Report on the Growth of Exotic Timber Trees in Various Districts' in Department of Agriculture, *Third Annual Report of the Secretary of Agriculture*, 1875, pp. 116–20.

15 Ferguson, 'Report on the Growth of Exotic Timber Trees', p. 117; *Argus*, 24 June 1867, p. 5.

16 Ferguson, 'Notes on Ornamental Planting: More Especially Grouping Ornamental Trees, Shrubs, and Flowers, as to Give a Better Effect to Landscape Scenery', Victorian Gardeners' Improvement Society, Essay Book, 2 February 1863, p. 140, MS 12521, SLV.

17 Ferguson, 'Notes on Ornamental Planting', 1863, pp. 134, 138–9.

18 William Ferguson, 'The Acclimatisation of Plants', *Australasian*, 14 September 1867, pp. 346–7.

19 Ferguson, 'Notes on Ornamental Planting', 1863, p. 138.

20 Paul Fox, 'Victorian Historic Gardens: Cultural Background and Issues of Interpretation', *Open to View: Historic Gardens and the Public*, pp. 7–8.

21 Veitch, 'Journal', 14 April 1866.

22 William Ferguson, 'The Aptitude of the Orange for Profitable Cultivation in Victoria', Victorian Gardeners' Mutual Improvement Society, Essay Book, 12 May 1862, p. 119, MS12521, SLV.

23 Ferguson, 'The Aptitude of the Orange', pp. 124, 128.

24 Veitch, 'Journal', 14 April 1866, p. 339.

25 Ferguson, 'The Aptitude of the Orange',

26 William Ferguson, 'Influence of Forests on Climate', *Age*, 26 September 1866, p. 7; Victorian Gardeners' Mutual Improvement Society, Minutes 19 November 1859–10 March 1873, 17 December 1866, p. 299, MS12521, SLV.

27 Ferguson, 'Notes on Ornamental Planting', 1863, p. 135.

28 William Ferguson, 'The Importance of Chemistry as Applicable to Horticulture and Agriculture', *Yeoman and Acclimatiser*, 4 July 1863, p. 619.

29 William Ferguson, 'Influence of Forests on Climate', p. 7.

30 William Ferguson, 'Influence of Forests on Climate', p. 7.

31 *Argus*, 21 February 1868, p. 6.

32 Ferguson, 'Report on the Growth of Exotic Timber Trees', p. 113.

33 'Kyneton Gardens', *Weekly Times*, 30 March 1872, p. 6; 'Kyneton Cemetery', *Weekly Times*, 14 December 1872, p. 7, reported 'the *Pinus insignis*, *Cupressus lambertiana*, *Cedrus deodara*, *Pinus pinaster* and *Cupressus macrocarpa* have succeeded best'. See also Richard Aitken, 'Horticultural Embellishments. Public Conferment from the Melbourne Botanic Garden, 1870', *Australian Garden History*, vol. 4, no. 4, January–February 1993, pp. 8–14.

34 L. T. Carron, *A History of Forestry in Australia*, p. 180; *Argus*, 25 August 1869, p. 5.

35 William Ferguson, 'Report from the Inspector of Forests', *Victorian Legislative Assembly, Votes and Proceedings*, vol. 1, 1871, p. 957.

36 'Bullarook Forest Private Nursery', *Town and Country* (Melbourne), 23 August 1873, p. 500.

37 Matthew Lindsay to Clement Hodgkinson, 7 September 1871, VPRS 44/P, Unit 280, File 71/D18842, PROV.

38 Ferguson, 'Report from the Inspector of Forests', *Victorian Legislative Assembly, Votes and Proceedings*, vol. 1, 1871, pp. 957–8; Francine Gilfedder, 'Guilfoyle Plan Rediscovered: Hamilton Botanic Gardens in 1881', *Journal of the Australian Garden History Society*, vol. 3, no. 2, September–October 1991, pp. 10–11; Richard Aitken, 'Picturesque but Instructive: William Guilfoyle's

First Decade at the Melbourne Botanic Gardens', *Journal of the Australian Garden History Society*, vol. 7, March–April 1996, p. 14.

39 William Ferguson to James Grant, President of Lands and Survey, 23 May 1867, VPRS 44/P, Unit 99, Application 49, PROV. I am indebted to Tom Darragh for this reference.

40 *Argus*, 4 November 1869, p. 5.

41 *Argus*, 19 May 1870, supplement, p. 1; 20 May 1870, pp. 5–6.

42 Charles Norton, *The Somerset Gazette and Gwyllehurst Messenger*, no. 6, 3 July 1867, Norton and Gill family papers, MS11382, SLV; Georgina Whitehead, *Civilising the City: A History of Melbourne's Public Gardens*, pp. 12, 92.

43 John Eales to Clement Hodgkinson, 5 May 1871, VPRS 44/P, Unit 279, File 71/Z5802, PROV.

44 Von Mueller to Chief Secretary, 10 June 1871, VPRS 44/P, Unit 279, File 71/Z7466, PROV.

45 Memo, 22 May 1871, VPRS 44/P, Unit 279, File 71/Y6613, PROV.

46 Von Mueller to Chief Secretary, 10 June 1871, VPRS 44/P, Unit 279, File 71/Z7466, PROV.

47 Clement Hodgkinson to Chief Secretary, n.d., attached to VPRS 44/P, Unit 279, File 71/Z7466, PROV.

48 *Leader*, 16 November 1872.

49 William Ferguson to Clement Hodgkinson, 21 February 1872, in Anthony Trollope, *Australia and New Zealand*, vol. 2, pp. 526–7.

50 *Daily Telegraph* (Melbourne), 12 July 1872, p. 3.

51 G. Schneider to J. J. Casey, 13 July 1872, VPRS 44/P, Unit 351, File 72/F14805, PROV.

52 A. R. Wallis, 'Report of the Present State of the Botanical Gardens', 20 March 1873, pp. 8–9, VPRS 44/P, Unit 750, File 73/K508S, PROV.

53 Henry Moreau to J. J. Casey, 13 July 1872, VPRS 44/P, Unit 351, File 72/F14805, PROV.

54 Ferguson to Clement Hodgkinson, 22 July 1872, PROV.

55 'A Report Concerning the Management of Melbourne Botanic Gardens', *Sydney Mail*, 24 September 1872, p. 360.

56 Ferguson to Clement Hodgkinson, 29 April 1872, VPRS 44/P, Unit 351, File 71/D24733, PROV.

57 William Ferguson, 'Report of the Inspector of State Forests to Clement Hodgkinson Esq. Inspector-General of Gardens, Parks and Reserves', *Report of the Inspector-General of Gardens, Parks and Reserves*, 1873 p. 27.

58 Ferguson, 'Report of the Inspector of State Forests', *Report of the Secretary of Agriculture*, 1873, p. 35; Ferguson, 'Report . . . to Clement Hodgkinson', 1873, p. 27.

59 Ferguson, 'Report of the Inspector of State Forests', *Report of the Secretary of Agriculture*, 1873, p. 35.

60 Ferguson, 'Report . . . to Clement Hodgkinson', 1873, pp. 27–8; Ferguson, 'Report of the Inspector of State Forests', *Report of the Secretary of Agriculture*, 1873, p. 36.

61 Ferguson, 'Report . . . to Clement Hodgkinson', 1873, pp. 29, 36; von Mueller to J. J. Casey, 26 June 1873, VPRS 44, Unit 750, File 73/12964, PROV.

62 *Australasian*, 6 January 1872, p. 22.

63 The firs were *Abies douglasii, A. menziesii, A. fraseri, A. albertina* and *A. cephalonica*; the pines were *Pinus ponderosa, P. insignis, P. tuberculata, P. excelsa* and *P. sabiniana*; and the cypress were *Cupressus lambertiana, C. lawsoniana, C. glauca, C. torulosa* and *C. goveniana*.

64 William Ferguson, 'Report of Superintendent of State Forestry', Victorian Department of Agriculture and Lands, *Third Annual Report of the Secretary of Agriculture*, 1875, p. 108.

65 Ferguson, 'Report of Superintendent of State Forestry', Victorian Department of Agriculture and Lands, *First Annual Report of the Secretary of Agriculture*, 1873, p. 37.

66 Ferguson, Evidence, 6 October 1886, Royal Commission on Vegetable Products, *Third Progress Report*, 1886, pp. 144–51.

67 Thomas Dunn, Evidence, 21 September 1887, Royal Commission on Vegetable Products, *Fifth Progress Report*, 1888, pp. 46–7.

68 'The Macedon State Nursery', *Australasian*, 4 July 1885, pp. 10–11; Angela Taylor, *A Forester's Log*, p. 142.

69 Ferguson, 'Report of Superintendent of State Forestry', *First Annual Report of the Secretary of Agriculture*, 1875, p. 36.

70 William Ferguson, 'Report of the Superintendent of State Nursery', Victorian Department of Agriculture and Lands, *First Annual Report of the Secretary of Agriculture*, 1873, p. 111.

71 William Ferguson, 'State Nurseries Superintendent's Report, State Nursery, Macedon, 4 February 1884', *Report for the Secretary for the Department of Agriculture for the Year 1883*, p. 9.

72 *Australasian*, 28 September 1878, p. 408.

73 Ferguson, 'State Nurseries Superintendent's Report, State Nursery, Macedon, 4 February 1884', *Report for the Secretary for the Department of Agriculture for the Year 1883*, p. 9.

74 *Australasian*, 28 September 1878, p. 408.

75 *Australasian*, 31 January 1885, p. 205.

76 *Leader*, 11 March 1882, p. 5.

77 Ferguson, 'State Nurseries Superintendent's Report', 1883, pp. 8–9.

78 William Ferguson, 'State Nurseries. Superintendent's Report 30 January 1885', *Report of the Secretary for the Department of Agriculture for the year 1884*, p. 19.

79 Ferguson, 'State Nurseries. Superintendent's Report 4 February 1884', p. 9.

80 *Colac Herald*, 15 October 1886, p. 2.

81 George Smith, Evidence, 18 June 1886, Royal Commission on Vegetable Products, *First Progress Report*, 1886, p. 109.

82 Ferguson, Evidence, 6 October 1886, Royal Commission on Vegetable Products, *Third Progress Report*, 1886, p. 153.

83 Ferguson, 'State Nurseries. Superintendent's Report 4 February 1884', p. 9.

84 Ferguson, 'State Nurseries. Superintendent's Report 30 January 1885', *Report for the Secretary for the Department of Agriculture for the Year 1884*, 1885, p. 17.

85 Angela Taylor, *A Forester's Log*, p. 141.

86 Ferguson, 'Report of the Inspector of State Forests', *First Annual Report of the Secretary of Agriculture*, 1873, p. 37.

87 Taylor, *A Forester's Log*, p. 141.

88 'State Forests. Foresters' Reports', *Report of the Secretary for the Department of Agriculture for the Year 1883*, *Votes and Proceedings of the Victorian Legislative Assembly*, vol. 2, no. 26, 1884, p. 13.

89 'State Forests. Foresters' Reports', 1884, p. 20.

90 *Australasian*, 31 May 1884, p. 683; Ferguson, 'State Nurseries. Superintendent's Report', 1884, p. 18.

91 *Australasian*, 29 November 1884, p. 1035.

92 Taylor, *A Forester's Log*, p. 142.

93 R. Wright, *The Bureaucrats' Domain: Space and the Public Interest in Victoria, 1836–84*, p. 223; on why the forest was to be reduced, see A. R. Wallis, 'Report on Cape Otway Forest', *Australasian*, 8 February 1879.

94 J. B. Gregory papers, private collection.

95 George Morrison Diary, 3 January 1880, MS312/2, item 6, Mitchell Library.

96 A. H. Lucas, *A. H. Lucas, Scientist: His Own Story*, p. 146. Gregory's father had been instrumental in securing a site for the Geelong Botanic Gardens before turning his attention to growing sugar in northern Australia (Alexander Thomson to J. A. Gregory, n.d. but *c.* 1850, Geelong Town Hall, sighted in tin trunk in the 1980s).

97 F. R. Moulds, *A Conflict of Interest*, p. 25.

98 The Vagabond, 'Colac District, no. 2', *Australasian*, 14 February 1885, supplement, p. 1; E. Bradford Burns, *Edweard Muybridge in Guatemala*, 1875, pp. 2, 16.

99 The Vagabond, 'The Otway Forest', *Australasian*, 28 February 1885, supplement, pp. 1–2; Fox, 'What's in a Historic Garden? The Villa Garden and the Landscape', *Papers Presented at the Historic Gardens Conference*, 1986, p. 15.

100 N. Houghton, *Beech Forest: A Century on the Ridge*, p. 8.

Botanical Appendix

Old Name	Revised Name	Common Name
Abies alba		Silver Fir
Abies albertina	*Picea glauca* var. *albertiana*	Alberta Spruce
Abies alcoquiana	*Picea alcoquiana*	Alcock's Spruce
Abies cephalonica		Greek Fir
Abies douglasii	*Pseudotsuga menziesii*	Douglas Fir
Abies excelsa	*Picea abies*	Norway Spruce, Common Spruce
Abies fraseri		Southern Balsam Fir, Fraser Fir
Abies grandis		Noble Fir
Abies menziesii	*Pseudotsuga menziesii*	Douglas Fir
Abies nobilis	*Abies procera*	Noble Fir
Abies polita	*Picea torano*	Tiger-tail Spruce
Abies webbiana	*Abies spectabilis*	Himalyan Fir
Acacia decurrens	Black Wattle	*Acacia glutinosa*
Acacia verricula	*Acacia longifolia*	Sydney Golden Wattle, Sallow Wattle, Golden Rods
Acacia lopantha		Cape Wattle
Acacia mearnsii		Black Wattle (korong)
Acacia melanoxylon		Blackwood
Acacia pycnantha		Golden Wattle
Akania lucens		Turnipwood
Amorphospermum antilogum		Mt Dryander Hardwood, Brown Pearwood
Aquilegia glandulosa	*Aralia japonica* *Fatsia japonica* ,	Paper Plant Fatsia
Araucaria bidwillii		Bunya Bunya Pine
Araucaria cunninghamii		Hoop Pine
Araucaria excelsa	*Araucaria heterophylla*	Norfolk Island Pine
Araucaria imbricata	*Araucaria araucana*	Monkey Puzzle
Arundo donax var. *versicolor*		Variegated Arundo
Asplenium australasicum		Bird's Nest Fern
Asplenium nidus		Bird's Nest Fern
Aucuba japonica		Aucuba
*Babiana tubiflora**		
Barklya syringifolia		Queensland Gold Blossom Tree
Biota meldensis	*Platycladus orientalis* 'Meldensis'	Bookleaf Cypress
Camellia 'Beali'		
Camellia 'Double White'		
Camellia 'Fimbriata'		
Camellia 'Imbricata'		
Catalpa syringifolia	*Catalpa speciosa*	Indian Bean Tree
Cedrus atlantica		Atlas Cedar
Cedrus deodara		Sacred Deodar, Sacred Cedar

Old Name	Revised Name	Common Name
Cedrus libani		Cedar of Lebanon
Ceratonia siliqua		Syrian Carob Bean
Chamaecyparis lawsoniana		Lawson's Cypress
Clematis aristata		Australian Clematis
Clematis patens 'Standishii'		
Croton 'Disraeli'	All the Crotons are most likely to be *Codiaeum variegatum* var. *pictum* cultivars	
Croton 'Lord Derby'		
Croton 'Wiseman'		
Croton disraeli		
Croton hookeri		
Croton maculatus katoni		
Croton ovalifolium		
Cryptomeria elegans	*Cryptomeria japonica* 'Elegans'	
Cryptomeria japonica		Japanese Cedar
Cupressus cashmeriana		Cashmerian Cypress
Cupressus funebris	*Chamaecyparis funebris*	Funeral Cypress
Cupressus glauca	*Cupressus lusitanica*	Mexican Cypress
Cupressus goveniana		Gowen Cypress
Cupressus lambertiana	*Cupressus macrocarpa*	Monterey Cypress
Cupressus macrocarpa		Monterey Cypress
Cupressus torulosa		Bhutan Cypress
Curcuma australasica		Australian Wild Turmeric
Dacrydium cupressinum		Rimu, Red Pine
Dacrydium franklinii	*Lagarostrobus franklinii*	Huon Pine
Dendrobium phalaenopsis	*Dendrobium bigibbum*	Cooktown Orchid
Dendrobium goldiei	*Dendrobium johannis*	(orchid)
Dendrobium sumneri		(orchid)
Dendrobium superbiens		(orchid)
Dendrobium tattonianum		Lord Egerton of Tatton's Dendrobe
Dianella tasmanica		Flax Lily
Digitalis lutea fucata	*Digitalis lutea* cultivar	
Diospyros lotus		Date Plum
Diploglottis cunninghamii		Australian Tamarind
Dracaena baptistii	*Cordyline terminalis* 'Baptisii'	
Dracaena ferrea rosea	*Cordyline terminalis*	
Dracaena guilfoylei		
Dracaena mooreana	*Dracaena monostachya*	
Dracaena regina	*Dracaena x reginae*	
Dracaena terminalis ferra	?*Cordyline fruticosa*	
*Elaeocarpus reedyi**		

Old Name	Revised Name	Common Name
*Elaeocarpus storckii**		(Fiji)
Epacris impressa		Flowering Heath
Epipogium gmelini		
Epipogium guilfoylei		(Orchid)
Eucalyptus amygdalina		
Eucalyptus ficifolia	*Corymbia ficifolia*	Red-flowering Gum
Eucalyptus obliqua		Messmate
Eucalyptus regnans		Mountain Ash
Eucalyptus rostrata	*Eucalyptus camaldulensis*	Red Gum
Eugenia jambolana	*Syzygium cumini*	Java Plum
*Eugenia melastomoides**		
Fagus cunninghamii	*Nothofagus cunninghamii*	Native Beech, Myrtle Beech
Ficus elastica		Rubber Tree
Ficus macrophylla		Moreton Bay Fig
Fuchsia fulgens		
Grevillea hilliana		White Silky Oak
Hakea obliqua		
Hibiscus lambertii	*Hibiscus rosa-sinensis* 'Lambertii'	
Hydrangea otaksa	*Hydrangea macrophylla* subsp. *macrophylla*	Wild Hydrangea
Inocarpus sp.	*Aniotum sp.*	
Jacaranda mimosaefolia	*Jacaranda mimosifolia*	Jacaranda
Juniperus excelsa		Grecian Juniper
Juniperus japonica	*Juniperus chinensis*	Chinese Juniper
Juniperus oxycedrus		Prickly Juniper
Juniperus recurva		Himalayan Weeping Juniper
Juniperus rigida		
Kentia wendlandiana	*Hydriastele wendlandiana*	(Palm)
Larix europaea	*Larix decidua*	European Larch
Leptospermum sp.		Tea-tree
Libocedrus chiliensis	*Austrocedrus chilensis*	
Lilium auratum		Golden-rayed Japanese Lily
Lilium speciosum		Japanese Lily
Liriodendron tulipifera		Tulip Tree
Livistona sp.		
Luculia gratissima		Luculia
Magnolia glauca	*Magnolia virginiana*	North American Sweet Bay
Magnolia grandiflora		Bull Bay
Magnolia macrophylla		Large-leaved Magnolia
Malus domestica 'Cox's Orange Pippin'		Apple
Mappa fanarai		
Mesembryanthemum sp.		Pigface, Pig's Face
Mucuna gigantea		Cow-itch Bean
Nelitris ingens	*Acmena ingens*	Scrub Myrtle
Nerium oleander		Oleander
Olea paniculata		Queensland Olive, Native Olive
Olearia argophylla		Native Musk, Musk Daisy-bush
Olearia gunniane	*Olearia phlogopappa*	Mr Gunn's Olearia, Alpine Daisy Bush
Osmanthus ilicifolius	*Osmanthus heterophyllus*	Chinese Holly
Oxalis hirtella	*Oxalis hirta*	
Paeonia moutan	*Paeonia suffruticosa*	Moutan, Tree Peony
Pancratium amboiense		
Petermannia cirrosa		
Petunia 'Matthieu'		
Philadelphus coronarius		Mock Orange
Phoenix canariensis		Canary Island Date Palm
Picea pindrow	*Abies pindrow*	Himalayan Spruce
Pinus austriaca	*Pinus nigra* subsp. *nigra*	Black Austrian Pine, Coriscan Pine
Pinus canariensis		Canary Island Pine
Pinus excelsa	*Pinus wallichiana*	Blue Pine, Himalayan Pine
Pinus filifolia	*Pinus montezumae*	Montezuma Pine
Pinus halepensis		Aleppo Pine
Pinus insignis	*Pinus radiata*	Monterey Pine, Radiata Pine
Pinus jeffreyi		Jeffrey Pine
Pinus laricio	*Pinus nigra* subsp. *laricio*	Corsican Pine
Pinus longifolia	*Pinus palustris*	Longleaf Pine
Pinus massoniana		
Pinus muricata		Bishop's Pine
Pinus pinaster		Maritime Pine
Pinus pinea		Italian Stone Pine
Pinus ponderosa		Ponderosa Pine, Western Yellow Pine
Pinus rigida		Pitch Pine
Pinus sabiniana		Digger Pine
Pinus sylvestris		Scots Pine, Scotch Pine
Pinus tuberculata	*Pinus attenuata*	Knob-cone Pine
Pittosporum rhombifolium	*Auranticarpa rhombifolia*	Diamond-leaf Laurel, Queensland Pittosporum
Platanus occidentalis		Western Plane
Platanus orientalis		Oriental Plane
Platycerium grande		Elkhorn Fern
Platycerium superbum		Staghorn Fern
Plumbago capensis	*Plumbago auriculata*	Cape of Good Hope Plumbago
Podocarpus andina	*Podocarpus andinus*	Plum-fruited Yew
Prunus avium 'Empress Eugenie'		Cherry
Prunus avium 'Governor Wood'		Cherry
Prunus avium 'Ohio Beauty'		Cherry

Old Name	Revised Name	Common Name
Prunus domestica 'Coe's Golden Drop'		Plum
Prunus domestica 'Ettiene'		Plum
Prunus domestica 'Guthrie's Late Green'		Plum
Prunus domestica 'Ickworth Imperatrice'		Plum
Prunus domestica 'Jefferson'		Plum
Prunus domestica 'Kirke's'		Plum
Prunus domestica 'Lawrence's Gage'		Plum
Prunus domestica 'Prince Englebert'		Plum
Prunus domestica 'Purple Gage'		Plum
Prunus domestica 'Rivers' Early Prolific'		Plum
Prunus domestica 'Washington'		Plum
Pyrus communis 'Beurres'		Pear
Pyrus communis 'Prince Albert'		Pear
Pyrus communis 'Winter Nelis'		Pear
Quercus macrolepis		Vallonea Oak (Vallonia)
Quercus suber		Cork Oak
Retinispora obtusa	*Chamaecyparis obtusa*	Hinoki Cypress
Retinospora lycopodioides	*Chamaecyparis obtusa* 'Lycopodioides'	
Retinospora pisifera	*Chamaecyparis pisifera*	Sawara Cypress
Rhododendron 'Alarm'		
Rhododendron 'Barclayana'		
Rhododendron 'Giganteum'		
Rhododendron 'John Waterer'		
Rhododendron 'Mirandum'		
Rhododendron 'Mrs John Waterer'		
Rhododendron 'Princess Alice'		
Rhododendron 'Sir Isaac Newton'		
Rhododendron 'Sir John Russell'		
Rhododendron 'Stella'		
Rhododendron dalhousiae		
Ricinus communis		Castor Oil Plant
Rosa 'Empereur du Maroc'		
Rosa 'General Washington'		

Old Name	Revised Name	Common Name
Rosa 'Isabella Gray'		
Rosa 'Prairie de Terre Noire'		
Salix caprea var. *pendula*	*Salix caprea*	'Kilmarnock' Kilmarnock Weeping Willow
Santalum acuminatum	Quandong (pidthegul)	
Seaforthia elegans	*Archontophoenix elegans*	
Strangea sp.		
Syzygium moorei		Lilly-pilly
Tapeinochilus sp.		
Taxodium sempervirens	*Sequoia sempervirens*	Coast Redwood
Taxus japonica	*Cephalotaxus harringtoniana*	'Fastigiata' Japanese yew
Tecoma jasminoides	*Pandorea jasminoides*	Bower Vine, Bower of Beauty
Thuja aurea	*Platycladus orientalis*	'Aureus' Golden spruce, Bookleaf Cypress
Thuja gigantea	*Thuja plicata*	Western Red Cedar
Thuja lobbii	*Thuja plicata*	Western Red Cedar
Thuja loetevirens*	*Thuja occidentalis*	White Cedar
Thuja variegata		Variegated cultivar of *Thuja occidentalis* or *Platycladus orientalis*
Thuja warrenga	*Thuja occidentalis* 'Wareana'	
Thujopsis dolabrata		Hiba Arbor-vitae
Tilia europea	*Tilia X europaea*	Linden, Common Lime
Torreya grandis		Japanese Stinking Cedar
Tritonia media	*Kniphofia sarmentosa*	
Ulmus parvifolia		Chinese Elm
Verbena 'Foxhunter'		
Victoria regia	*Victoria amazonica*	South American Waterlily, Giant Amazon Lily
Weinmannia biagiana		Flowering Belum Wood
Wellingtonia gigantea	*Sequoiadendron giganteum*	Giant Redwood, Big Tree, Californian Redwood
Wigandia caracasana		Caracas Big Leaf
Xanthorrhoea sp.		Grass Tree, Blackboy

All botanical names in this book are included in this Botanical Appendix in the form they appeared in the books, lists and catalogues of the time. Since the Nineteenth Century many plant names have been revised by Botanists and thus the currently accepted name has been given if it has changed. Names marked with an asterix could not be found in the literature at present. Please note that common names vary from place to place and over time.

Select Bibliography

Manuscripts

Archer, William H., Papers, University of Melbourne Archives.

Australian Autograph Collection, State Library of Victoria.

Bendigo Council Archives.

Black, Niel, Papers, State Library of Victoria.

Gregory, John B., Papers, Private Collection.

Guilfoyle, William R., Papers, University of Melbourne Archives.

Hooker, Joseph D., Correspondence, Royal Botanic Gardens, Kew.

Hutton, Barney, Papers on Thomas Lang, Private Collection.

Lang, Thomas, List of Plants Received into Lang's Nursery, Ballarat Historical Parks Association.

Macarthur, William, Papers, Mitchell Library.

Morrison, George E., Papers, Mitchell Library.

Nicoll, Henry, Papers, State Library of Victoria.

Norton and Gill Families, Papers, State Library of Victoria.

Pescott, R. M., Papers, Archives of the Royal Botanic Gardens, Melbourne.

Sinclair, James, Every Man his Own Gardener, State Library of Victoria.

Victorian Gardeners' Mutual Improvement Society, Papers, State Library of Victoria.

Victorian Public Record Series 44/P, Department of Crown Lands and Survey: Inward Registered and Unregistered Correspondence, Public Records Office, Victoria.

Newspapers

Argus, 1850–1880, 1908, 1912.

Australasian, 1867–1886, 1896.

Australasian Town and Country Journal, 1873–1876.

Ballarat Star, 1858–1866.

Ballarat Times, 1860.

Bendigo Advertiser, 1878.

Colac Herald, 1886.

Daily Telegraph (Melbourne), 1872.

Geelong Advertiser, 1860–1875.

Geelong Chronicle, 1864.

Geelong Register, 1867.

Gippsland Times, 1880–1881.

Kyneton Guardian, 1876–1880, 1893.

Lancefield Examiner, 1876.

Lancefield Mercury and West Bourke Agricultural Record, 1876.

Leader (Melbourne), 1869–1881.

Portland Guardian, 1865.

Sydney Mail, 1872–1873.

Town and Country (Melbourne), 1873–1875.

Warragul Guardian, 1880.

Weekly Times, 1872–1881.

Yeoman and Acclimatiser, 1859–1864.

Horticultural Journals

Botanist, The: Containing Accurately Coloured Figures of Tender and Hardy Ornamental Plants with Scientific Description, 1838–1846.

Curtis's Botanical Magazine, 1810–1880.

Floral World, 1869–1876.

Florist, Fruitist and Garden Miscellany, 1851–1861.

Florist and Pomologist: A Pictorial Monthly Magazine of Flowers, Fruit and General Horticulture, 1862–1879.

Garden, The, 1876.

Garden Gazette, 1902–1903.

Gardeners' Chronicle and Agricultural Gazette, 1848–1874.

Gardeners' Chronicle, 1875–1896.

Gardener's Magazine, 1826–1844.

Loddiges Botanical Cabinet, 1817–1833.

Victorian Agricultural and Horticultural Gazette, 1857–1861.

Other Journals

Annales des Sciences Naturelles, second series, 1838.

Phonetic Journal, 1848–1849, 1851–1854, 1857–1859.

Nursery Catalogues

Bunce, Daniel. *Catalogue of Seeds and Plants Indigenous and Exotic, Cultivated and On Sale at Denmark Hill Nursery, Newtown Road, Hobart Town*. Mulini Press, Canberra, *c.* 1994.

—— *Catalogue of Plants under Cultivation in the Botanical Gardens*. Thomas Brown, Geelong, 1860.

Guilfoyle, Michael. *Catalogue of Plants for Sale by Michael Guilfoyle, Nursery and Seedsman, Exotic Nursery, Double Bay, New South Head Road*. Kemp & Fairfax, Sydney, 1851.

Guilfoyle, Michael and Sons. *Catalogue of Ornamental Trees, Shrubs, Fruit Trees, Bulbs, Plants & Climbers*. Reading & Wellbank, Sydney, 1866.

Thomas Lang & Company. *List of Flowering Bulbs and Tubers Cultivated by Thomas Lang & Company*, no. 16. Heath & Cordell, Melbourne, 1867.

—— *List of Coniferous Trees, Japanese Plants, Hardy Trees and Shrubs, Climbers, Greenhouse Plants, Herbaceous Plants, Roses, Fruit Trees and Hedge Plants*, no. 17. Heath & Cordell, Melbourne, 1867.

—— *Catalogue of Plants Cultivated for Sale 1868*, no. 20. Heath & Cordell, Melbourne, 1868.

—— *Catalogue of Plants Cultivated for Sale by Thomas Lang & Company*. Massina & Company, Melbourne, 1870.

—— *Special List for 1872 of Apples on Majetin Stocks, also List of Apples on Northern Spy Stocks, List of Prize Gooseberries, and Abridged List of Fruit Trees*, no. 37. Clarson, Massina & Co., Melbourne, 1871.

—— *Catalogue of Flowering Bulbs, Tubers Cultivated by Thomas Lang & Co.*, no. 38. Clarson, Massina & Co., Melbourne, 1872.

—— *Catalogue of Plants Cultivated for Sale by Thomas Lang, Nursery, Seedsmen, & Florist*, no. 39. Clarson, Massina & Co., Melbourne, 1872.

Rule, John J. *Catalogue of Plants Cultivated for Sale by John J. Rule at the Victoria Nurseries, Church Street Richmond*. W. H. Williams, Melbourne, 1857.

Writings of Daniel Bunce

Bunce, Daniel. *Manual of Practical Gardening Adapted to the Climate of Van Diemen's Land: Containing Plain and Familiar Directions for the Management of the Kitchen, Fruit and Flower Garden, Nursery, Greenhouse and Forcing Department for Every Month of the Year*. William Gore Elliston, Hobart Town, 1838.

—— 'Journal of a Naturalist', *Argus*, 25 December 1849, p. 2; 7 March 1850, p. 2; 11 March 1850, p. 2; 14 March 1850, p. 2; 16 March 1850, p. 2; 22 March 1850, p. 2; 28 March 1850, p. 2; 30 March 1850, p. 2; 4 April 1850, p. 2; 6 April 1850, p. 2; 19 April 1850, p. 2; 24 April 1850, p. 2; 4 May 1850, p. 2; 13 May 1850, p. 2; 20 May 1850, p. 2.

—— Letter, *Argus*, 14 February 1850, p. 2.

—— Letter, *Argus*, 21 February 1850, p. 2.

—— Letter, *Argus*, 28 February 1850, p. 2.

—— *Hortus Victoriensis. A Catalogue of the Most Generally Known Flora of the Colony of Victoria with their Linnaean Classification and General Remarks.* Daniel Harrison, Melbourne, 1851.

—— *Language of the Aborigines of the Colony of Victoria and Other Districts.* Daniel Harrison, Melbourne, 1851.

—— 'Victoria Diggings, Anderson's Creek', *Argus*, 20 December 1851.

—— 'Indigenous Plants', *The Rural Magazine*, 1 May 1855, pp. 18–20; 1 June 1855, pp. 32–4; 1 July 1855, pp. 66–7; 1 August 1855, pp. 84–6; 1 September 1855, pp. 104–5; 1 October 1855, pp. 121–2.

—— 'Journal of a Naturalist', *The Rural Magazine*, 1 May 1855, pp. 20–23; 1 June 1855, pp. 35–9; 1 July 1855, pp. 62–6; 1 August 1855, pp. 77–81; 1 September 1855, pp. 93–6; 1 October 1855, pp. 117–19.

—— 'Tree Planting in Victoria Parade', *The Rural Magazine*, 1 May 1855, pp. 25–6.

—— 'Planting of Trees in Towns', *Agricultural and Horticultural Gazette*, 23 June 1861, pp. 79–80.

—— *Travels with Dr Leichhardt*. Oxford University Press, Melbourne, 1979.

Writings of William Ferguson

Ferguson, William. 'Aptitude of Roses for Pot Culture in Victoria', *Victorian Agricultural and Horticultural Gazette*, 28 May 1861, pp. 66–7.

—— 'Notes on Ornamental Planting. Read before the Horticultural Improvement Association of the Western District', *Victorian Agricultural and Horticultural Gazette*, 14 August 1861, pp. 102–3.

—— 'The Aptitude of the Orange for Profitable Cultivation in Victoria', Victorian Gardeners' Mutual Improvement Society, Essay Book, 12 May 1862, pp. 119–30.

—— 'Notes on Ornamental Planting: More Especially Grouping Ornamental Trees, Shrubs, and Flowers, as to Give a Better Effect to Landscape Scenery', Victorian Gardeners' Mutual Improvement Society, Essay Book, 2 February 1863, pp. 131–42.

—— 'Trees Best Adapted for Ornamental Planting', *Argus*, 7 March 1865, p. 5.

—— 'Shrubs Best Adapted for Planting in Victoria', *Argus*, 11 April 1865, p. 4.

—— 'Influence of Forests on Climate', *Age*, 26 September 1866, p. 7.

—— 'The Acclimatisation of Plants', *Australasian*, 14 September 1867, pp. 346–7.

—— 'Report of the Inspector of Forests for 1870', *Votes and Proceedings of Victorian Legislative Assembly*, vol. 1, no. 9, 1871, pp. 957–8.

—— 'To Clement Hodgkinson 21 February 1872', in Anthony Trollope, *Australia and New Zealand*, vol. 2, Chapman & Hall, London, 1873.

—— 'Report of the Inspector of State Forests, 1 June 1873', *Report of the Secretary for Agriculture*. John Ferres, Melbourne, 1873, pp. 35–7.

—— 'Report of the Inspector of State Forests, 21 August 1873', *Report of the Inspector-General of Gardens, Parks and Reserves*. John Ferres, Melbourne, 1873, pp. 27–9.

—— 'Plants Adapted for Live Fences', *Department of Lands and Agriculture, Report of the Secretary for Agriculture in which is Appended the Report of the Inspector-General of Gardens, Parks and Reserves*. John Ferres, Melbourne, 1873, pp. 73–6.

—— 'Report on the Growth of Exotic Timber Trees in Various Districts of Victoria', Department of Lands and Agriculture, *Third Annual Report of the Secretary of Agriculture*. George Skinner, Melbourne, 1875, pp. 113–23.

—— 'Report of the Superintendent of State Nursery', Department of Lands and Agriculture, *Third Annual Report of the Secretary for Agriculture*. George Skinner, Melbourne, 1875, pp. 73–6.

—— 'The Cape Otway Beech Forest', *Australasian*, 24 February 1883, p. 250.

—— 'State Nurseries: Superintendent's Report. State Nursery, Macedon, 4 February 1884', *Report of the Secretary for the Department of Agriculture for the Year 1883, Votes and Proceedings of the Victorian Legislative Assembly*, vol. 2, no. 26, 1884, pp. 9–10.

—— 'State Nurseries: Superintendent's Report. 30 January 1885', *Report of the Secretary for the Department of Agriculture for the Year 1884, Votes and Proceedings of the Victorian Legislative Assembly*, vol. 3, no. 34, 1885, pp. 16–19.

—— 'Report to Secretary of Agriculture, 22 January 1885', *Australasian*, 31 January 1885, p. 205.

—— Evidence, 6 October 1886, Royal Commission on Vegetable Products, *Third Progress Report*, 1886, pp. 144–51.

Writings of William Guilfoyle

Guilfoyle, W. R. 'A Botanical Tour Among the South Sea Islands', *Journal of Botany, British and Foreign*, vol. 7, 1869, pp. 117–36.

—— 'Sydney Botanic Gardens', *Leader*, 28 May 1870, pp. 7–8.

—— 'Vegetation and Scenery of the Tweed River', *Sydney Mail*, 14 September 1872, p. 329.

—— 'The Tweed River and District from the Top of Mount Warning', *Australasian Town and Country Journal*, 17 May 1873, p. 625.

—— 'Monthly Report of the Curator of the Botanical and Domain Gardens', *Report of the Inspector-General of Parks and Gardens*. John Ferres, Melbourne, 1873, pp. 16–26.

—— 'Notes on the Dracaena and Cordyline', *Weekly Times*, 23 January 1875, p. 6; 30 January 1875, p. 6.

—— *Annual Report on the Melbourne Botanic Gardens with a Plan of the Garden*. George Skinner, Melbourne, 1875.

—— (attrib.), 'Notes from the Botanic Gardens', *Australasian*, 10 January 1880, p. 58; 24 January 1880, p. 122; 31 January 1880, p. 154; 7 February 1880, p. 185; 28 February 1880, p. 281; 3 April 1880, p. 441; 3 July 1880, p. 28; 21 October 1880, p. 9; 25 December 1880, p. 827; *Weekly Times*, 27 November 1880, p. 11.

—— *The ABC of Botany*. S. Mullen, Melbourne, 1880.

—— *Catalogue of Plants Under Cultivation in the Melbourne Botanic Gardens, Alphabetically Arranged*. John Ferres, Melbourne, 1883.

—— *Australian Botany for the Use of Schools*. George Robertson, Melbourne, 1884.

—— 'Some Glimpses of Some Botanical Gardens and their Conservatories 11 August 1893' in Australian Vegetation. Articles, Lectures etc., unpublished.

—— *Fibres from Plants Indigenous and Introduced Eligible for Industrial Culture and Experiment in Victoria*. R. S. Brain, Melbourne, 1894.

—— 'Magnolias and Allied Plants in the Botanic Gardens', *Garden Gazette*, September 1902, pp. 42–3.

—— 'Notes from the Botanic Gardens', *Garden Gazette*, December 1902, p. 118.

—— 'Notes on Palms', *Garden Gazette*, December 1902, pp. 104–5.

—— 'Rockwork', *Garden Gazette*, February 1903, pp. 158–61.

—— 'New Zealand's Wonderland', *Argus*, 25 April 1908, p. 6.

—— 'Sydney Botanic Gardens', *Australasian*, 4 September 1909, p. 587.

—— Report on the Modelling and Development of the Colac Botanic Gardens, unpublished report, 1910.

—— *Australian Plants Suitable for Gardens, Parks, Timber Reserves etc*. Whitcombe & Tombs, Melbourne, 1911.

Writings of Thomas Lang

Lang, Thomas. 'Melons', *Victorian Agricultural and Horticultural Gazette*, 21 July 1858, pp. 58–9.

—— 'Eastern Municipal Trees', *Ballarat Star*, 7 November 1860, p. 3.

—— 'On Wardian or Plant Cases', *Ballarat Star*, 9 April 1862, supplement, p. 1.

—— 'Practical Jottings', *Kyneton Guardian*, 5 January, p. 4; 31 January, p. 4; 28 February, p. 4; 6 April, p. 4; 2 May, p. 4; 1 June, p. 4; 4 July, p. 4; 3 August, p. 4; 31 August, p. 4; 2 November, p. 4; 5 December 1893, p. 4.

—— *Phonetic Printing or the Reformation of Printing*. E. W. Cole, Melbourne, 1895.

Writings of Josiah Mitchell

Mitchell, Josiah. 'The Application of Known Principles of Cultivation in This Colony', Victorian Gardeners' Mutual Improvement Society, Essay Book, 6 February 1860, pp. 1–4.

—— 'Healthy and High Cultivation. How It Only Partially Prevents the Attacks of Insects', Victorian Gardeners' Mutual Improvement Society, Essay Book, 16 December 1861, pp. 1–4.

—— 'The Advantages from Shading the Ground with Green Crops', *Yeoman and Acclimatiser*, 17 January 1863, p. 239.

—— 'Exhaustion of the Soils', *Yeoman and Acclimatiser*, 7 February 1863, p. 289.

—— 'Report on the Present Condition of the Experimental Farm', *Argus*, 3 October 1863, p. 6.

—— 'Report of the Tenant of the Experimental Farm', *Fifth Annual Report: Presented by the Council to the Board of Agriculture*. Wilson & McKinnon, Melbourne, 1864, pp. 22–3.

—— 'Experimental Farm Report', *Sixth Annual Report: Presented by the Council to the Board of Agriculture*. John Ferres, Melbourne, 1865, pp. 28–9.

—— 'Report of the Lessee of the Experimental Farm', *Seventh Annual Report: Presented by the Council to the Board of Agriculture*. John Ferres, Melbourne, 1866, pp. 29–33.

—— 'Lecture on the Rotation of Crops at the New Presbyterian Church Brunswick', *Seventh Annual Report: Presented by the Council to the Board of Agriculture*. John Ferres, Melbourne, 1866, pp. 33–42.

—— 'Report of the Lessee of the Experimental Farm', *Eighth Annual Report: Presented by the Council to the Board of Agriculture*. John Ferres, Melbourne, 1867, pp. 28–33.

—— 'Report of the Lessee of the Experimental Farm', *Ninth Annual Report: Presented by the Council to the Board of Agriculture*. Stillwell & Knight, Melbourne, 1868, pp. 42–6.

—— 'Report of the Lessee of the Experimental Farm', *Tenth Annual Report: Presented by the Council to the Board of Agriculture*. Mason, Firth & Co., Melbourne, 1869, pp. 34–8.

—— 'Report of the Lessee of the Experimental Farm', *Eleventh Annual Report: Presented by the Council to the Board of Agriculture*. Mason, Firth & M'Cutcheon, Melbourne, 1870, pp. 58–64.

—— 'What is Rational Agriculture?', *Leader*, 14 May 1870, pp. 6–7.

—— 'The Sydney Intercolonial Exhibition', *Leader*, 24 September 1870, pp. 7–8.

—— 'The Sydney Exhibition', *Leader*, 22 October 1870, p. 7.

—— 'The Orange Groves of Parramatta', *Leader*, 29 October 1870, p. 7.

—— 'Orange Culture', *Second Annual Report of the Secretary for Agriculture*. John Ferres, Melbourne, 1874, pp. 172–7.

—— 'Pasturelands', *Kyneton Guardian*, 6 September 1876, pp. 2–3.

Mitchell, Josiah, Greig, William and Sangster, William, 'Report of the Board of Inquiry upon the Botanical Gardens', *Australasian*, 6 January 1872, pp. 26–7.

Mitchell, Josiah, et al., 'Judges' Report on Prize Farms in the Smeaton Agricultural District', *Annual Third Report of the Secretary for Agriculture*. George Skinner, Melbourne, 1875, pp. 211–22.

Mitchell, Josiah ('Hodden Grey'), 'Clods', *Australasian*, 9 October 1880, p. 472; 23 October 1880, pp. 536–7.

Books and Articles

Aitken, Richard. 'Horticultural Embellishments: Public Conferment from the Melbourne Botanic Garden, 1870', *Australian Garden History*, vol. 4, no. 4, January–February 1993, pp. 8–14.

—— 'Picturesque but Instructive: William Guilfoyle's First Decade at the Melbourne Botanic Gardens', *Australian Garden History*, vol. 7, no. 5, March–April 1996, pp. 6–18.

Aitken, Richard, and Looker, Michael (eds). *The Oxford Companion to Australian Gardens*. Oxford University Press, Melbourne, 2002.

Alcock, Rutherford. *The Capital of the Tycoon: A Narrative of a Three Years' Residence in Japan*. Longman, Green, Longman, Roberts & Green, London, 1863.

Allan, Mea. *William Robertson 1838–1935: Father of the English Flower Garden*. Faber & Faber, London, 1982.

Aurousseau, M. (ed.). *The Letters of F. W. Ludwig Leichhardt*. Hakluyt Society, London, 1968, 3 vols.

Bacchus, W. H. 'A Description of some Victorian and other Australian Grasses', *Second Annual Report of the Secretary for Agriculture*. John Ferres, Melbourne, 1874, pp. 126–49.

Bate, Weston. *The Lucky City: The First Generation at Ballarat 1851–1901*. Melbourne University Press, Melbourne, 1978.

Bean, W. J. *Trees and Shrubs Hardy in the British Isles*. John Murray, London, 1980, 4 vols.

Benezit, E. *Dictionnaire des Peintres, Sculptures, Desinateurs et Graveurs*. Grund, Paris, 1999.

Billis, R. V. and Kenyon, A. S. *Pastoral Pioneers of Port Phillip*. Stockland Press, Melbourne, 1974.

Brenchley, Julius. *Jottings during the Cruise of the Curaçao: Among the South Sea Islands in 1865*. Longman, Green & Co., London, 1873.

Bride, T. F. (ed.). *Letters from Victorian Pioneers*. Currey O'Neil, Melbourne, 1983.

Brookes, Margaret and Barley, Richard. *Plants Listed in Nursery Catalogues in Victoria 1855–1889*. Law Printer, Melbourne, 1992.

Brownhill, Walter Randolph. *History of Geelong and Corio Bay*. Wilkie & Co., Melbourne, 1955.

Burke, Edmund. *Choice Pieces: Including On the Sublime and the Beautiful*. Alexander Murray, London, 1871.

Burns, E. Bradford. *Edweard Muybridge in Guatemala, 1875: The Photographer as Social Recorder*. University of California Press, Berkeley, 1986.

Burns, T. E. and Skemp, J. R. (eds). *Van Diemen's Land Correspondents: Letters from R. C. Gunn, R. W. Laurence, Jorgen Jorgenson, Sir John Franklin and others to Sir William Hooker, 1827–1849*. Queen Victoria Museum, Launceston, 1961.

Carron, L. T. *A History of Forestry in Australia*. Australian National University Press, Canberra, 1985.

Cavanagh, Tony. 'New Holland Exotics: Australian Plants Cultivated in England and Europe from 1771', *Australian Garden History*, vol. 2, no. 3, November–December 1990, pp. 7–10.

Clarke, Michael. *Clarke of Rupertswood 1831–1879: The Life and Times of William John Clarke First Baronet of Rupertswood*. Australian Scholarly Publishing, Melbourne, 1995.

Cohn, Helen and Maroske, Sara. 'Relief from Duties of Minor Importance: The Removal of Baron von Mueller from the Directorship of the Royal Botanic Gardens', *Victorian Historical Journal*, vol. 67, no. 1, April 1996, pp. 113–15.

Cole, T. C. *Cole's Gardening in Victoria: Containing Full Descriptions for the Formation and General Management of a Good Garden Together with a Comprehensive Calendar for the Operation of Each Month of the Year*. W. Fairfax & Co., Melbourne, 1860.

Conway, Hazel. *People's Parks: The Design and Development of Victorian Parks in Britain.* Cambridge University Press, Cambridge, 1991.

Council of the Board of Agriculture. *Annual Reports 1861–70.* Government Printer, Melbourne, 1861–1870.

Daniels, Stephen. *Humphry Repton: Landscape and the Geography of Georgian England.* Yale University Press, New Haven, 1999.

Davis, Joseph Barnard. *On Synostotic Crania among Aboriginal Races of Man.* De Erven Loosjes, Haarlem, 1865.

—— *Thesaurus Craniorum: Catalogue of the Skulls of Various Races of Man in the Collection of Joseph Barnard Davis.* Taylor & Francis, London, 1867.

Desmond, Ray. *A Celebration of Flowers: Two Hundred Years of Curtis's Botanical Magazine.* Royal Botanic Gardens, Kew & Collingridge Books, London, 1987.

—— *Dictionary of British and Irish Botanists and Horticulturalists: Including Plant Collectors, Flower Painters and Garden Designers.* Taylor & Francis & Natural History Museum, London, 1994.

Evans, William (ed.). *Diary of a Welsh Swagman 1869–1894.* Pan Macmillan, Melbourne, 1995.

Fitzgerald, Robert David. *Australian Orchids.* Thomas Richards, Sydney, 1882–1893.

Foljambe, C. G. S. *Three Years on the Australian Station.* Hatchard & Co., London, 1868.

Foster, John. *Victorian Picturesque: The Colonial Gardens of William Sangster.* History Department, University of Melbourne, Parkville, 1989.

Fox, Paul, 'Daniel Bunce: Gardener and Botanical Explorer', *Australian Garden History*, vol. 1, no. 2, August–September 1989, pp. 7–11.

—— 'Discovering Port Phillip', in Jennifer Phipps, *La Trobe and his Circle: An Exhibition to Mark the 150th Anniversary of the Arrival of Victoria's First Lieutenant Governor.* Council of the State Library of Victoria, Melbourne, 1989, pp. 41–50.

—— 'In Search of Birds and Beetles: Scientific Imagination and New Guinea', *Meanjin*, vol. 49, no. 4, summer 1990, pp. 676–88.

—— 'Over the Garden Fence', *Historic Environment*, vol. 4, no. 3, 1985, pp. 29–36.

—— 'Portraits of Oceania', *Portraits of Oceania.* Art Gallery of New South Wales, Sydney, 1997, pp. 23–28.

—— 'Puzzling Landscape', in Sean Pickersgill (ed.), *On What Ground(s)?.* Society of Architectural Historians of Australia and New Zealand, Adelaide, 1997, pp. 34–41.

—— 'The Simla of the South', *Australian Garden History*, vol. 6, no. 4, January–February 1995, pp. 10–14.

—— 'Victorian Historic Gardens: Cultural Background and Issues of Interpretation', *Open to View. Historic Gardens and the Public. Proceedings of the Ninth Annual Conference of the Australian Garden History Society*, Australian Garden History Society, Melbourne, 1990, pp. 6–13.

—— 'What's in a Historic Garden? The Villa Garden and the Landscape', *Papers Presented at the Historic Gardens Conference Melbourne 1986*, Ministry for Planning and the Environment and Historic Buildings Council Victoria, n.d., pp. 5–17.

—— Images of the Mind: Worlds Within Gardens. Master of Landscape Architecture minor thesis, University of Melbourne, 1980.

Fox, Paul and Kerr, Joan, 'Thomas Foster Chuck' in Joan Kerr (ed.), *The Dictionary of Australian Artists: Painters, Sketchers, Photographers and Engravers to 1870*. Oxford University Press, Melbourne, 1992.

Garnett, T. R. *Man of Roses: Alister Clark of Glenara and his Family*. Kangaroo Press, Kenthurst, 1990.

Gilbert, Lionel. *The Royal Botanic Gardens, Sydney: A History 1816–1985*. Oxford University Press, Melbourne, 1986.

Gilfedder, Francine, 'Guilfoyle Plan Rediscovered: Hamilton Botanic Gardens in 1881', *Australian Garden History*, vol. 3, no. 2, September–October 1991, pp. 10–11.

—— 'Sowing the Seeds: The Early Nursery Industry in the Macedon Ranges', *Australian Garden History*, vol. 6, no. 4, January–February 1995, pp. 18–21.

Gordon, George and Glendinning, Robert. *The Pinetum: Being a Synopsis of all the Conifers at Present Known, with Descriptions, History and Synonyms, and Comprising One Hundred New Kinds*. Henry Bohn, London, 1858.

Gorer, Richard. *The Development of Garden Flowers*. Eyre & Spottiswood, London, 1970.

—— *The Flower Garden in England*. B. T. Batesford, London, 1975.

Gray, H. R., 'State Forests of Empire: Victoria', *Empire Forestry Journal*, vol. 14, 1935, pp. 235–49.

Griffiths, D. A., 'A Garden on the Edge of China: Hong Kong, 1848', *Garden History*, vol. 16, no. 2, autumn 1988, pp. 189–98.

Hadfield, Miles. *A History of British Gardening*. John Murray, London, third edition, 1979.

Hadfield, Miles, Harling, Robert, and Highton, Leonie (eds). *British Gardeners: A Biographical Dictionary*. A. Zwemmer Ltd., London, 1980.

Hawker, John, 'Early Plantings of William Guilfoyle', *Australian Garden History*, vol. 7, no. 5, March–April 1996, pp. 19–20.

Hawks, F. L. *Narrative of an Expedition of an American Squadron to the China Seas and Japan in the years 1852, 1853, 1854 under the command of Commodore M. C. Perry, United States Navy: Compiled from the Original Notes and Journals of Commodore Perry and his Officers, at his Request and his supervision by F. L. Hawks of the Government of the United States.* Beverly Tucker, Washington, 1856, 4 vols.

Heriz-Smith, S., 'The Veitch Nurseries of Killerton and Exeter *c.* 1780 to 1863', *Garden History*, vol. 16, no. 1, spring 1988, pp. 41–57; vol. 16, no. 2, autumn 1988, pp. 174–88.

Hooker, Joseph Dalton. *The Rhododendrons of Sikkim-Himalaya: Being an Account, Botanical and Geographic of Rhododendrons Recently Discovered in the Mountains of the Eastern Himalaya from Drawings and Descriptions Made on the Spot during a Government Mission to that Country.* Reeve & Co., London, 1849.

Houghton, N. *Beech Forest: A Century on the Ridge.* Ken Jenkin, Geelong, 1994.

Hoyles, Martin. *The Story of Gardening.* Journeyman Press, London, 1991.

Hull, William. *Remarks on the Probable Origin and Antiquity of the Aborigines of New South Wales: Deduced from Certain of their Customs, Superstitions, and Existing Caves and Drawings, in Connection with those of the Nations of Antiquity.* William Clarke, Melbourne, 1846.

Humbert, Aimé. *Le Japon Illustré.* Librairie de L. Hachette & Co., Paris, 1870, 2 vols.

Hutton, H. B., 'Thomas Lang, Nurseryman', *Australian Garden Journal*, vol. 4, no. 4, April 1985, pp. 94–6; vol. 4, no. 5, June 1985, pp. 131–3.

—— 'The Introduction of Rhododendrons to Victoria', *Historic Environment*, vol. 4, no. 3, 1985, pp. 37–41.

Jacquin, Nikolaus Joseph von. *Oxalis: Monographia Iconibus Illustrata.* Christian Fridericum Wappla, Vienna, 1794.

James, H. A. *Hand-Book of Australian Horticulture.* Turner & Henderson, Sydney, 1892.

Jekyll, Gertrude. *Colour in the Flower Garden.* Country Life & George Newness, London, 1908.

John Patrick Pty. Ltd. in association with Allom Lovell and Associates Pty. Ltd. Glenara, Bulla: Conservation Study and Management Plan, July 1996, unpublished report.

Johnson, James. *The Chemistry of Common Life.* Blackwood & Sons, London, 1856, 2 vols.

Jones, George. *Growing Together: A Gardening History of Geelong—Extending to Colac and Camperdown*. List Print, Geelong, 1984.

Kellaway, Carlotta, 'Useful Documentary Sources for Researching Gardens', *Papers Presented at the Historic Gardens Conference*, 1986, pp. 67–72, n.p.

Kemp, Edward. *How to Lay Out a Garden: Intended as a General Guide in Choosing, Forming, or Improving an Estate*. John Wiley & Son, New York, 1889.

Krussmann, Gerd. *Rhododendrons: Their History, Geographical Distribution, Hybridisation and Culture*. Ward Lock, London, 1970.

Kynaston, Edward. *A Man on Edge: A Life of Baron Sir Ferdinand von Mueller*. Allen Lane, Melbourne, 1981.

Leach, Helen. *Cultivating Myths: Fiction, Fact & Fashion in Garden History*. Random House, Auckland, 2000.

Loudon, J. C. *Observations on Laying out Farms in the Scotch Style Adapted to England: Comprising an Account of the Introduction of the Berwickshire Husbandary into Middlesex and Oxfordshire with Remarks on the Importance of this System to the Central Improvement of Landed Property*. John Harding, London, 1812.

—— *An Encyclopaedia of Gardening: Comprising the Theory and Practice of Horticulture, Floriculture, Arboriculture and Landscape Gardening*. Longman, Brown, Green & Longman, London, 1850.

Lucas, A. H. *A. H. Lucas, Scientist: His Own Story*. Angus & Robertson, Sydney, 1937.

McBryde, Isabel (ed.). *Records of Times Past: Ethnohistorical Essays on the Culture and Ecology of the New England Tribes*. Australian Institute of Aboriginal Studies, Canberra, 1978.

McCraken, Donal F. *Gardens of Empire: Botanical Institutions of the Victorian British Empire*. Leicester University Press, London, 1997.

MacGillivray, John. *The Narrative of HMS Rattlesnake*. T. & W. Boone, London, 1852.

McIntosh, Charles. *Flora and Pomona or the British Fruit Garden*. J. Rider, London, 1829.

MacLeod, Roy and Rehbock, Phiilip F. (eds). *Darwin's Laboratory: Evolutionary Theory and Natural History in the Pacific*. University of Hawai'i Press, Honolulu, 1994.

MacMillan, David. *A Squatter Went to Sea*. Currawong Publishing Co., Sydney, 1957.

—— *The Book of the Garden*. Blackwood & Sons, Edinburgh, 1853.

Maroske, Sara, 'Planting the Melbourne General Cemetery: The Contribution of Ferdinand von Mueller', *Australian Garden History*, vol. 2, no. 5, March–April 1991, pp. 3–7.

Massola, A. 'Two Aboriginal Legends of the Ballarat District', *Victorian Naturalist*, vol. 79, no. 4, August 1962, pp. 110–12.

Milbourne, Jean. *Mount Macedon: Its History and Grandeur 1836–1978*. Cambridge Press, Bendigo, 1981.

Millias, J. G. *Rhododendrons: In which Is Set Forth an Account of all Species of the Genus Rhododendron Including Azalea and the Various Hybrids*. Lothian, London, 1917.

Moore, Henry Byron. *A Brief Report on the Land System*. John Ferres, Melbourne, 1868.

Moulds, Francis Robert. *The Dynamic Forest: A History of Forestry and Forest Industries in Victoria*. Lynedoch Publications, Melbourne, 1991.

Moulds, F. R. and Burns M. J. *From Little Seeds: A History of the Macedon State Nursery 1872–1995*. Forests Service, Department of Natural Resources and Environment, Melbourne, 1997.

Mueller, Ferdinand von. *Descriptive Notes on Papuan Plants*. Government Printer, Melbourne, 1875–1890.

Neale, Anne, 'Edward La Trobe Bateman', *Australian Garden History*, vol. 9, no. 4, January–February 1998, p. 24.

—— 'Ornamental Gardening and Architecture: The Private Gardens of E. L. Bateman', in Sean Pickersgill (ed.), *On What Ground(s)?*, Society of Architectural Historians of Australia and New Zealand, Adelaide, 1997, pp. 178–81.

Noble, F. H. O. and Morgan, R. *Speed the Plough: A History of the Royal Agricultural Society of Victoria*. Wilkie & Co. Ltd., Melbourne, 1981.

'Papers Relative to Botanic Gardens', *Votes and Proceedings, New South Wales Legislative Council*, 1854, vol. 2, pp. 1231–97.

Paul, William. *The Rose Garden in Two Divisions*. Sherwood, Gilbert & Piper, Edinburgh, 1848.

Paxton, Joseph. *Paxton's Botanical Dictionary: Comprising the Names, History and Culture of All Plants Known in Britain; with a Full Explanation of Technical Terms*. Bradbury, Evans & Co., London, 1868.

Pescott, E. E., 'The Pioneers of Horticulture in Victoria', *Victorian Historical Magazine*, vol. 18, no. 1, February 1940, pp. 127–38.

—— 'The Writings of Daniel Bunce, 1813–1872', *The Victorian Historical Magazine*, vol. 23, no. 3, September 1950, pp. 115–25.

Pescott, R. T. M. *W. R. Guilfoyle 1840–1912: The Master of Landscaping*. Oxford University Press, Melbourne, 1974.

—— *The Royal Botanic Gardens, Melbourne: A History from 1854 to 1970.* Oxford University Press, Melbourne, 1982.

'Petition of T.W. Sheperd and M. Guilfoyle', *Votes and Proceedings of the NSW Legislative Council*, 1854, vol. 2, pp. 1295–7.

Polya, Rosemary. *Nineteenth Century Plant Nursery Catalogues of South East Australia: A Bibliography.* La Trobe University Library, Bundoora, 1981.

Randell, J. O. *Pastoral Settlement in Northern Victoria: The Coliban District.* Queensberry Hill Press, Melbourne, 1979.

Ravenscroft, Edward. *The Pinetum Britannicum: A Descriptive Account of Hardy Cultivated Trees Cultivated in Great Britain.* W. Blackwood & Sons, Edinburgh, 1884, 3 vols.

Reid, John (ed.). *When Memory Turns the Key: The History of the Shire of Romsey.* Joval Publications, Bacchus Marsh, 1992.

'Report of the Trustees, Public Library, Museums and National Gallery of Victoria for 1883', *Votes and Proceedings of the Victorian Legislative Council*, vol. 2, no. 36, 1884.

Rivers, Thomas. *The Rose Amateur's Guide: Containing Ample Description of all the Fine Leading Varieties of Roses, Regularly Classed in their Respective Families; their History, and Mode of Culture.* Longman, Brown, Green & Longman, London, 1846.

Robinson, William. *The Subtropical Garden: Or Beauty of Form in the Flower Garden.* John Murray, London, 1871.

—— *The Wild Garden: Or our Groves and Shrubberies Made Beautiful by the Naturalism of Hardy Exotic Plants. With a Chapter on the Garden of British Wild Flowers.* Scholar Press, London, 1977.

Rougetel, Hazel Le, 'The First Rose Grower in England', *Country Life*, 25 June 1981.

Royal Commission into Vegetable Products. *Progress Report of the Royal Commission on Vegetable Products.* Robert Brain, Melbourne, 1886–91, 9 vols.

Sander, F. *Reichenbachia: Orchids Illustrated and Described.* H. Sotheran & Co., London, 1888, 4 vols.

Sayce, Joseph, 'Report of Curator of Government House Domain with Photo-Lithographed Design and Notes Explanatory Thereof', *Report of the Secretary for Agriculture*, John Ferres, Melbourne, 1873, pp. 19–25.

—— 'Notes Relative to the More Important Parts of the Design for the Government House Gardens and the Domain Gardens', *Report of the Secretary for Agriculture*, John Ferres, Melbourne, 1873, pp. 25–34.

Scott, Hew (ed.). *Fasti Ecclesiae Scoticanae.* vol. 3, Synod of Glasgow and Ayr, 1920.

Seeman, Berthold. *Flora Vitiensis: A Description of the Plants of Viti or Fiji Islands.* L. Reeve & Co., London, 1865–73.

Select Committee on the Botanic Gardens, Minutes of Evidence 10 August 1855, *Votes and Proceedings, New South Wales Legislative Council*, 1855, vol. 1, pp. 1135–79.

Shephard, Sue. *Seeds of Fortune: A Gardening Dynasty.* Bloomsbury, London, 2003.

Short, P. S. (ed.). *History of Systematic Botany in Australasia: Proceedings of a Symposium held at the University of Melbourne 25–27 May 1988.* Australian Systematic Botany Society, Melbourne, 1990.

Siebold, Philipp Franz von. *Flora Japonica, sive Plantae quas in Imperio Japonico Collegit, Descripsit, ex parte in ipsis Locus Pingendas Curavit.* Lugduni Batavorum, Leiden, 1835–70, 2 vols.

Sinclair, James. *Gardener's Magazine and Journal of Rural Economy.* Slater, Williams & Hodgson, Melbourne, 1855–56.

Smith, C. H. J. *Parks and Pleasure Grounds: Or Practical Notes on Country Residences, Villas, Public Parks and Gardens.* Reeve & Co., London, 1852.

Spencer, Roger, 'Fashions in Street Tree Planting in Victoria', *Landscape Australia*, November 1986, pp. 304–308.

Sponberg, Stephen A. *A Reunion of Trees: The Discovery of Exotic Plants and their Introduction into North American and European Landscapes.* Harvard University Press, Cambridge, 1990.

Stackhouse, Jennifer. *Mr Macleay's Garden.* Historic Houses Trust of New South Wales, Sydney, 1981.

Stanbridge, W. E., 'General Characteristics, Astronomy, and Mythology of the Tribes in Central Parts of Victoria', *Ethnographical Society Transactions*, vol. 1, 1861, pp. 286–304.

Steenis, C. G. G. J. van (ed.). *Flora Malesiana.* vol. 1, Noordhoff-Kolff N.V., Jakarta, 1950.

Stephen, Leslie and Lee, Sidney (eds). *Dictionary of National Biography.* vols 3, 8, 19, London, Oxford University Press, 1968.

Synan, Peter. *Gippsland's Lucky City. A History of Sale.* City of Sale, Sale, 1994.

Tanner, Howard (ed.). *Converting the Wilderness: The Art of Gardening in Colonial Australia.* Landridge Press, Sydney, 1979.

—— *Architects of Australia.* Macmillan, Melbourne, 1981.

Taylor, Angela. *A Forester's Log: The Story of John La Gerche and the Ballarat-Creswick State Forest 1882–1897.* Melbourne University Press, Melbourne, 1998.

Treen, W. H. *The Majetin v Apple Blight.* A. L. Henriques, Melbourne, 1871.

Trollope, Anthony. *Australia and New Zealand*. Chapman & Hall, London, 1873, 2 vols.

Veitch, James Herbert. *A Traveller's Notes of a Tour through India, Malaysia, Japan, Corea, the Australian Colonies and New Zealand during 1891–1893*. James Veitch & Sons, London, 1896.

Veitch, James. *Hortus Veitchii: A History of the Rise and Progress of the Nurseries of Messrs James Veitch and Sons, Together with an Account of the Botanical Collectors*. James Veitch & Sons, London, 1906.

Victorian Forests Commission. *Macedon: Forest Nursery Centenary 1873–1973*. n.d.

Waite, Deborah B. *Artefacts from the Solomon Islands in the Julius L. Brenchley Collection*. British Museum Publications, London, 1987.

Wallis, A. R., 'Memorandum by the Secretary for Agriculture Relative to Works in the Government House Domain prior to 1st July 1873', *Report of the Inspector-General of Parks and Gardens*, John Ferres, Melbourne, 1873, pp. 12–15.

Ward, Nathaniel. *On the Growth of Plants in Closely Glazed Cases*. Van Voorst, London, 1852.

Watts, Peter. *Historic Gardens of Victoria: A Reconnaissance*. Oxford University Press, Melbourne, 1983.

—— 'What did Guilfoyle Really Design?', *Australian Garden History*, summer 1982, no. 3, pp. 8–12.

Webster, E. M. *Whirlwinds in the Plain: Ludwig Leichhardt: Friends, Foes and History*. Melbourne University Press, Melbourne, 1980.

Williams, B. S. *The Orchid Grower's Manual: Containing Descriptions of the Best Species and Varieties of Orchidaceous Plants in Cultivation*. Victoria & Paradise Nurseries, London, 1894.

Willis, Margaret. *By Their Fruits: A Life of Ferdinand von Mueller, Botanist and Explorer*. Angus & Robertson, Sydney, 1949.

Whitehead, Georgina. *Civilising the City: A History of Melbourne's Public Gardens*. State Library of Victoria, Melbourne, 1997.

Wright, Raymond, 'A Troubled Start: The Domain, Melbourne, 1872–73', *Victorian Historical Journal*, vol. 53, nos. 2–3, May–August 1982, pp. 138–51.

—— 'Dispensed With': A. R. Wallis, First Secretary for Agriculture in Victoria 1827–1882', *Research Project Series 150*, Department of Agriculture, Melbourne, 1982.

—— *The Bureaucrats' Domain: Space and the Public Interest in Victoria, 1836–84*. Oxford University Press, Melbourne, 1989.

Zola, Nelly and Gott, Beth. *Koorie Plants, Koorie People: Traditional Aboriginal Fibre and Healing Plants of Victoria*. Globe Press, Melbourne, 1992.

List of Illustrations

Index

THE MIEGUNYAH PRESS

This book was designed and typeset by Hamish Freeman and Klarissa Pfisterer
The text was set in 10¼ point Minion
with 4¼ points of leading
The text is printed on 128 gsm silk art

This book was edited by Jenny Lee

One thousand five hundred copies of this edition
were printed in Australia by BPA Print Group